POLITICAL THOUGHT AND HISTORY

John Pocock is arguably the most original and imaginative historian of ideas of modern times. Over the past half-century he has created an audience for his work which is truly global, and he has marked the way in which the history of political thought is studied as deeply and personally as any historian of the period. The essays in this major new collection are selected from a lifetime of thinking about political thought, and how we should study it in history. What in fact does it mean to write the history of a political society, and what kind of political thought is this? Professor Pocock emphasizes both the theory and practice of political thought considered as action in history, and the political theory of historiography considered as a form of political thought. Together these essays constitute a collection that any serious student of politics and intellectual history needs to possess.

PROFESSOR JOHN POCOCK, Honorary Fellow of St John's College, Cambridge, is the Harry C. Black Professor of History Emeritus at the Johns Hopkins University. His many seminal works on intellectual history include *The Ancient Constitution and the Feudal Law* (1957, second edition 1987), *Politics, Language and Time* (1971), *The Machiavellian Moment* (1975), *Virtue, Commerce and History* (1985), *Barbarism and Religion* (1999) and *The Discovery of Islands* (2005). He has edited *The Political Works of James Harrington* (1977) and Burke's *Reflections on the Revolution in France* (1987), as well as the collaborative study *The Varieties of British Political Thought* (1995).

Professor Pocock is a Corresponding Fellow of the British Academy and of the Royal Historical Society, and a member of both the American Academy of Arts and Sciences and the American Philosophical Society.

POLITICAL THOUGHT AND HISTORY

Essays on Theory and Method

J. G. A. POCOCK

CAMBRIDGE
UNIVERSITY PRESS

University Printing House, Cambridge CB2 8BS, United Kingdom

Cambridge University Press is part of the University of Cambridge.

It furthers the University's mission by disseminating knowledge in the pursuit of education, learning and research at the highest international levels of excellence.

www.cambridge.org
Information on this title: www.cambridge.org/9780521714068

First published 2009
3rd printing 2011

A catalogue record for this publication is available from the British Library

Library of Congress Cataloguing in Publication data
Pocock, J. G. A. (John Greville Agard), 1924–
Political thought and history : essays on theory and method / J. G. A. Pocock.
p. cm.
Includes index.
ISBN 978-0-521-88657-4 (hardback) – ISBN 978-0-521-71406-8 (pbk.)
1. Political science. 2. Political science – History. I. Title.
JA71.P58 2008
320 – dc22 2008027834

ISBN 978-0-521-71406-8 Paperback

Contents

PART II: HISTORY AS POLITICAL THOUGHT

Preface

(1)

I present this selection from essays written during the past half-century as a possibly useful contribution, first to reflection on method and second to recent intellectual history. A certain method, or procedure, for defining political thought and studying its history – alternatively, for studying it in history – has been formed and practised during that period, at Cambridge and other universities, and is so far associated with the first of these that it is often known by its name (perhaps with increasing confidence as one moves away from Cambridge itself). A time has come when several of its best-known practitioners are beginning to retire from active teaching, and while it will certainly continue to be practised in intellectual history, its location and purposes may be expected to change. Since my involvement in the genesis of this method (and my own retirement from teaching, though not from intellectual productivity) somewhat antedate those of others, I would like to make use of this moment to present some essays which indicate what I have taken (and still take) this method and its intimations to be, and further indicate how these intimations have changed my work and given it a direction of its own. Some aspects of this presentation are necessarily autobiographical and support the ego of the author; but I have tried to present the ego as acting in a historical context that is still operating but has changed during its own history. What I recover of my past work, and say of it in a more recent present, is intended as a contribution to the method I have mentioned.

As I have recalled in other essays,[1] and in chapters 2 and 8 below, I date the genesis of the 'Cambridge method' from 1949–50, when, as a research

[1] 'Present at the Creation: With Laslett to the Lost Worlds', *International Journal of Public Affairs* (Chiba University, Japan), 2 (2006), pp. 7–17; 'Foundations and Moments', in Annabel Brett and James Tully (eds.), *Rethinking the Foundations of Modern Political Thought* (Cambridge: Cambridge University Press, 2006), pp. 37–49.

student supervised by Herbert Butterfield, I became aware of the work of Peter Laslett. As is hardly necessary to repeat, he separated the context in which Filmer wrote *Patriarcha* from that in which it was published with his other works many years later, and the context in which Locke wrote the *Treatises of Government* some years before the revolution of 1688–9 from that in which he published them after it. There is no need to retrace the steps, taken by Laslett and others, by which these researches became the foundation of an understanding of 'political thought' as a multiplicity of language acts performed by language users in historical contexts. I first attempted to theorize this approach in an essay of 1962, republished here as chapter 1, but originally published in circumstances which locate it in the contexts of Laslett's extraordinary trajectory and Cambridge intellectual history during the 1950s. As early as 1949–50, however, research I undertook in pursuit of suggestions made by Butterfield in *The Englishman and His History*[2] had shown that the publication of Filmer's works in 1679–80 had led to controversy in two kinds: the philosophical debate over the origins of society and government, of which Locke's *Two Treatises* were part; and the historical debate over the origins of English common law and parliament,[3] in which the adversaries of Filmer were counter-attacked by Robert Brady. The study of the latter debate led to my doctoral dissertation in 1952 and its enlargement into *The Ancient Constitution and the Feudal Law* five years later.

What I had begun to see was, first, that political argument – part of what is loosely termed 'political thought' – had been conducted in a plurality of languages, and had consisted in a plurality of language acts, all coming together to constitute the 'history of political thought'; second, that one at least of these 'languages' had been a language of historical argument, joining with others to constitute a discourse of history, or 'historiography'. I therefore opened up a gap between 'political thought' and 'political theory' or 'philosophy',[4] and at the same time began to think of history/historiography as a form of 'political thought' and a constituent of its history. I consider that my role as a practitioner of the 'Cambridge method' has been to pursue its intimations in the latter direction. In historical research and synthesis,

[2] Cambridge: Cambridge University Press, 1944. I have never found difficulty in reconciling this work with his *The Whig Interpretation of History*, since the word 'Whig' is differently used and bears different meanings in the two essays.

[3] This arose from the inclusion among Filmer's essays of *The Freeholder's Grand Inquest*, which has since been ascribed to another author. It was assumed to be Filmer's at the time of which I write.

[4] I contributed a chapter on 'Theory in History' to the *Oxford Handbook of Political Theory* (2006). When I was asked to contribute a similar chapter to the *Oxford Handbook of Political Philosophy*, I did not know how to reply.

I have sometimes suggested,[5] where Quentin Skinner and Richard Tuck have remained concerned with the state and political philosophy in the seventeenth century, I have chosen – from *The Machiavellian Moment* in 1975 to the continuing series *Barbarism and Religion*, begun in 1999 – to pursue the themes of civil society and historiography into the eighteenth. It was American scholars – Caroline Robbins and Bernard Bailyn – who first showed me the way through the impact of commerce on political thought before and after 1700 and 1776, and recently in Cambridge I have found Istvan Hont and Michael Sonenscher[6] travelling far ahead of me on roads I once thought I knew.

The volume to which this is a preface is concerned with relations between history and political theory. The first part, 'Political thought as history', begins (chapter 1) with my first attempt to provide a method for studying the one as the other, and proceeds (3 and 4) to formulate theories of how language is organized in history in terms intended to produce, first, an experimental politics of language, and second, as uncontentious a relationship between philosopher and historian as could be hoped for when one had to share the academy with the followers of the late Leo Strauss. (Among my intentions in selecting these essays has been to recall incidents in recent intellectual history, especially in the United States, where I have practised the history of political thought.) My career as political theorist belonged chiefly to the 1970s; in the 1980s I find myself (chapters 5–7) developing a method for studying political thought as history, and determining what kind of history it was.

In Part II, 'History as political thought', the essays pursue a road on which I have found fewer companions: the attempt to consider history – not philosophy of history, but historiography; Oakeshott's practical history, capable of discovering the limits beyond which it ceases to be practical – as a form of political thought: first, a way in which the political society furnishes one more way in which it can be thought about, second, a way of thinking about a society by narrating it in the multiple contexts of historical circumstance and change. My interest in the history of historiography seems to have begun (1962) as early as that in the historiography of political

[5] See, e.g., the essays cited in note 1 above, and chapter 8 in this volume.

[6] Istvan Hont and Michael Ignatieff (eds.), *Wealth and Virtue: The Shaping of Political Economy in the Scottish Enlightenment* (Cambridge: Cambridge University Press, 1983); Hont, *Jealousy of Trade; international competition and the nation-state in historical perspective* (Cambridge, MA: The Belknap Press of Harvard University Press, 2005); Michael Sonenscher, *Before the Deluge: Public Debt, Inequality, and the Intellectual Origins of the French Revolution* (Princeton: Princeton University Press, 2007).

thought, and the first two essays in this section were written at the University of Canterbury, where I taught before leaving New Zealand for the United States in 1966. Both reflect my deep if limited involvement with the thought of Michael Oakeshott, which I used for my own purposes in ways of which neither he nor his committed followers would have approved, and both make mention of a project in which I have had no Western followers at all:[7] that of including an elementary account of ancient Chinese political philosophy in undergraduate courses in the history of political thought.

Nearly twenty years separate them from those that follow, in which I take up the subject of historiography as political thought, in the terms used to describe it a few sentences earlier than this. These, the last three in the volume (chapters 9–13), inquire in what sense the historian of a society may be its citizen, participant in it through recounting and re-narrating its history, which she or he shares with those who do not recount and need not think of it. They suggest ways in which the society may generate narratives of its history, commonly originating as myths but later entailing ways in which they may be queried, verified and re-narrated, as the society discovers its past to be contested, contestable, and above all multidimensional: a history which has gone on in contexts which there may be no end of discovering. I take it to be an exercise of the sovereignty, autonomy or self-command of a civil society that it can narrate, re-narrate and interpret its history, with the consequence that it recognizes sovereignty even in this sense to be contestable, conditional and in short historical; and I oppose my argument to the impulse, inherent in the ideology of globalized post-modernity, to assert that because the autonomous society, and the autonomous self, exist in more relationships than they can define or control, they do not and should not have the ability to relate their pasts and enact their futures. I incline to see having a history as more important than having an identity, the ability to criticize and re-narrate one's history as a means of navigating Oakeshott's bottomless and boundless sea.[8] But this presupposes citizenship; one must feel oneself in some sense participant in the history one takes part in relating. There are those who have good cause to

[7] See 'Ritual, Language, Power: an essay on the apparent political meanings of ancient Chinese philosophy', originally published in *Political Science* (Victoria University of Wellington), 16.1 (1964); republished in J. G. A. Pocock, *Politics, Language and Time: essays on political thought and history* (New York: Atheneum, 1971; Chicago: University of Chicago Press, 1989), pp. 42–79. Translated into Japanese by Takahiro Nakajima, in *Todai Journal of Chinese Philosophy* (University of Tokyo), 7 (1993), pp. 1–45.

[8] These arguments are developed in several chapters of J. G. A. Pocock, *The Discovery of Islands: essays in British history* (Cambridge: Cambridge University Press, 2005).

see themselves as merely subject and 'subaltern' to history, and I endeavour in chapter 12 to imagine what history could be written of, for or by them. It may be that the societies that can have histories in my sense are few in number, and that many others see the histories we have as oppressing them in the history they have been denied. How then do we retain ours while doing justice to them? By waiting until they write histories as we do, and ours and theirs can be read in the contexts all create for one another? They may not desire to exist in the condition of multi-contextuality – so much a product of our history and our historiography – and we appear meanwhile to be going through a second Enlightenment, in which not the sacred but the self is targeted for deconstruction, and the particular society and its history are denied autonomy. This tendency is strong enough to be resisted in these essays. They are concerned with the contested attainment of autonomous histories, which must now be seen as passing into the histories of others, deflecting and even denying their growth; but we shall not assist them in attaining their own autonomy by denying it to ourselves.

(II)

A number of essays that form part of this enterprise have been omitted from the present volume, partly in order to set limits to its bulk, but more importantly because they are available in collections still in print. They may indeed be better known to readers than many of the essays republished here; but for that very reason it may be worth noting and describing them, so that it may be seen what place they have in the history of this inquiry. *Politics, Language and Time*,[9] published in 1971, contains an introductory and a valedictory essay: 'Languages and their implications: the transformation of the study of political thought' (pp. 3–41), and 'On the non-revolutionary character of paradigms: a self-criticism and afterpiece' (pp. 273–91). The keyword 'paradigms', appearing in the second title, indicates the theme of the initial essay. I was at that time greatly intrigued by Thomas S. Kuhn's *The Structure of Scientific Revolutions*,[10] and in particular by his concept of the paradigm: a mental and linguistic construct, capable of appearing with dramatic suddenness, which not only supplied the answers to questions, but determined what questions and kinds of questions should be asked – to the exclusion and occlusion of others – and so dictated the course of

[9] See note 7 above.
[10] Thomas S. Kuhn, *The Structure of Scientific Revolutions* (Chicago: University of Chicago Press, 1962).

scientific inquiry, and even the structure and character of communities of scientific inquirers, until such time as the 'paradigm' should disintegrate and be replaced by another, in a process dramatic enough to deserve the name of 'revolution'.

Kuhn's scenario was obviously a highly political one, and I was encouraged to believe that the notion of the 'paradigm' would prove applicable to the inquiry I was conducting into the rise, transformation and disappearance of political 'languages'. A new 'language', it seemed plausible, might dictate a new concept of politics and of the political community itself. I continue to find this believable, and the word 'paradigm' valuable, in certain cases: above all, of course, the transformation of English political thought that came about in the decades following 1688, when it became accepted that politics could be understood only as the politics of a commercial society. It can be no surprise to readers that I have come to see this as a profound change in the history of political thought, and in my own pursuit of that history. On this occasion at least, a 'paradigm revolution' may be said to have occurred, and in *The Machiavellian Moment* (1975) and *Virtue, Commerce and History* (1985), I pursued its consequences into the eighteenth century. An association between my methodological writings and Kuhn's work is therefore proper;[11] but as early as 1971 I was doubtful about carrying it too far, and knew that these doubts were shared by Kuhn himself.[12] They arose from an awareness that his chief concern, the scientific community, though it has its own politics and interacts with the politics of others, differs radically from what may be termed the political community and interacts differently with the controlling language structures, or 'paradigms', both communities generate in pursuing their purposes. The political community is not essentially, though it is incidentally, a community of inquiry, and the 'paradigms' it from time to time generates to define it as a community dealing with certain problems, and having a certain structure, operate within a multiplicity of problem-situations so great that no one 'paradigm' can long succeed in excluding or occluding its alternatives. It follows that many 'paradigms' must co-exist, and need not though they often will compete, in defining the community, its problems and its methods. They will be linguistically and culturally diverse, like those of

[11] John Burrow, *A History of Histories: epics, chronicles, romances and inquiries from Herodotus and Thucydides to the twentieth century* (London: Allen Lane, 2007), pp. 498–9.

[12] I may be permitted to recall that I sent him a presentation copy of *Politics, Language and Time*, inscribed 'in acknowledgment of a debt he probably does not wish acknowledged'. At the time of his death years later, I heard that he agreed with me in maintaining a distance, though one not unbridgable, between his concerns and mine.

which I became aware as outcomes of the Filmerian controversy, and for this reason among others, the Kuhnian concept of a community so closely controlled by its paradigms that their replacement must have the character of a revolution will be needed only in specific circumstances. The word 'paradigm' thus loses force as a noun, though it may continue to be useful in adjectival or adverbial form. There will be so many competitors for the role of paradigm that we are interested in each only within the limits to which it is successful. It is easier to write the discursive history of a political community if we assume that it is always exposed to new linguistic possibilities. For this reason the Kuhnian paradigm is a starting point in these methodological exercises, not a continuing tool; still less a 'paradigm' in its own right. At the date of *Politics, Language and Time* I was, however confusedly, as much indebted to Oakeshott as to him; as much and no more.

How far a given political community is open to the alternatives its paradigms seek to occlude is, of course, a matter for investigation; but the historian's assumption that alternatives will always be present has, no less 'of course', politically normative implications. The essay on 'the non-revolutionary character of paradigms' was less the direct challenge to Kuhn it may have appeared than a product of the 1960s: a period during which a great deal of revolutionary sentiment, if little enough revolutionary action, had led to demands for transparence, that is for language which could demonstrate its freedom from imposed preconditions. Like others who held posts on American campuses during that decade, I had had my troubles with self-appointed Red Guards and their very small-scale cultural revolutions, and there was ready to hand the massive literature of Cold War post-historicist and anti-revolutionary argument: Popper, Polanyi, Talmon, Berlin and in his own way Oakeshott. In this essay I fell back on what still seems to me the fact rather than the argument that historical inquiry is anti-paradigmatic, in the sense that it multiplies without theoretical limitation the problem-situations, contingencies and contexts in which any historical occurrence may have been situated, and therefore performs the liberal-conservative function of warning the ruler on the one hand, and the revolutionary on the other, that there is always more going on than either can understand or control.

Virtue, Commerce and History (1985)[13] was less concerned with presenting specimens of the new historiography than its predecessor; its purpose

[13] J. G. A. Pocock, *Virtue, Commerce and History: essays on political thought and history, chiefly in the eighteenth century* (Cambridge: Cambridge University Press, 1985).

was to pursue a history of anglophone political thought through the eighteenth century. I prefaced it with a methodological 'Introduction: the state of the art' (pp. 1–34) because I wished to show how far method and theory had progressed, and what might be the agenda for their further development. In particular, I wished to press beyond the establishment of 'what an author was doing', in Quentin Skinner's famous phrase of 1978[14] – in other words, how the author's 'intentions' shaped and were shaped by the language context in which they were expressed – to the question of 'what he/she turned out to have done'; from illocution to allocution, to borrow language once again from Skinner. What this was, and how it came to be, involved not only the shaping of *parole* by *langue*; one must also inquire how authors were understood by readers, and how the response of the latter both shaped and was shaped by the original author's speech act. Here there yawned before me a series of caverns signposted '*Rezeptiongeschichte*' and 'reader response theory', at the end of which there was said to lurk a minotaur ingeminating 'the death of the author'. I did not find it necessary to explore them; 'the state of the art' was limited to the pursuit of two enterprises. One – here foreshadowed in chapters 3 and 4 – was the elaboration of the relations between speech act performer, respondent and language context into a simple but necessary politics of speech, intended to illuminate what might happen when speech was performed at familiar levels of literacy, probably those of an early-modern print culture. Out of this grew the second enterprise. Author, respondent and language context were visibly engaged in processes of innovation and interpretation, in which actions had consequences other than those intended, and *parole* and *langue* underwent change intended and unintended; new language-worlds might appear, either gradually or suddenly, and even Kuhn's paradigmatic revolution was a possibility not to be dismissed. The community or competition of political speech I had tried to outline was involved in making history by its intended actions, but in history some actions had not been intended. I was formulating a theoretical historiography of political discourse over consecutive periods of time (necessarily confined to occurring in specific political cultures), which I went on to elaborate in what are now chapters 6 and 7, as well as in various works of history.

A further group of essays not included because currently available has as its centre 'The treaty between histories' (2001 and 2006),[15] to which could

[14] Quentin Skinner, *The Foundations of Modern Political Thought*, 1: *The Renaissance* (Cambridge: Cambridge University Press, 1978), p. xi.

[15] In Andrew Sharp and Paul McHugh (eds.), *Histories, Power and Loss: uses of the past – a New Zealand commentary* (Wellington: Bridget Williams Books, 2001), pp. 75–96; and in Julia Rudolph (ed.), *History and Nation* (Lewisburg, PA: Bucknell University Press, 2006), pp. 137–65.

be added several chapters from *The Discovery of Islands*.[16] These pursue in various directions themes raised in Part II of this volume, culminating in chapter 13. I argue that a political community with any degree of autonomy will generate narratives of its past, modifying them as it performs new actions and suffers new experiences in the present. There is consequently a close relation between its historiography and its sovereignty: the capacity to declare what its past has been is important to the latter, as is that to declare what its future shall be. It is obvious that these narratives may be no more than myths of continuity; but it is also probable that they will be contested and criticized, first by alternative and conflicting narratives arising in the political process that generates the historiography, second by discovered interactions and commonalties between the community's history and those of others close to it, and third (chapter 12) by voices arising from those within it who have been excluded from its politics and are now asserting narratives of their own. If the community desires to remain an actor in the management of these contests, it must learn to narrate them with conflicting voices, thus declaring its sovereignty as the history of a sovereignty – and an identity – contested, challenged and open-endedly problematic. A problematic sovereignty (and historiography) does not cease to be a sovereignty; the problem is the sovereignty because peculiar to the community; but in our present ideological climate, radical criticism and economic globalization seize upon every modification of a community's history as a means of denying its autonomy. Like *The Discovery of Islands*, this volume is intended to argue against this tendency.

In 'The treaty between histories', I extrapolated from the recent history of New Zealand (where 'the Treaty' has a specific meaning) to imagine the case of a single polity where sovereignty is shared between two peoples, one narrating of itself a history of the familiar Anglo-European kind, the other giving mythical expression to an animist world-view, such as a modern Maori scholar has declared to be rather a way of ordering a world than of narrating a history.[17] I argued that the sharing of sovereignty between two such peoples must be very carefully negotiated between others who might comprehend each other's world-view but could not be expected to share it. I also argued, however, that the latter people must find themselves affirming their unhistorical world-view in a universe made inescapably historical by the sheer fact of contact with the former, and therefore negotiating less with

[16] Pocock, *The Discovery of Islands*, chs. 13, 14, 16, 17.

[17] Te Maire Tau, '*Matauranga Maori* as an Epistemology', in Sharp and McHugh, *Histories, Power and Loss*, pp. 61–74; 'The Death of Knowledge: ghosts on the plains', *New Zealand Journal of History*, 35.2 (2001), pp. 131–52.

the other's history than with history itself. I have considerable confidence in Maori capacity to do this. *Political Thought and History* therefore ends with two adjurations: one, that we cannot learn others' histories unless the others (and we) write both for others and for themselves, which will not be easy; second, that we should attend to the possibility that the concept 'history' itself has lexical and contextual limits. The Second Enlightenment will probably try to abolish all these distinctions, but will probably fail.

Acknowledgments

These essays have been lightly edited, in one or two cases to sharpen the argument; but none has been rewritten and the originals are accessible. I have also experimented, in editing them, with ways of dealing with the gender bias of English pronouns, though no solution is altogether satisfactory. For this I ask the reader's understanding. A few additions to the footnotes are enclosed in square brackets.

My thanks to Katherine Moran for her very careful and helpful preparation of the typescript, and to the following publishers for permission to reprint: Blackwell Publishers (chapters 1 and 12); Random House Ltd (chapter 3); Princeton University Press (chapter 4); Johns Hopkins University Press (chapter 5); the University of California Press (chapter 7); Duke University Press (chapter 8); the Publication Office of the University of the South Pacific (chapter 11); the editors of *Historical Research*, University of London (chapter 13). Chapters 6, 9 and 10 were originally published by Cambridge University Press.

PART I

Political thought as history

CHAPTER I

The history of political thought: a methodological inquiry

In this article I shall attempt to make a theoretical statement of what it is we study when we claim to be studying the history of political thought, and to draw from this statement some inferences about how the study thus defined might be undertaken.

The history of political thought is an established and flourishing discipline, but the terms on which it is established and flourishes appear to be conventional and traditional. At the level of academic inquiry, it is often useful to submit a tradition to examination and make it yield some theoretical account of itself; and it may happen that a tradition of thought is shown to contain some vaguenesses and inconsistencies, whose removal could have been achieved in no other way. When I suggest that certain improvements could be carried out in this discipline if a more precise theoretical formulation were adopted of its subject-matter and methods, I shall not be suggesting that this, or any other, formulation is the only basis on which the discipline can be effectively carried on. But a political scientist may further be interested in the relations between the political activities, institutions and traditions of a society and the terms in which that political complex is from time to time expressed and commented on, and in the uses to which those terms are put; in short, in the functions within a political society of what may be called its language (or languages) of politics.

When I say that the history of political thought is at present a traditional form of study, I mean that it consists of the study of such thinkers about politics as have become and remained the objects of historical attention; and that our reasons for studying them, and the character of the attention we pay them, are such as have grown up in the course of our historical experience. These writers and their ideas do not form the subject-matter of a single consistent science. Simply, there is a body of thinkers to whom we have

[Published in Peter Laslett and W. G. Runciman (eds.), *Philosophy, Politics and Society*, 2nd ser. (Oxford: Blackwell, 1962), pp. 183–202.]

grown into the habit of paying attention, and a number of viewpoints from which they appear interesting to us. These thinkers, from these viewpoints – now from one, now from another – we study; doing so is a traditional piece of behaviour, and they and their study form a tradition, or part of a tradition, which, in Oakeshott's parlance,[1] we get to know.

Since it can be accepted that there is no one set of assumptions from which alone it is proper to approach the history of political thought, there must consequently be an indefinite number of approaches which we may make; and what these are is determined less by ourselves, independently choosing a line of inquiry, than by the social and intellectual traditions in which we conduct our thinking. The traditionalist attitude consists in accepting (1) the indefinite variety of these possible approaches, (2) that there is no *a priori* reason for preferring any one of them to others, (3) that we can never hope to rid ourselves entirely of the simultaneous presence in our thoughts of more than one of the different sets of assumptions and interests on which they are founded. In this field as in others, the traditionalist acknowledges that the subject-matter of his study forms a tradition in which he is involved, and that his own approach to it is determined by this and other traditions; he settles down to conduct his thinking from within a pattern of inheritance over which he has not perfect control.

This situation is one in which reasonably satisfactory intellectual activity can be carried on. But to say that a historian does his thinking within a tradition is to say that he does it within an inheritance of intellectual positions which can never be reduced to a single pattern of coherence and cannot even be completely distinguished from one another. The more fully we accept this, the clearer should the necessity become to distinguish between the various positions of which our tradition consists with as great a degree of precision as can be managed – meaning by the term 'precision' that precision which knows the limits of its own preciseness. To accept that our position is a traditional one is to accept that there are and must be limits on our power to clarify our proceedings, but it obviously does not mean that we should not clarify what we are trying to do at any given moment to the limits of our ability, or seek for means of pushing those limits back. The defect of the traditionalist definition of an intellectual inquiry, however, is that it says nothing about the means by which this clarification may be attempted. If means of doing this are not found, confusions will occur which may lead,

[1] See Michael Oakeshott, 'Political Education', in Peter Laslett (ed.), *Philosophy, Politics and Society* (Oxford: Blackwell, 1956). [This was the first volume of the series in the second of which this essay appeared.]

paradoxically enough, as easily in the direction of intellectual vagueness and pretension as in that of the conservative and empirical caution which it is generally the design of the traditionalist definition to produce.

This is peculiarly the case with the tradition of thought we call the history of political ideas, because that tradition is a tradition of intellectualizing; and there is a two-way relationship between confusions of thought about how others did their thinking and confusions of thought about why and how we are thinking about them. To define what I mean by 'a tradition of intellectualizing', I shall adopt the Burkean-Oakeshottian characterization of political theorizing as an activity of 'abstraction, or abridgment, from a tradition'. In this usage 'tradition' now refers to a 'tradition of behaviour', meaning the whole complex of ways of behaving, talking and thinking in politics which we inherit from a social past. From this 'tradition of behaviour' political thought forms a series of 'abstractions' or 'abridgments'; the sense in which it is desirable to define this series as itself a 'tradition' has been given earlier and does not for the present concern us. From a 'tradition of behaviour', then, theorists perform acts of abstraction; the study of political thought is the study of what takes place when they do this.

There are at least two approaches to this study. Political thought may be regarded as an aspect of social behaviour, of the ways in which humans behave towards each other and towards the institutions of their society; or it may be regarded as an aspect of intellectuality, of their attempts to gain understanding of their experience and environment. Abstractions are made for a medley of purposes, varying between the rhetorical and the scientific. Indeed, in political as in other forms of social thought, it is never possible to isolate one of the two functions of abstraction decisively from the other. To solve a theoretical problem may have practical implications and, conversely, to state and solve a practical problem may raise new problems of wider generality. However much the conservative may deplore the fact, the human mind does pursue implications from the theoretical to the practical and from the practical to the theoretical; and no one knows where the process of abstraction may lead, which one is beginning (perhaps) with a clear and limited purpose in view.

Abstractions point to further abstractions and the level of thought shifts constantly between the theoretical and the practical. The same piece of thought may be viewed, simultaneously, as an act of political persuasion and as an incident in the pursuit of understanding; the arguments and concepts are repeated, after very short intervals, for purposes more theoretical, or more practical, than those for which they were just now employed. A philosophy reappears as an ideology; a party slogan as a heuristic device of high scientific value. It becomes important, then, that we do not make *a priori* assumptions about the character of political thought – as we do when we dismiss a piece of theoretical writing by representing it as a piece of persuasion on behalf of a group – and that we possess means of distinguishing between the different functions which political thought may be performing, and of following the history of concepts and abstractions as they move from one employment to another.

It may therefore be expected that the political thought appearing in a given society over a period – and the same may well be true of the political thought of a given individual – will prove on inspection to exist on a number of different levels of abstraction, varying with the character of the problems which it is intended to solve. This will confront the historian with no insoluble conundrum. It is perfectly possible, by the ordinary methods of historical reconstruction, to determine the level of abstraction on which a particular piece of thinking took place. But it does mean that the only assumptions we can make *in advance* about that level will be selective ones. We can choose to concern ourselves only with political thought at a certain level of abstraction; we cannot assume in advance that political thought in actual fact took place only on that level. The strictly historical task before us is plainly that of determining by investigation on what levels of abstraction thought did take place.

But the historian of political thought is all too often diverted from carrying out this task, and what diverts him may be termed the indefinite rationality of his subject. The act of disengagement, of 'abstraction from a tradition', is simultaneously an act of intellectual reorganization, and the writers whose thought he studies had all, in varying degrees, a tendency to become philosophers – that is, to organize their thought towards higher states of rational coherence. To this process, once embarked upon, there is no known end, and our effort to understand the philosopher's thought must be an effort not only to follow it, but actually to assist it, in its indefinite progress towards higher states of organization. Consequently, the historian of political thought is commonly engaged both in strictly historical reconstruction and in a kind of philosophical reconstruction – one seeks to understand past political thought by raising it to ever higher levels of generality and abstraction.

As a result, the history of political thought has a constant tendency to become philosophy. The historian has a further professional motive pressing in this direction: the need to find a narrative theme around which to organize the piece of history which one is studying. One may be writing a history of political thought in a certain period, embracing a number of thinkers who developed their political ideas in the attempt to deal with a number of problems at a number of different levels of abstraction; and one desires to make a single coherent story out of it all. One has already, as we have seen, a tendency to study each thinker at a high level of abstraction; and by interpreting all their thought at a high common level, one discovers certain general assumptions which all adopted, or by their attitude towards which each can be interpreted.

The history of political thought in this period now becomes the history of these assumptions: of the various consequences that were deduced from them, of the various attitudes that were adopted towards them, and of the various modifications that were introduced into them, so that perhaps by the end of the period they are shown to have become significantly unlike what they were at its beginning. The history of political thought – in this no doubt resembling that of other forms of organized thought – has in this way a tendency to become the history of mutations in the cardinal assumptions (perhaps unconscious ones) on which it can be shown to have been based. If the term 'philosophy' may be used for thought which leads to the establishment or modification of cardinal assumptions, the history being written will be philosophical history; and if the set of assumptions whose history is being traced can be shown to have been cardinal not only to the political thought of an age, but to all or several of its modes of organized thought, they may properly be termed its *Weltanschauung* and the history being written will be *Weltanschauungsgeschichte*.

In this way, the tradition which is the object of study has been condensed into a single narrative, taking place at a high level of abstraction. It must next be asked whether the process described furnishes valid historical explanations. The answer must depend on the criteria we adopt; but a good test of the value of a piece of history expressed in highly abstract terms is to ask whether its abstractions correspond to realities actually experienced, to things which some identifiable Alcibiades really did or suffered. If the assumptions on which changes in thought are supposed to rest are represented as such that nobody was aware of making them, it will be difficult to submit the model to verification. But if it can independently be shown that these assumptions were consciously formulated from time to time, then what was an explanatory model will begin to appear a history of events which actually occurred. We may write the history of thought in terms of abstractions at any level of generality, no matter how high, so long as we can provide independent verification that the abstractions we employ were employed in the relevant field, at the relevant time, by thinkers included in our story. We may write in terms of mutations occurring in the *Weltanschauung*, of a continuing dialogue between more or less stable systems of philosophy, or cardinal ideas in the stable vocabulary of political theory; and whenever the explanations we construct are found to be historically valid, historical understanding will be enriched.

Yet it is impossible to be wholly satisfied with the process of thought so far described. If political thought is 'abstraction from a tradition', that abstraction may be carried to many different levels of theoretical generality; and we have so far depicted a historian capable of verifying whether political thought did in fact take place at the level of abstraction at which one has chosen to explain it, but not of starting one's inquiries by empirically ascertaining the level at which it was taking place. The choice of a level of abstraction is determined by the need to give as completely rational an explanation as possible of the piece of thought with which one is concerned; the level one chooses will therefore tend to be high, and to rise. One selects the assumptions on the basis of which the piece of thought can be explained with maximum rational coherence, and then seeks to show that they were in use at the relevant period and were employed by the thinker or thinkers one is studying.

If this is the only method we are capable of adopting, we may be at a loss when confronted with the possibility that the piece of thought in question may be as well or better explained on assumptions which do not endow it with maximum rational coherence. There are passages in the writings of Burke (let us suppose) which can be explained by assuming them to be based on presumptions which are to be found explicit in the writings of Hume. Our historian embraces this mode of explanation, with the consequence that one presents Burke's thought in these passages as being systematic political philosophy of the same order as the relevant passages from Hume. This method predisposes us to accept the idea that Burke's political thought can best be explained as political philosophy. But now let it be suggested that the same passages in Burke can be no less plausibly explained as grounded on assumptions of a different order of generality – assumptions made by lawyers about institutions and practice, for example, rather than assumptions made by philosophers about thought and action; and let it be further suggested that though this explanation does not provide Burke's thought with maximum rational coherence, it is capable of a higher degree of historical verification than the explanation which does.

The historian we have hitherto imagined is poorly placed for taking part in this discussion, because not yet capable of adopting a method which recognizes that there are different levels of abstraction at which thought takes place and different degrees of rational coherence with which it can be explained; still less one which permits us to discriminate between these levels as a matter of historical inquiry. One is as yet the prisoner of a method which condemns one to explain political thought only in so far as it can be presented as systematic political theory or philosophy. When one writes of political thinking as a series of events taking place in history, one will treat them as taking place in, and explicable only by reference to, a context of events consisting of the thinking of theorists or philosophers. In the case we have been supposing,[2] one will present Burke's thinking as he did as the effect, or in some other way the historical consequence, of Hume's thinking as *he* did; and the political thought of a society over a given period will appear historically intelligible only as a sequence of thought-patterns exchanged among its political theorists or philosophers.

There seems to be general agreement that political thought, at whatever level of abstraction or systematization, is a mode of discussing certain aspects of social experience. If this is so, it becomes important to distinguish between the approaches made to this subject by the philosopher and the historian. The philosopher is interested in the thought produced in so far as it can be explained in strict rationality, and in establishing the limits within which this can be done. The historian is interested in men thinking about politics just as in them fighting or farming or doing anything else, namely as individuals behaving in a society, whose recorded behaviour can be studied by the method of historical reconstruction, in order to show what manner of world they lived in and why they behaved in it as they did. He or she is concerned with the relation between experience and thought, between the tradition of behaviour in a society and the abstraction from it of concepts which are used in attempts to understand and influence it; but may easily fail to pursue the historian's proper function by confusing it with that of the philosopher.

A historian who attempts to explain thought only by endowing it with the highest attainable rational coherence is condemned to study it only at the highest attainable level of abstraction from the traditions, or transmitted experience, of the society in which it went on; he is not well placed to study the actual process of abstraction which produced it. In short, if thought be defined as a series of abstractions from experience, or from a

[2] Which may be located in empirical reality; see F. Meinecke, *Die Enstehung des Historismus*, 2nd edn, (Munich, 1946), Part 1, ch. 6; and G. H. Sabine, *A History of Political Theory* (New York, 1945), ch. 29.

tradition, thinking may be defined as the activity of producing and using those abstractions, and it is this activity of thinking which the historian who confuses himself with the philosopher is disqualifying himself from studying properly. To put it another way, he is disqualifying himself from studying the relations between thinking and experience.

We may now see why he is vulnerable to the attacks of those who deny that there is any significant relation between political activity and political theory – between the tradition of behaviour and the concepts abstracted from it. This kind of attack, though frequently launched, is not always easy to understand precisely. In many cases, of course, what is intended is a piece of conservative polemic. The launcher of the attack presupposes that he is in the presence of an opponent who takes a more sanguine – and therefore more dangerous – view than he does of the extent to which political concepts can be used to criticize and modify the tradition of behaviour from which they have been abstracted; he therefore sets out to emphasize the limitations on the extent to which they can be so used.

The situation becomes more complex, however, when the attack is launched in the course of a debate between historians. Here the argument appears, at least initially, to be concerned with motivation and causation. One historian will accuse another of exaggerating the extent to which men's actions in a political context are motivated by the theories which they have formed from that context and the extent to which these theories, even supposing that they motivate men's actions, in fact determine the course which they take. Such a critic will ask whether the individual's actions must not be understood 'more' by reference to the determining influence of the historical situation in which they were carried out than by reference to the theoretical principles on which they were said to be founded.

Now many arguments between historians, as to whether one historical factor or cause was 'more important' than another, are undeniably meaningless. If $5 \times 3 = 15$, it is vain to contend that 5 is 'more important' than 3 in making 15 on the grounds that 5 is greater than 3. The only question worth discussing is whether it is possible to construct a satisfactory explanation of the process without taking the factor in question into account. It is unlikely that this will be impossible. If one constructs an explanation of a political action in such a way as to lay all the emphasis on the situational factors determining it, one can easily explain it in such a way as to make no reference necessary to any theoretical principles which may have been expressed during its course. One may even succeed in refuting in this way any explanation which supposes that they either motivated its inception or determined its outcome.

It is still perfectly possible that expressions of principle were frequently put forward in the course of the action, and absorbed much of the time and energy of those engaged in bringing it to completion. At this point we shall find them spoken of as 'propaganda', 'rationalizations', 'myths' and so forth – vaguely dismissive language designed to indicate that, whatever part they played in the story, it is not worth considering. But from what standpoint is it not worth considering? One or more explanations of the action may be constructed without taking it into account, and a historian may legitimately say that he is interested only in those aspects of the action which can be explained in this way. But the expressions of principle happened; they form part of the action and modify by their presence its total character. They must have borne some relation to its course, and though a historian may not wish to explore that relation and may be satisfied with an explanation of the action that omits it, one is not entitled to say that there was no such relation or that this explanation may not be modified by the construction of an explanation which includes it.[3]

What historiography requires at this point is the ability to explore the different possible relations which theorizing may bear to experience and action. But the anti-ideological interpreter tends to suppose that when he has refuted the suggestion that theory stands in a certain relation to action, he has refuted the suggestion that there is any relation between the two at all. As a historian he can be convicted of methodological naivety. Employing, in none too sophisticated a manner, the concepts of motive and cause, he refutes the suggestion that theory was, by itself, a sufficient motive to explain the inception of an action or a sufficient cause to explain its outcome, and supposes that he has deprived it of any place in the story whatever. Men in politics, he asserts, learn from experience 'and not' from theory – as if their theoretical formulations of experience could be pronounced in advance to play no part whatever in the way they learn from it. As a political theorist, he is oversimplifying the thesis of conservative empiricism, which is designed to refute, and does refute, any theory of politics contending that the concepts abstracted from a tradition suffice either to justify men in seeking to annul and replace that tradition or to explain the actions which they take within it. To deny that concepts may be isolated and shown to play a determining role in politics is not to deny that

[3] It can be contended that the word 'explanation' should be used only when an account of the action is constructed in purely causal terms. If this is so, and if all mention of the role of ideas is omitted, then an account of the action which included ideas only in some other capacity – e.g. that of bringing out the subjective significance of the action to those taking part in it – would have to be called by some name other than 'explanation'.

they play any role whatever; yet the anti-ideological interpreter not only supposes that it is, but often has difficulty in believing that the student of ideas in the political process is not, automatically, assigning a determining role to them.[4]

This error – that of supposing that theory can bear only one relation to action, so that if it does not bear this relation it does not bear any – is only the counterpart of the error earlier assigned to the historian of political thought: that of supposing that theory could only be studied at the highest attainable level of abstraction from experience. If the latter insisted on studying thought, as it accompanied experience and action, only in the form of systematic theory and philosophy, the former was hardly to blame for supposing that thought could accompany the activity of politics only in the detached role of a normative and programmatic guide. When he had, understandably, rejected this account of its behaviour, no alternative was offered him, and it was not his fault if his relations with the historian of ideas degenerated into a scholastic comedy of cross-purposes.

If this is the situation in which the historiography of political thought largely finds itself at the present time, it is not, as has been demonstrated, incompatible with the gaining of valid and valuable results in countless particular investigations. It does mean, however, that confusions and frustrations may arise, and efforts be misdirected and wasted, because there is an area of inquiry over which we do not have adequate methodological control. Our capacities might be increased, then, if our methods were to be refined; and for this purpose it would seem that we need means of discriminating between the different relations which concepts abstracted from a tradition of behaviour may bear (a) to that tradition, and (b) to the behaviour, stemming from it, with which they are associated.

There are two distinguishable fields of study here: what takes place when concepts are abstracted from a tradition, and what takes place when they are employed in action within that tradition. In the former, we are concerned with an activity of thinking, i.e. abstracting; in the latter, with an activity of political action. It may be asserted that the historian of thought is concerned with the activity of thinking rather than with that of action, and that consequently some modification is required of the demand, often put

[4] The present writer once published a study of some aspects of English political controversy in the 1680s and pointed out that there was a logical connexion between certain views of certain writers and certain defences of the Revolution of 1688. A reviewer accused him of exaggerating the role of the former ideas in *causing* the Revolution – and, being challenged, refused to withdraw; apparently because he was unable to conceive that any other assertion could be made about them. [I cannot now recall, and will not attempt to discover, who this reviewer was.]

forward, that the political thought of a Bodin or a Burke should be studied in the context of practical activity in which it took shape and which it was designed to influence. Certainly, much (though not all) political thinking does take shape in an immediate practical context, and when this is the case it must be studied accordingly.

But there is an evident difference between the intellectual content of a piece of thinking, and the role it was designed to play, or actually did play, in influencing political action. We must not confuse the motive behind an idea with its source, or suppose that when we have found the intention with which a particular piece of thought was constructed, we have adequately explained it. One may wish to justify a particular action, to persuade others to adopt or approve it, and this will doubtless do much to determine the content of the argument. But it is an error, not uncommon among historians, to suppose that men are at entire liberty to find and put forward exactly the rationalizations they need. How a man justifies his actions is determined by factors not at his command, and what they are must be ascertained by studying both the situation in which he is placed and the tradition within which he acts. And this is an inquiry distinguishable from that entailed in the study of how the arguments he advances affect the situation which they are intended to influence.

As a rough division of labour, then, it is for the historian of action to investigate how ideas, beliefs and arguments help us to understand the actions of men in particular situations; for the historian of thought to study the activity of thinking, of conceptualizing, of abstracting ideas from particular situations and traditions. (The historian of Bodin or Burke, of course, may need to cast himself in both these roles; all the more reason why they should not be confused.) The historian of thought will be perpetually interested in thought as it takes shape under the pressure of immediate events, but this interest will not be exclusive. One is more likely to take as one's main concern the relatively stable concepts which are regularly employed in the political thought of relatively stable societies, and to spend most of one's time studying how these are abstracted from traditions of behaviour, employed to criticize them and finally incorporated in them. Once one has taken this turn, one will tend to be concerned with thought as the language of tradition, rather than with action, though as one moves towards studying how traditional concepts are employed and modified in particular situations of action, one will approach the point where one's work shades into that of the historian of action as it is modified by thought. On the whole, however, one will tend to approach the history of political thought through studying the regular employment of relatively stable concepts; and it may seem as though this entailed the arbitrary choice of a certain level of abstraction from experience and tradition. But because one is investigating the process of abstraction itself, one is in a position to judge of the level to which it has been carried and to relate it to the social and traditional context from which it began; the choice is not an arbitrary one.

Any stable and articulate society possesses concepts with which to discuss its political affairs, and associates these to form groups or languages. There is no reason to suppose that a society will have only one such language; we may rather expect to find several, differing in the departments of social activity from which they originate, the uses to which they are put and the modifications which they undergo. Some originate in the technical vocabulary of one of society's institutionalized modes of regulating public affairs. Western political thought has been conducted largely in the vocabulary of law, Confucian Chinese in that of ritual. Others originate in the vocabulary of some social process which has become relevant to politics: theology in an ecclesiastical society, land tenure in a feudal society, technology in an industrial society.

As such vocabularies are increasingly used out of their original contexts, there may grow up corresponding languages of theory, designed to explain and defend their use in their new setting and relate them to terms of other origin similarly employed, and even languages of philosophy, designed to defend or criticize the ethical and logical intelligibility of the use of all these terms. But the advent of, say, a vocabulary of legal philosophy need not supersede the use in political discussion of the vocabulary of institutional law which the former was developed to defend; some political argument will be conducted at an institutional, some at a philosophical, level of abstraction. A comparable development occurs with the concepts used to denote the sources of legitimacy in a society, or to express the society's sense of its continuity with those sources; but here the process of abstraction produces different results. The criticism of a traditional account of society's continuity results in the writing of history. We reach a point at which a society possesses both a body of political theory and a manner of interpreting its history, yet where its traditions continue to be related, perhaps on more than one level of critical sophistication, as means of defending or denying the legitimacy of political behaviour, and thus figure among the modes in which its political thought is conducted.[5]

[5] See further J. G. A. Pocock, 'The Origins of Study of the Past: a comparative approach', *Comparative Studies in Society and History*, 4.2 (1962). [Chapter 9 in this volume.]

A society's political thought is built up largely in this way, by the adoption of technical vocabularies from different aspects of its social and cultural traditions and by the development of specialized languages in which to explain and defend the use of the former as means of discussing politics. We might call the former traditional languages, the latter theoretical languages, and it is tempting to add that political philosophy is never more than a theoretical language of a special kind, a second-order mode of discussing the intelligibility of all the other languages which may be in use. To say this, however, would be – from the historian's point of view – to underestimate the significance of political philosophy in the classical sense, which is found when a thinker mobilizes the principal moral and metaphysical ideas known to him with the intention of bringing political experience under their control and explaining it by their means.

Analysts may, indeed, hold that philosophers of this kind achieve no more than a critique and restatement of the political ideas traditional in their societies. But the historian must stress, first, that a tradition of this kind of philosophizing may provide a society with one of its languages of political discussion, and second, that it does not originate simply in the attempt to make existing languages more intelligible. A tradition of moral and metaphysical thinking may originate independently of political discussion and then be applied to it. Here, then, are at least two ways in which a language may develop capable of making statements about politics of greater generality than can normally be achieved by the simple adaptation of terms from other departments of social activity.

Once such languages have developed, thought about politics may become an autonomous theoretical activity and assume such forms as political philosophy or political science; and it may be supposed that the historian of political thought is the historian of these forms of autonomous theory. But once we define political thought as the language of political discussion, this cannot be so. For the practical and the theoretical are not separable, and the same political question may be discussed, at one and the same time, in a vocabulary adapted from social tradition and a vocabulary specialized for making universal statements about political association as such. When vocabularies of the latter kind appear, their claims may be investigated by the relevant methodologists, and it may be necessary to conduct this investigation historically – i.e. by tracing the development of their claims to elucidate certain types of problem. But the historian we are supposing is not a methodologist and there is no reason why we should confine ourselves to those branches of political thought which have been said to be autonomous theoretical sciences. A mode of political discussion for which this claim can be made is not intrinsically more interesting than one for which it cannot. We are interested in the presence of both in the vocabulary of a certain society, and in the relation of both to that society's traditions and developing experience.

The historian might approach the political thought of a society by observing, first, what modes of criticizing or defending the legitimacy of political behaviour were in existence, to what symbols or principles they referred, and in what language and by what forms of argument they sought to achieve their purposes. In late seventeenth-century England, for example, political behaviour could be discussed by reference to events which had occurred in three historical areas. First there was English constitutional history, whose authority as a guide in present affairs rested on certain ideas about legal continuity, themselves derived from the structure of English law and landed property. Then there was Old and New Testament history, deriving its authority from the ideas and procedures of the Christian church. Finally there was Greco-Roman history, whose authority arose from the ideas of Latin humanism. In addition to all these there was a body of classical political theory and philosophy, common to the thinkers of Western Europe generally, deriving its vocabulary from civilian and scholastic sources and from the arguments of this tradition's more recent critics. In studying the possession and use by Englishmen of these four distinctive modes of political argument, a historian would be doing work akin to that of Raymond Firth when he studied the use made by Tikopia of the traditions belonging to their several lineages, and the part these play in maintaining social solidarity or furthering social conflict.[6]

One would be studying the elements of its social structure and cultural traditions which a society chooses to keep in mind for purposes of validating social behaviour, and the language and ideas which are employed to see that these purposes are achieved. In studying the conceptualization of elements from a tradition, one would be conducting a systematic exploration in historical terms of what we have been meaning by 'abstraction from a tradition' – for merely to repeat, negatively, that political thought can only be such a form of abstraction is, in the last analysis, no more than conservative polemic. This historian is analysing the vague and compendious term 'tradition' into some of its elements, and noting which of them give rise to articulate languages which are themselves transmitted and used for purposes of discussion. No doubt, much of what a tradition most effectively transmits is inarticulate and unorganized, and it will be proper

[6] Raymond Firth, *Tikopia Tradition and History* (Wellington, 1961).

for the historian who so desires to follow Oakeshott in emphasizing the importance of the unspoken in shaping the tradition on which thought is a commentary. But the business of the historian of thought is to study the emergence and the role of the organizing concepts employed by society, and the knowledge that this role has necessary limitations need not deter us.

At this point in our studies, we are investigating how the ideas, in which consciousness of a tradition becomes articulate, were abstracted from that tradition, and are particularly concerned with the relationship between thought and the structure of society. Knowing of what elements in that structure men were conscious, and in what terms their consciousness was expressed, we are in a position to criticize the not uncommon fallacies which are committed when historians, assuming that political thought must be the 'reflection' of a social structure or political situation, construct a model of that structure or situation and proceed to explain the thought as in accordance with the model, though often unable to offer more than a vague congruency or parallelism in support of their claims. Our historian may agree that thought 'reflects' society and its interests. But we have made it our business to see how the process of 'reflection' takes place, and how far language is from a simple mirror of unmediated experience or aspiration.

We are, to put it in other terms, investigating the stereotypes of various elements in its structure and traditions with which a society conducts its political thinking. All stereotypes are, more or less, obsolete or otherwise inadequate; the historian gets used to the fact that the models of itself with which a society does its thinking often seem wholly unconvincing to a historian, seeking to understand that society from the standpoint of a later time. Eighteenth-century England was not governed solely by corruption and parties, but eighteenth-century Englishmen – and not only political propagandists – regularly talked and wrote as if it was. Why were these assumptions generally accepted? There is a gap between thinking and experience; but it is the business of the historian of political ideas to inhabit that gap and try to understand its significance. All stereotypes are, more or less, satisfactory as means to understanding and action; but we do not know why until we understand their history.

But not all the concepts used in a society's political discussion, or the languages based upon them, consist of simple stereotypes abstracted direct from society's structure and traditions. We have seen that the process of abstraction is a complex one, and that languages of increasing theoretical generality are built up from older traditional languages or intruded into the tradition from other sources. This is how a society's political thought comes to be conducted on more than one level of abstraction and to consist of languages of more than one degree of theoretical generality. The historian we are imagining has to cope with the situation that results and endeavour to render it intelligible; and this is the point at which, as we saw earlier, one encounters the temptation to search for underlying assumptions of the utmost theoretical generality on which all the varying languages in use can with equal satisfactoriness be explained. Given that this is a dangerous procedure – unless one can provide independent verification that these assumptions were in use as widely as the interpretation implies – we must now show how our ideal historian may escape adopting it.

To begin with, since one has grown familiar with the different languages of discussion that were in use, and the different levels of abstraction which they normally implied, one will be able to ascertain in which language and on which level a given controversy was conducted or a given thinker developed his or her ideas. One will be able to join Burke and Macaulay in considering whether the Revolution of 1688 was justified more in terms of historical precedent or of abstract political theory, and to consider whether Burke's traditionalism was based on a common lawyer's vision of immemorial custom or a German romantic's vision of the unfolding national *Geist*. It is of some importance to be able to interpret thought by placing it in the tradition of discourse to which it rightfully belongs; and this is so for two reasons. In the first place, it enables us to interpret thought as social behaviour, to observe the mind acting with relation to its society, that society's traditions and its fellow-inhabitants of that society. In the second place, it is of assistance in rendering thought intelligible to be able to identify the concepts which the thinker was handling and the language in which he was communicating with his fellow-men; what he was talking about and what he was taken to mean.

But as language employed in political discussion comes to be of increasing theoretical generality, so the persuasive success of the thinker's arguments comes to rest less on success in invoking traditional symbols than on the rational coherence of the statements being made in some field of political discourse where statements of wide theoretical generality are taken to be possible. Here, sooner or later, our historian must abandon the role of a student of thought as the language of a society, and become a student of thought as philosophy – i.e. in its capacity for making intelligible general statements. The advantage at this point of the approach we have supposed is this. Being familiar with the language of discussion which the thinker is employing one knows – one has 'got to know' – how it is normally employed and the degree of theoretical generality of the assumptions which it normally implies. Now, either by some technique of analysis or by some acquired familiarity with the way in which a particular theorist's mind works, one may attempt a reconstruction of the latter's thought to the extent to which it possesses rational completeness. In this way one may form an estimate of the degree and kind of theoretical generality with which the traditional language is being employed by the thinker one is studying – as well as of the problem the thinker was using it to solve and the prepossessions with which she or he was approaching the problem. The historian can now consider the level of abstraction on which the thinker's language tends to make one operate, and the level of abstraction on which the thinker's preoccupations tend to make one use one's language. We can now give some precision of meaning to the vague phrase: every thinker operates within a tradition; we can study the demands which thinker and tradition make upon each other.

If the traditional language which the thinker employs is one specialized for use upon the highest attainable level of generality, and the thinker's preoccupations impel him to operate on a similarly high level, then the historian's problems will be few and the method by which one interprets his subject's thought will be close to that by which a philosopher might interpret it. But it is implicit in the picture of political thought which has been given here, and in the definition of such thought as 'abstraction from a tradition', that this will not always happen and cannot be expected to go on happening for long. There may be a tradition of philosophical discussion of politics in a society; this tradition may be self-developing and need not be regarded as a mere analytical commentary on other modes of discussing politics. But in any complex society it is probable that politics will be discussed in too many languages and on too many levels of abstraction, and will raise too many problems directing thought to some particular language and level, to make it safe to predict that even the philosopher will succeed, any more than we ourselves do, in keeping thought at any one level of theoretical generality. To the extent that this is so, it will be found desirable to study political philosophy in the context of a tradition, consisting of a number of languages used in a given society for the discussion of politics; and the only alternative to anatomizing that tradition in the socio-linguistic way that has been suggested, seems to be the attempt to study it by converting it into a philosophy that has probably grown out of it or grown up in it.

CHAPTER 2

Working on ideas in time

It is easier to describe a style than to isolate and examine a specific piece of work in it. If the historian's life is a continuity, it must consist of the constant shaping of a pattern of thinking and inquiring, and this is especially true when his work involves, as mine does, a high concentration of theory. But to describe either the growth of a personal style, or moments in such a growth, cannot be done without yielding in some degree to the seductions of autobiography. The only justification I can claim for this is that my work has proved, somewhat against my will and certainly to my surprise, formally historicist. For over twenty years I have been increasingly interested in the ways in which men in political societies find and explore languages for conceptualizing their lives in such structures, and in the ways in which these languages carry patterns of thought about the continuity of society and politics in time and in history.

I see that this interest has since its beginnings been intimately related to a sense of my own position first between two cultures and then *vis-à-vis* a third – those of New Zealand, Britain and America – each with its own distinctive sense of a past, and between two academic disciplines, history and political science, each with its way of looking at the generation of ideas by men in society. A possible formula would be: I locate others in social time – this is history; I study how others located themselves in time – the study of historiography; this is related to the way in which I locate myself in time – the element of historicism. Yet this might mislead. I have always rather disliked historicism in the sense of the romantic self-creation of an identity in the historical flux because of its irrational and illiberal potentialities, and have tried to practise it only in the sense of a self-disciplined criticism of the historically given. In current intellectual fashion, it is considered both false and reactionary to assert that one can locate oneself in time by formal academic inquiry; but Apollo is alive and

[Published in L. P. Curtis Jr (ed.), *The Historian's Workshop* (New York: Knopf, 1971), pp. 153–65.]

living closer to his brother Dionysus than the maenads of California and New York imagine. What I wish to present, therefore, is far from being the record of another boring struggle for identity. I cannot offer any account of my work which is not an account of the long-term working out of a partly personal perspective; but the proportion between ego and cosmos has to be a proportion, and the perspective I aim to describe originates not merely in a personal and cultural problem, but in the need to practise certain self-testing intellectual disciplines. It is with the academic respectability of what I am doing that the readers of this book should be concerned.

The late Sir James Hight, under whom I studied in 1942–5, was a figure deserving and receiving veneration in what was then Canterbury University College in the University of New Zealand and is now (as he always held it should be) the University of Canterbury. He was not a very original teacher, but some indefinable grace of personality made it impossible to be in his presence for five minutes without knowing what scholarship was. Among his more easily identifiable achievements was the introduction, among the offerings of the department of history which he headed with one assistant, of courses in a subject known as political science. This statement is intended to exert a certain exotic charm upon American readers, but at the same time it has some functional importance: many of the themes I wish to treat contain the idea of the traversing of wide distances, both between cultures and between disciplines, and the successful establishment of homes and settlements upon distant shores. The two courses in political science – it fell to me in after years to enlarge, not to say explode, this syllabus into a full-scale departmental offering – each lasting for an academic year, consisted of a general survey of some notable contemporary governments (fewer in those days) and a historical survey of political philosophy of the kind still prescribed in many famous universities and wearily termed 'Plato to Nato' by my friends at Cambridge to this day. *In illo tempore* it consisted to all intents and purposes of a reading of the classic work of G. H. Sabine.[1]

Today, I find myself rather strongly committed to the view that Sabine's book is obsolete. His *History of Political Theory* does not seem to me to be a history at all, in the sense that it is not the history of any isolable and continuous human activity. And as a corollary, I insist, in both writing and teaching, that it is not possible to write any piece of the history of political thinking by his method of chronologically arranging philosophical systems. Nevertheless, I always urge students to read him; his book is a great American classic, an ideal among survey histories; and I see no reason why a

[1] G. H. Sabine, *History of Political Theory* (New York, 1937).

beginner even today should not get from him the sudden sense of discovery which I had during a course of evening lectures in 1943. I spent much of my time filling a large exercise book with a conflation of Hight's lecture notes and Sabine's survey, and as I wrote on and on, I had the sensation, still recoverable, of growing into something, like a snake feeling its new skin. I was, I suppose, discovering the tradition which it was to be my business to criticize; but the stages by which I discovered the need for such criticism and the techniques of it, like so many of the crucial moments in intellectual autobiography, evade recall. In that year, however, I can say that I acquired an enduring sympathy for the phenomenon of political discourse itself, for the intellect's attempt to construct an intelligible world out of the materials of political experience. But though my approach to the study of politics has remained a humanist one, and I select for study that aspect of politics in which it can be seen as an agent transforming human consciousness, a curious fact is that I have never seen the activities of the politicized consciousness primarily as the construction of a world-view, or become more than an amateur of political philosophy. What I suspect to be an incorrigibly rhetorical and verbal cast of mind has made me adhere to middle high politics, to those upper levels of political discourse where are generated many intellectual activities in addition to philosophy proper.

Four or five years later, when I was preparing to leave Canterbury to pursue a research degree at Cambridge, I had an honours degree in history and had taught it for over two years. I do not remember teaching much political thought during that time, yet when I sat down to propose a thesis subject in a letter from New Zealand to the Cambridge Board of Research Studies, it did not occur to me to propose one outside the history of thought. There are those for whom this is an independent subdiscipline – not long ago a publisher's representative tried in vain to sell me a new survey volume in intellectual history – but this had not figured in my work at Canterbury. I knew well enough that much in the history of political thought passed by the name of philosophy, but I had never taken a course in that subject, though I might have listened to the teaching of A. N. Prior if I had. During my honours year, I had listened with fascination to the lectures which Karl Popper, who passed the war years at Canterbury, was then developing into *The Open Society and Its Enemies*; but while these constituted a major intellectual experience, it was to be years before I saw the relevance of Popper's teaching to my own work. What I heard then seemed to me – as it was meant to – an account of disciplined inquiry which one need not be a philosopher to follow, and as for its stimulating my concern with intellectual history, I could see well enough that Popper's thought was inadequate history even if it was superb philosophy of method. If I search for other reasons why the direction of my interests was already irreversible, one other circumstance comes to mind that is relevant to what I am trying to say.

Imaginative writing in New Zealand, during the late thirties and forties, was not only more alive than it had ever been before, but a good deal more to my taste than it has ever been since. The poets and critics of the day (Allen Curnow, Rex Fairburn, Denis Glover), though they regarded themselves as a hard-drinking crew of iconoclasts, appear in retrospect somewhat Georgian, perhaps because an education at the fag-end of a transplanted English style – which I shared – had given them a concern with literary tradition and its relation to the environment that subsequent educational democratization has led many to insist presents no problem at all. Theirs was a pastoral landscape, its soil eroded by too many real sheep; and they explored the theme of the creative imagination confronting a land where human occupancy was not more than a thousand years old and English civilization with its books not more than a hundred. 'The land was ours before we were the land's' tended to become a statement in the present tense, and it was possible to make distinctions among the imagination of South Pacific islanders like ourselves and those of the English, fed by a sense of tradition even when quarrelling with it, the Americans, for whom settlement in a new land went with a series of revolutionary transformations and compulsive commitments, or even the Australians, with whom a populist nationalism maintained a mythology of the Outback which we did not share. New Zealand culture seemed sure to remain oceanic, transitory, looking obliquely toward its derivations, and the problem was that of making some sort of harmony and vitality for oneself in these conditions. History and myth, which we were told to consider necessities, were, irrevocably, other people's; we were not going to generate much of our own, and the fact of poetry was there to remind us that the creative imagination existed and must find ways of working.

The poetry written in this style is still very much in my bones, and since it clearly presented the problem of the historical imagination in an unhistoric land, I suspect that it had a good deal to do with shaping the interests I describe.[2] When about this time I read Toynbee, I recall writing a juvenile essay in which I employed *yang* and *yin* to denote, respectively, the historical and poetic imagination – it is a curious fact that most of those who have written histories of New Zealand have also written poetry, though I

[2] [See further J. G. A. Pocock, *The Discovery of Islands: essays on British history* (Cambridge, 2005).]

have done neither – and the unhistoric landscape, neither humanized by cultivation nor devastated by extraction, which the plains and mountains of the South Island imprinted on the eye. A year or two later I was to find the intensely humanized landscape of southern England actually oppressive; I wanted to get back to the shingle rivers; and yet *yang*, if my construction had any meaning, was giving me an enduring interest in the intellectual, imaginative, and mythical representations of history which were other people's. There was a solution to be found in eclecticism, if the methods of selection and study could be made strong enough to build on.

When, at any rate, I considered what to propose as a Cambridge dissertation, all that occurred to me had to do with the mythical element in historical thought. I was rash enough to toy with the notion of studying myth in the philosophy of Marx, but by great good fortune, and as a result of thought processes of which I can remember nothing at all, suggested instead that I should write about anti-Normanism in the thought of the English Levellers. I heard that I had been accepted and that Herbert Butterfield was to be my supervisor; I wrote to him from Canterbury, and he replied that a good deal had been done on anti-Normanism, but that there were some interesting manifestations of rather similar thought of a conservative and royalist kind from the later seventeenth century. He thought I might be interested in studying them.

The work I then began to do was ultimately published under the title of *The Ancient Constitution and the Feudal Law*.[3] It is further described as 'a study of English historical thought in the seventeenth century', but I find it important to stress that 'historical thought' is not the same thing as 'historiography'. One of the book's heroes, Robert Brady, seems to have sensed this when he observed in the preface to his *An Introduction to the Old English History*, 'Histories I know are written after another manner.' He meant to differentiate between his critical and interpretative (and political and polemical) writings and the construction of formal written narratives, and though this distinction can no longer be upheld, it has been a central theme of my work that the beginnings and growth of historical consciousness are often to be found not in the writings of works formally entitled 'histories', but in the modes of thought which entail an image of a past and its relation to the present.

On one level, it can be said that the work I have been doing ever since has been directed at discovering how these conceptualized 'pasts' arise, and how

[3] J. G. A. Pocock, *The Ancient Constitution and the Feudal Law* (Cambridge, 1957, and New York, 1967). Reissued with a retrospect, Cambridge, 1987.

thought about their relationship to the present attains a degree of critical autonomy which makes it what we call 'history'. I indeed think that Western historical consciousness has developed through the increase of this kind of critical ability, at least as much as through the formulation of Augustinian or Hegelian philosophies of history. But there are other levels. One of the most important thought-modes through which images of the past and its relation to the present arise and are criticized is thought directed at political legitimation. The sources of authority in a political society may be located in the past, or they may be said to consist in its continuity. In either case, where there is a sense of institutional structure and an argument concerning what is legitimate and what are the sources of legitimacy, there can arise a critical reconstruction so drastic that the past is discovered to have existed in its own right and not as a mere extension of the authority structure of the present. This, as Butterfield had pointed out before I began work, had happened in seventeenth-century England; and at one time I thought of calling my book, in a pastiche of the seventeenth-century manner, *Historico-politicus Anglicanus*.

In other words, I was still engaged in the study of political thought, of which historical thought might be a branch and historical consciousness a product; but this raised the further question, what is political thought? In the mode I was studying, it was neither political theory nor political philosophy, though it might be immanent in both; and what I was able to learn about the concept of ideology seemed to me no more accurate as a description of its character. Though I doubt if I knew it at this period, I was in need of new concepts and theories for defining the phenomena which occurred, the activity which went on, when men in political societies engaged in systematic discourse and debate about political society as they knew it and as part of their life in it. I was on the way to formulating such concepts when I realized, as I increasingly did, that the mode of thought with which I was mainly concerned could be characterized as a rhetoric, a universe of discourse, a language. Englishmen of the seventeenth century were litigious animals; they spent much time in the courts of common law, which regulated their property system, their social structure, and its distribution of power. They consequently spoke of all these things – and in speaking, identified and administered them – in the language of the common law. This language was more than a regulative terminology; it was heavy with assumptions, and these were applied, both consciously and unconsciously, to the social and political complex about which it was used. The central assumption was that law was custom, and custom immemorial; the social and political complex was therefore assumed to be immemorial in the same way and on the same grounds. In this way arose the concept and myth of the ancient constitution, against which the most original scholars of the seventeenth century developed their energetic criticisms. At a later date I was able to identify this language, and the consequences of using it, in the works of Edmund Burke; not only did it play a cardinal role in the formulation of some of Burke's most important thoughts, but Burke himself could be seen explicitly alluding to the existence of the common-law language of politics as a fact in the making of English history.[4]

What I was coming to see was that the history of political ideas, the history of political thought considered as an activity, could very conveniently be treated as the history of political language or languages. Various conceptual vocabularies, styles of discourse or modes of thought exist, in varying degrees of formalization, in the structure of a political society. They are used by the inhabitants of that society to articulate the various utterances – the emphasis here is on the more highly formalized types of utterance – to which men are moved in the course of political life. These languages originate in various ways – the common-law language is a case of one formed out of the specialized vocabulary of a governing institution – and their content varies both explicitly and implicitly. It can be shown that any political language carries assumptions and implications in excess of those which can be made articulate at any one moment, and a significant part of what we call political theory consists less in attempts to erect a consistent theory of politics than in attempts to follow up and explore the implications which, under the stress of political debate, action, and choice, the language articulating a society to itself has been seen to possess. These implications may carry the mind, and specialize its workings, in many directions. The common-law language was particularly rich in implications suggesting the past of society, and clearly not all political languages will carry implications of that sort; but it also carried implications concerning the nature and limits of political action and knowledge; and it is remarkable how often political languages carry such implications, suggesting also, as these did, ideas concerning time as the dimension or continuum of action and knowledge.

My style of work, then, is one in which I identify languages of political conceptualization, select patterns of implication which they may bear, and try to trace the working out of these implications in the history of thought. It requires both historical sensitivity and sensitivity to patterns of political

[4] ['Burke and the Ancient Constitution: a problem in the history of ideas', *Historical Journal*, 3.2 (1960); reprinted in *Politics, Language and Time: essays on political thought and history* (New York, 1971; Chicago, 1989), pp. 202–32.]

behaviour – conceptualization, argument, and theorizing all being forms of political behaviour of a rather special sort. But since the root concept of the whole proceeding as I have experienced and described its growth is that of language, it requires above all a sensitivity to language of a kind which links it to the criticism of literature on one flank, as its political character links it to the criticism of the other. The beginnings of my interest in these matters, as I have attempted to depict them in the foregoing autobiographical case study – the reading of Sabine and so on – lay, it seems, in a high sensibility to language as the bearer of thought which stopped short of becoming an interest in the formalization of thought that might have made a philosopher of me.

Historians, I think with J. H. Hexter, are and should be rhetoricians rather than logicians. Needless to say, rhetoricians have to be logical. I have been helped as a historian, whatever it might have done to me as a philosopher, by exposure to that school of the fifties which held that philosophy could be no more than a working out of the possibilities of language. This, and the teachings of Popper concerning the logic of inquiry, have counterpointed, in a way perhaps confused, but to me fruitful, an earlier enthusiasm for the writings of R. G. Collingwood. It will be recalled that Collingwood was understood to say that all history was the history of thought and that the aim of the historian was to rethink the thoughts of the men he was studying. Plainly, this is easier to accept when the history one is studying *is* the history of thought as an overt and formal activity, and I am certain that a Collingwoodian adolescence helped me greatly later on in formulating the idea of effecting re-entry into the linguistic universes of the past. But at the same time I was always fully aware that total recall was beyond the historian's powers, and that he 'rethought' the ideas of men in the past by erecting an explanatory structure through which he could restate them in a language of his own designed to reconstruct, and in that sense to clarify, the language in which they had been stated. Popper, stressing that every scientific hypothesis entailed a statement of the conditions of its own validity, and T. D. Weldon, proclaiming that the business of the philosopher was to make statements about statements, in various ways assisted the formulation of the idea that the historian of thought aimed at finding out what had been said and restating it in language which defined the language in which it had been said. But I divert attention from the logical structure of the original statement to its rhetorical and socio-linguistic context, as I think any historian must do. That context – the linguistic universe – has to be reconstructed historically; and if any language structure consists of an indefinite number of possible meanings, implications, and consequences, of which no speaker at a given moment can be fully aware, the historian has an alarming degree of liberty as to the direction in which he will pursue the possible meanings and consequences of what the speaker said. He must not only reconstruct; he must also select and assume.

At another level, I was aided throughout by the fact that as a student I had been enormously interested in acting – though happily never good enough to fail at it – and had thought a great deal about doctrines of the mask and the anti-self. The actor constructs, out of and at some distance from his own personality and that of Shakespeare's Hamlet, a Hamlet through whom he mediates and communicates between Shakespeare and his audience, while remaining himself an indestructibly original contributor to the communication. Since those days, of course, the theatre, like so much else, has gone in for the abolition of individuality, but this is a tedious if necessary interlude through which we must make our way. Apollo and Dionysus are both gods of the theatre, and the Apollonian view of acting, which I learned, has left me with an ineradicable conviction that historical reconstruction is possible through mask-like structures of explanation which communicate as they conventionalize, as well as with an absolute refusal of philosophies which aver that communication is impossible and the self non-existent. Even a bad actor knows better than that. He knows that his distinctness from the work he creates is what relates him to it, so that the cruder forms of alienation have little meaning for him; and this has considerable relevance to what goes on in the 'workshop' of the kind of historian I am describing.

The historian of theory spends his time absorbing other people's theoretical language and reproducing it in a language of his own designed to reveal its historical character. The historical events he studies are events in the history of conceptualization. His characteristic workshop activity, then, is reading, thinking, and writing aimed at carrying himself and his readers back from the concept as articulated to the process of conceptualization, and at finding out what it was that happened, what events in human consciousness occurred, when and as conceptualization and articulation took place. There are not many ancillary skills to this, and their role, while at any time it may prove important, is not constant or continuous. For this reason, such a historian will not surround himself with apparatus. He needs, of course, access to the best library he can find, since the keys to what he is looking for may often be found in writings so obscure that even he has come upon them by accident (he will probably prefer open stacks to the best system of information retrieval that can be designed); but he may well end by basing his pattern of explanation on a quite limited selection of sources, and – if he knows how to do it properly – he may do no more with these sources than sit and read, sit and think, sit and write.

In the very complex process of combining abstractions so that they become a recognizable account of the process of abstraction as occurring in historic reality, it is above all the historian's use of his own language that must keep the relations between abstraction and reality clearly visible, and his account of these relations a piece of history. For this reason, the task of learning to think in this way draws very close indeed to the task of learning to write; it is in the construction of sustained explanatory prose that the Collingwoodian process of rethinking takes place. Historians, especially in America, are traditionally supposed to surround themselves with stacks and files of note cards, but I do not think I have ever used one. Instead, I read – books, microfilms, manuscripts or whatever – and as I read, I try to digest what I read into the constantly growing and changing patterns of re-presentation and explanation which I have to develop and expound. Pieces of detective work aimed at finding out who wrote it and when, or whether there was an earlier version, sometimes come my way, but they are ancillary tasks; the individuals of my story are paradigms rather than people, concepts whose changing use is best traced by constructing models of long-term change. Theory is prior to narrative – or rather, there is a constant process of devising, using, and improving such models of change that takes place in the sustained refinement of the inner rhetoric of one's teaching, writing, and thinking. This is another reason why it would be virtually impossible to write the history of an isolated piece of work from start to finish; each is a thread in a constantly reworked pattern.

A lesson I had to learn early – the earlier one learns it the better – was that much of the process of digestion and rearrangement of ideas, alteration and sharpening of perspectives, takes place in the supposedly irrational subconscious. The circuits of the brain must learn to carry great stores of highly verbalized and conceptualized information which can be recovered – and recovered, so to speak, with the right one of a thousand facets uppermost – at a moment's notice. I sometimes, though not often, spend weeks translating, or simply transcribing, passages of an important book which is not in my permanent possession. To perturbed enquirers who want to know why I am not making photocopies instead, I reply that I am getting the structure and movement of the book's argument into my bones, and that this is not a process which can be mechanized. What matters is not simply what the brain does with the information after it has been loaded into it, but the shape in which the information is processed while it is being loaded; and my apparently antiquated procedure may at times be the most efficient way of processing information while on the in-channels.

'Processing the verbiage *in situ*', as the Archfiend Belphegor calls it in Michael Ayrton's splendid *Tittivulus*,[5] renders the pattern of my working life at once simple and complex. When I feel ready to begin interpreting an author, a controversy or the history of a cluster of modes of thought, I sit down with an untidy sufficiency of books and notes, the beginnings of an expository pattern in my brain, and begin writing. Like most writers, I have a number of physical fads: the paper must be soft, the ink blue and the nib metal. I cannot construct decent prose on a typewriter, and there has come to be an association in my mind between the unwinding of a skein of thought and the long, essentially unbroken, looped and twisted line of regular cursive hand-writing. I must cast about once or twice for a suitable rhetorical exordium, and then the patterns will begin to develop as the sentences and paragraphs take shape.

This means that the units of thought, if such a term has any meaning, are lengthy passages of expository prose. One does not – at least I do not – revise one's written argument as one goes along, clause by clause or sentence by sentence, filling the page with emendations and refinements. If the work is going well, the prose comes of itself. I go on writing until my argument seems to have lost its way or run out of steam; to say that I know when this has happened because the pen falls from my nerveless hand would be to exaggerate, but a strong physical disinclination to go on writing is one of the symptoms. I now go back to the last point at which the argument seems to me to have been running authoritatively, and begin again at the top of that page of the manuscript, throwing away several (sometimes many) sheets of clearly written, carefully composed, uncorrected handwriting. If I do this several times and am still bogged down in the same section of the argument, I am aware that there is something wrong at a level deeper than I had realized.

I was years learning to master this syndrome – it is much more than a technique. When I wrote my first article for a professional journal, I sat every day for eight weeks in my room in a council house in an unpleasant place in the north of England, surrounded by a growing pile of discarded manuscript, none of which I dared throw away, and wondering in all seriousness whether I was heading for a nervous breakdown. I think people have suffered worse than breakdown in similar circumstances. The terrifying element in such an experience is not that you suddenly become aware

[5] [Michael Ayrton, *Tittivulus, or The Verbiage Demon* (London, Max Reinhardt, 1953).]

that you are writing nonsense. Your prose and your thought seem as clear and as close-textured as they did before, you cannot find a logical flaw in what you have written, and yet the effort to continue creating what is, after all, an impersonal extension of your self becomes more and more intolerable until you physically cannot go on. *Es geht nicht.* If you try again and again, and each time reach the same point of self-exhausting clarity about the same stage in your argument, the experience is much more frightening than mere bewilderment or confusion can ever be. It is the contrast between the apparent clarity of your thought and its exhaustion and failure that is intolerable, and here you must – like a mystic whose meditation has gone wrong – break off altogether, and resist the first impulse to start again. I am convinced, though I cannot prove it, that scholars have driven themselves to suicide by going back for one more try at a recalcitrant piece of writing.

Once you have learned to break off and go away from the work for hours or days or longer, the unconscious processes of digestion, aided a little by carefully timed thrusts and pressures from the conscious levels, may be left to do the rearrangement of your thoughts for you. I use the word rearrangement, though it is rather a weak term for what goes on, to indicate that it is a new pattern which is needed and must be allowed – and trusted – to emerge. There is an awareness of sudden release – accompanied sometimes, in my experience, by a physical sensation that the locus of tension has shifted from the forehead to the diaphragm – which signals the return of creativity and a strong and confident impulse to begin writing again. At this point it will usually be found that the concepts and data have rearranged themselves to form a pattern with the potential for growth in it that was lacking before. Sometimes one discovers that what was at the end should have been at the beginning, or vice versa. The order of analysis is not the order of exposition, but the transformation from thought that was clear but sterile to thought that is concrete and fertile is more radical than the foregoing words indicate. I can only compare it to the transition from negative to positive in photographic development. Each image is as clear as the other, but only one inhabits the same daylight as yourself. And this is also the moment – to resume the Collingwoodian exposition – at which another man's thought has become your own, and you have begun to expound it in a way which constitutes historical interpretation. You are both identified with and detached from it. There is a *paradoxe sur le comédien* to be used in understanding historiography, and the actor in a university theatre has not been useless to the historian of political thought.

The workshop I have described is, defiantly, that of a latter-day scribe: a man, that is, employing highly sophisticated scribal techniques to interpret the thought of men who lived and wrote in early Gutenberg cultures. I do not work on ideas or writers before 1500 or after 1800, though these limitations are in part accidental and do not seem to me rigorously dictated by my techniques. It may well be, however, that these methods would be less appropriate to study of the thought of men who were not primarily writers of books. I do not claim to know the inwardness – the almost tactile reality – of the thought revealed in newspaper editorials or the television techniques of African demagogues, and my friends who ask me why I do not conduct content analyses with the aid of computers may well be making a point of substance with regard to these or other structures of verbal communication.

If I can think only as I write, it is possible that I can only deal adequately with the thought of men for whom the same was true. But this would not matter very much. The Gutenberg era was a great era in the history of human thought, and in any but a totally barbarized future we shall constantly be going back to it, in search not merely of its thought-patterns, but of its structures of individuality. And to study it as it was is a mode of being valid for the electronic here and now; the inhabitant of my workshop is no Luddite. The fact that men in the Gutenberg era wrote their books with their own hands before they were printed – even Franklin's philosophy was probably not set up direct from a tray of type – should remind us that in a complex culture many historical levels may be present and operative together, and the gloomiest vision possible of an electronic future does not depict a world in which books will vanish. They will survive, and methods of study not unlike my own will survive, because they are necessities for the survival of individuality. An ability to criticize tradition enabled Renaissance man to locate himself in the time flow, and the survival of individuality under electronic bombardment will depend on the development of means of holding up the incessant stream of communication and giving ourselves time to think. Books will survive, it might be said, as spanners in the networks; the printed page and the printed book are the most reliable means yet devised of ensuring that we have the chance to take a second and third look at what someone is trying to sell us. It is for this reason that one historian in his highly unmechanized workshop is able to regard himself as a modern man and a reasonably militant one – a code-breaker.

CHAPTER 3

Verbalizing a political act: towards a politics of speech

In this paper I propose to talk about both the verbalization *of* a political act and verbalization itself *as* a political act. I shall not withhold a measure of sympathy from those who feel that there are simply too many words floating around already, and that the nöosphere is in danger of becoming as badly polluted as the atmosphere, biosphere, and geosphere. A man in Los Angeles said to me: 'You're under no obligation to verbalize your life-style'; and on the way down life's staircase since, it has occurred to me that the proper answer would have been: 'A very strong inner compulsion at least; and I suspect that Thomas Hobbes could even have found an obligation.' There have been schools of political philosophy whose doctrine was founded on the rejection of the word; I think I know of two such in ancient China. The Confucians held that shared patterns of ritualized behaviour communicated and internalized values more harmoniously and with fewer contradictions than did verbal imperatives; while the Taoists withdrew in disgust from the monstrous edifice of fictions, confusions, and lies which words entailed, to pursue an anti-politics of transcendence.[1] But it seems that both schools were reacting, from different sides, against the discovery that it was next to impossible to construct any verbal statement in terms such that it could not be refuted or distorted. Refutability was to the Confucians a stumbling-block and to the Taoists foolishness; but there has been enough of Karl Popper in my upbringing to commit me to the view that refutability *macht frei*. I shall in due course argue that it is the imperfect character of verbal statements which renders them answerable and human communication possible, and that there may be said to exist a Hobbesian kind of obligation to verbalize my acts toward my

[Published in *Political Theory*, 1.1 (1973), pp. 27–44. An earlier version was delivered to the Conference for the Study of Political Thought, meeting at the Graduate Center of the City University of New York in April 1971.]

[1] J. G. A. Pocock, *Politics, Language and Time: essays on political thought and history* (New York: Atheneum, 1971; Chicago: University of Chicago Press, 1989), ch. 2.

neighbour so that he may have the opportunity of answering them; and I shall say this in the context of a consideration of politics itself as a language-system and language itself as a political system. I ought also to say at this stage that I do not claim competence in theoretical linguistics and that those who have such competence may well be able to correct me. And although my politics will initially develop as a classical structure of shared power, I shall – in order to make it quite clear that it is power that is being shared – start with a consideration of words as actions and as acts of power towards persons.

Shakespeare's Brutus declares – and it is significant that he does so in a soliloquy:

> Between the acting of a dreadful thing
> And the first motion, all the interim is
> Like a phantasma or a hideous dream
> (*Julius Caesar*, II.i.63–5)

R. G. Collingwood[2] argued with characteristic ingenuity that 'the acting' meant the initial conception and 'the first motion' the first step in actual performance. The point need not be settled in order to realize its significance, which is that the framing of the intention is part of the total process of the act. English treason law, of which Shakespeare will have been thinking, used to insist that to 'compass or imagine' the death of the king was as treasonable as to kill him, and the point was not entirely unsound; but the law used further to insist on two witnesses to an overt act as proof even of the compassing or imagining. Words, however, might well be taken as proof of the act of intention, and this step takes us near the heart of the complexities of our subject. But unless some zealous agent has bugged the garden where Brutus utters his soliloquy, he is not at this moment acting by communicating his intention to others; he is talking to himself. Given the ambiguity of speech as both expression and communication, both a private and a public act, it is appropriate to begin a study of the politics of verbalization with a man in a moment of self-communion.

The words quoted indicate to us what Brutus is doing. He is trying to escape from a hideous dream by verbalizing his action to himself, and this means two things: verbalizing his intention to act, and verbalizing the quality of the act he intends (which is, *inter alia*, to provide it with a rationale). Under the first aspect, verbalization is immediately performative: by saying 'I intend to kill Caesar', Brutus confirms – he completes forming – that

[2] R. G. Collingwood, *The New Leviathan* (Oxford: Clarendon Press, 1942), p. 97.

intention, and this performance is part of a series of performances which constitute the totality of the act of killing Caesar. It is at present part of the hideous dream that Brutus does not know for sure that he is really going to kill Caesar, or that he really intends or wants to kill him, until he hears himself say that he intends to do so. This is why he is talking to himself; the communication is part of the performance. But under the second aspect, verbalization is much more complex though still in part performative. Brutus may now say: 'I intend to kill Caesar because he is a tyrant', and this utterance is more than simply explanatory or justificatory. 'Caesar is a tyrant' is an assertion, an act of definition, not the simple recital of a previously accepted datum. In defining Caesar as a tyrant, Brutus is not only justifying the act he intends, but is also qualifying it; he is saying that to kill Caesar is to kill a tyrant, so that what he intends when he says 'I intend' is 'to kill a tyrant'. The statement 'Caesar is a tyrant' and the implication 'it is right to kill tyrants' are both present and may perhaps be articulated and further explored; but equally they may be left behind, embedded in the structure of the utterance in such a way that it will become increasingly hard to go back and examine them. Brutus may subconsciously intend to make it hard for himself to do this, given that throughout the utterance he is engaged in burning his boats. But the assertions and the assumptions he is found to have been making are in no case separate from the formation of an intention by verbalization. In qualifying the intention, they help make it by making it what it is, and so form part of – and help form – both the immediate and the prospective performance, even though none of them by itself may constitute a performative statement.

But the intention and the performance require, to give them meaning, the sort of qualifying context which the words invoke; they require it for reasons lying deeper than even the need for justification. In using so potent a word as 'tyrant', Brutus invokes a whole world of reference structures, into which his other words, his intended act, and his verbalized state of consciousness now enter in such a way that it qualifies them all; so that 'Caesar', 'kill', 'intend' and even 'I' take on new meanings retrodictively as they enter the world that 'tyrant' invokes. Because of the magic quality of speech, the worlds you invoke are very likely to appear around you. Speech acts of this kind are notoriously difficult to revoke – not least so, perhaps, as Brutus may very well intend, when uttered in soliloquy. For the hideous dream, they substitute what is verbalized and presented as a terrible reality.

Brutus is using language; he is communicating with a hearer, who happens to be himself. He is acting upon himself – the first person 'I' – by forming his intention as an act of verbalization; but this he does by communicating information concerning that intention to a second person – himself as hearer – who is in turn acted upon by being made the receiver of information which is bound, as it is intended, to modify his perceptions of the world. In archaic and formal English, a communication of information was sometimes introduced by the imperative verb 'Know that', and the message would follow; the imperative left no doubt that to inform might be to act upon and to command. If we imagine Brutus communicating his intention to a second person existing independently – let us say his wife – the situation would be complicated by the immediacy of her self-willed responses, which would immediately modify Brutus's perception of his intention through perceiving her perception of it. But let us not exaggerate the scale of this complication; in the first place, Brutus's message would be designed to predetermine Portia's response to it; and, in the second place, I used to give a lecture entitled 'Playback, or you never know who's listening', with the theme that in any message you had always one auditor – yourself – whose responses might be those you could least determine or predict. Meanwhile, at a distance, a third person – Caesar – is being acted upon in two ways: he is being defined in the imparted perceptions of the first and second persons (a) as the object of an intended act, 'killing'; and (b) as the sort of person, 'tyrant', who qualifies the act as the sort of act it is henceforth intended and understood to be. Verbalizations, we now see, act upon people – and so constitute acts of power – in at least two ways: either by informing them and so modifying their perceptions, or by defining them and so modifying the ways in which they are perceived by others. Either of these acts of power may be entirely unilateral and arbitrary: performed, that is, by the will of one person only.

In discussing verbalization *of* an act as part of the act performed, we have also begun discussing verbalization *as* an act or performance – indeed, an assertion of power – in its own right; that is to say, we have examined the relation of 'means' to 'ends' in examining the intention as part of the action. We will also be considering the relation of 'theory' to 'practice' if we imagine Brutus pausing – as he does pause – to explore and clarify the meanings and implications of the words he is using; but to set up this relation as a worthwhile problem we shall have to suppose that clarification of language may become an intended act distinguishable from the intended act which the language has been verbalizing. If we imagine primary verbalizations of intent which constitute practice and concerning which the former are made, then theory must be seen as re-entering the complex of verbalization, intention, communication, and action which constitutes what we call practice. But, in introducing the distinction between first-order and second-order verbalizations, we have introduced another problem, of equal if not greater importance.

Brutus's language is not his own. He would be unable to talk about it if it were composed purely and exclusively of his declarations of his intentions. He has been asserting, or defining, his intentions, his role, and the roles of second and third persons, and acting upon all three, in a language which he has not made, but which consists largely of the sedimentation and institutionalization of speech acts performed by other persons, upon other persons, and with other intentions.[3] Very complex processes of assumption, mediation, and conventionalization have gone on to bring this language to him as a structure of givens, and, as a result, it is usually not possible to say with simple factuality what their authors intended the speech acts originally fed into the language to effect; who meant what by them. For this very reason, Brutus's language is not his own; he did not make it and he does not know who did, and given – what for a variety of reasons we must concede – that there is much implicit in language which becomes explicit only when it is explored after being used, a consequence for Brutus is that, in willing to impose a variety of roles upon himself and others, he is discovered to have been entering into a most complex collaborative fiction with co-authors whose names, intentions, and communicative devices are removed from him along an ever-receding series of mediations. Each of us speaks with many voices, like a tribal shaman in whom the ancestor ghosts are all talking at once; when we speak, we are not sure who is talking or what is being said, and our acts of power in communication are not wholly our own. Theory may be said to consist in attempts to answer questions of this order, to decide what power is being exercised over us when we seek to exercise it.

At this point, it becomes possible – though only, I think, on Platonic, puritan, romantic or existentialist grounds – to accuse Brutus of bad faith. To assert his intention, role or identity in language made up of others' assertions of their intentions, roles and identities is to allow his act of power to be taken over by the ghosts and to disguise their power as his; he is accepting a false identity, subjecting himself to an alien power, and allowing it to be supposed that the alien agency is his active self. To reduce speech acts to acts of power is to point toward this result, because power is desperately hard to reconcile with fiction or with identification with another. I cannot say that another's power is my power; I may indeed own that another's power is to be treated *as if* it were my power, but how I come

[3] P. L. Berger and T. Luckmann, *The Social Construction of Reality* (New York: Doubleday, 1966).

to perform this is one of the darkest mysteries in *Leviathan* (I, 16). Brutus, then, is saying 'this is mine' when actually what he is saying is another's. He is performing a fiction. But the accusation of bad faith is valid only if he does not know or will not admit that he is performing a fiction or that the conditions of utterance are such that the fiction he intends to perform cannot be the fiction he is performing. The language he uses is not of his own making; it has been made by others. But if he knows to the full what others have intended – or, to telescope the whole series of mediations in a single metaphor, what is intended – by the language he uses, then he knows to the full what the action is that he intends by means of fiction to perform; whereas if – as is far more probable – he knows that he does not know fully what his language means, then he knows that he does not know the full meaning of the act he intends; and theory becomes the honest exploration of the limits of his intention and action, the pursuit of the Socratic and Confucian wisdom of 'knowing what one does not know'. It is, of course, difficult to be, or to endure being, as conscious of one's medium as this; but it is mere intellectual snobbery, posing as anti-intellectualism, to pretend that the number of people who can be so is insignificant.

At this level, too, what appeared to be Brutus's disguising of others' power as his own may become his acceptance of others' power as a qualification and limitation of his own. I want next to put forward a picture of language operating, as a two-way communication system, to transform the unilateral assertion of power in action into the shared exercise of power in a polity. I shall be saying that there is polity where people succeed in communicating – that is, in making and replying to statements in such a way that there is some not too remotely discernible relationship and continuity of medium between statement, reply, and counter-reply – and I shall postpone consideration of the somewhat too easily rhetorized situations which exist when this is not the case.

I shall continue to assume that humans communicate by means of language, and that language consists of a number of already formed and institutionalized structures. These embody and perform speech acts, but they perform the intentions of the user only through words formed by sedimentation and institutionalization of the utterances performed by others whose identities and intentions may no longer be precisely known. There is a double sense, then, in which the words that perform my acts are not my own: in the first place, they are words used by others and only borrowed by me, and in the second place, they have been institutionalized to the point where they cannot finally be reduced to the speech acts of known individuals. My acts, therefore, have been preinstitutionalized; they must be performed by institutionalized means. But language-structures which have been institutionalized are available for use by more than one person, operating with more than one purpose and in more than one situation; they are never free from ambiguity in the sense that they can never be reduced to the performance of any one person's intention. To perform my speech act I must borrow another's, and he was in exactly the same predicament; all verbalized action is mediated. But next, institutionalization makes my language available to the person to or about whom I speak for purposes of reply and refutation; he can, as we put it, answer me in my terms. Communication rests upon ambiguity. From the premise of institutionalization, it follows both that we can never fully understand one another (or even ourselves) and that we can always answer one another (and in soliloquy, we can answer ourselves). There is a certain refraction and recalcitrance in the medium which ensures that the language I bend to perform my own acts can be bent back in the performance of others' acts against me, without ceasing to be available for my counter-replication. Language gives me power, but power which I cannot fully control or prevent others from sharing. In performing a verbalized act of power, I enter upon a polity of shared power.

Two incidents in *Alice Through the Looking Glass* (chs. 4 and 9) would seem to be making this point. Humpty Dumpty, as is well known, avers that 'when I use a word, it means what I want it to mean, neither more nor less . . . The question is who is to be master, that's all'. This poor being is in the linguistic equivalent of a Hobbesian state of nature; it has not occurred to him that words subject to one person's totally arbitrary control may become unintelligible to those hearing them, and so of very little use for purposes even of mastery. As his conversation with Alice develops, he is increasingly unable to retain the master's posture and is forced to resort to obfuscation. 'Impenetrability! That's what I say.' Finally Alice gets tired of him and simply walks away, and as she does so he falls off his wall. At a later stage in the story, the Red Queen remarks, 'When you've said a thing, that fixes it and you must take the consequences.' Without going too deeply into her use of the word 'fixes', we can interpret her as meaning that to use language at all, you must make commitments. You have not merely performed upon yourself; you are inescapably perceived as having performed in ways defined by others' acceptances of the words you have used. You have performed upon them, but the means by which you have performed are in some degree not at your power but at theirs. An act of power verbalized is, in this perspective, an act of power mediated and mitigated.

There is, of course, one fairly evident possible flaw in this presentation, and I will come to that. First, however, I need to explore some further theoretical implications of the perspective in which language is seen as uncontrolled by any single or isolable agency; we rest this assertion on the premise that language is institutional. Institutionalization breeds ambivalence, or rather multivalence. Where Humpty Dumpty went wrong was in averring that his words meant what he wanted them to mean, 'neither more nor less'. In language, it must be declared, we have to be content with saying both less and more than we mean: less, because our language will never immediately convey our meaning or perform our acts of power; more because it will always convey messages and involve us in consequences other than those we intended. And it is our willingness to be involved in these unintended consequences, to commit ourselves to what others may make of our words, our intentions, our performances, and our *esse* as *percipi*, that makes communication and even action possible. I am clearly not presenting language as a neutrally objective medium, though I will at need argue from these premises that there are neutral and objective operations that can be performed with it. This theory of language is essentially Clausewitzian. Clausewitz perceived that it was the relative non-conductivity of the medium in which violence was conducted that made it conceivable that war might be conducted as an intelligent, and so intelligible, communicative, political mode of behaviour. Because there were frictions between my intention and its performance – because, that is, I was not Humpty Dumpty – I had a problem in relating means to ends. To that problem I might intelligently address myself; my adversary, perceiving and interpreting my actions, might infer from them what my ends and means were; and I might direct my actions towards him as messages of a special sort designed to influence his will, as he might do to me. We entered the chess-playing stage, of seeking to impose strategies on one another by means of symbolic communications which were also acts of power; and none of this would have been possible had either of us possessed the power of immediately performing our intentions. Because there were frictions in the medium, we were compelled to accept mediation of our acts; because the acts and the frictions were observed and utilized by two mutually perceptive intelligences, they became modalities of communication and neither intelligence could exclude its adversary from the medium or the mediation.

It now becomes possible to regard verbalization as a singularly effective device for introducing frictions into a medium and thus rendering it communicative. Language is an effective medium for political communication and action, on this interpretation, not because it is neutral but because it is relatively uncontrollable and so hard to monopolize. Whatever biases I impart to the medium, it is hard for me to prevent others not merely from imparting their own biases but actually from using my imparted biases to construct and impart their own. We thus have to devise strategies, and in observing one another's strategies, we begin to communicate. If we reach the point of uttering statements about the medium, its frictions and our strategies in making use of these, which are not merely moves in the power game but clarificatory utterances simultaneously usable by both players, we have reached the point of theory – of making utterances about utterances which possess a certain objectivity that permits them to perform a further mediatory and communicative function. The institutionalized speech-structures which the language polity requires us to employ carry a certain load of utterances of this secondary kind, which have themselves been institutionalized.

I am aware that the emphasis I am laying upon interposing frictions in the way of action will have a conservative ring in some ears, and since my intentions are only incidentally conservative, if at all, I feel slightly apologetic about this. I do think it desirable to slow down the action to the point where it can be conceptualized and criticized and we can relate ourselves to it; I have anti-McLuhanist preferences, and if this be conservatism, make the most of it; but my main concern is for the preservation of a structure of two-way communication, which appears to me a necessary feature of any form of human freedom, and I am stressing the introduction of frictions into the medium with that end in view – and equally, I am seeking to slow down the power act so that it ceases to be immediate and unmediated. This is why I prefer my politics verbalized. But I am also probably exposing myself to what has lately become the accusation of pluralism in stressing that mediation has to go through the medium of a relatively slow-changing authority-structure, and the time has come to show that I am under no illusions about the tendency of institutionalized authority to get out of hand and become power – either somebody's or nobody's. So far I have been dealing with a language polity and talking in terms of the classical politics, which is the appropriate vocabulary to use when we believe ourselves to have equals; the players of my language game are performing the linguistic equivalent of Aristotle's 'ruling and being ruled'. It is now desirable to examine the linguistics of unshared power.

When I said there was a flaw in the theory of the language polity, I had in mind that Humpty Dumpty need not be an isolated eccentric sitting on a wall. He may command the services of all the king's horses and all the king's men; and he may use them to convey, and to compel acceptance of, his arbitrarily varied speech acts. The two-way character of communication will be entirely lost when there are those who have the meaning of their words decided entirely for them, and reply to the speech acts of those in command of the language only, if at all, in terms which the latter have determined and to which they impart nothing of their own. When we define the situation as precisely as that, we can ask whether it ever exists in definitional purity in the real world; but there is an impressive array of rhetoric to remind us that real-world situations can come close to it. We therefore need to understand both the linguistics of this situation and the linguistics of getting out of it.

If the point is reached where I exist, even in my own perceptions, solely as defined in terms set by others, my condition may be called that of the slave. My masters may be visible or invisible, personal or impersonal. There may be some identifiable Humpty Dumpty with power to fix or change the language at will; there may be some institutionalized language independent of any will now existing, but permitting some to perform all the speech acts and others only to suffer them; or I may, as in *1984*, find myself subject to an invisible but highly effective bureaucracy of manipulators who maintain their power by varying the entire language structure in directions and at moments that cannot be predicted. What I know is that speech acts are being performed on me, and that I am performing none of them myself. Now let it be assumed that I begin to liberate myself from this slavery, and that I do so partly by the performance of speech acts which begin to be my own in the sense that they perform my intentions and I intend their performance. The questions now arise: how do I acquire the linguistic resources to perform these acts and on whom do I perform them?

There is an important body of theory which says: I must acquire the linguistic means of liberation from my former master; and I will acquire them by using, in the world of experience into which he has thrust me, the means of verbalizing that experience which he has imposed upon me, but which can no longer be used as a means of such verbalization without setting off conceptual consequences unforeseen and undesired by him. Something has happened, unintended by the master, in the material world which my speech verbalizes; we proceed to provide a theory of change in the world, brought about in consequence of the relationship between me and my master, which will explain and predict how this unintended result happens. But if it is to be asserted that my self-liberating speech act is a simple reversal of his speech acts towards me, simply my expropriation of his language defining me in order to perform my definition of my self, the master must be locked into the relationship between us in such a way that he cannot move from it or redefine it; his language must imprison him as rigorously as does the same language when imposed upon me. He may be allowed to find new ways of enjoining me to consider myself a slave, or tell me the outright lie that I am not a slave if this can have the sole and exclusive result of manipulating me to remain one; but if he is able to perform any speech act the effect of which is that I become other than a slave, then I am no longer liberating myself by the simple negation of his language that enslaves me. On the other hand, if I am doing this I am not engaging in two-way communication with him. Essentially, I am talking about myself to myself, and if I say anything to him it is probably said in order that I may hear myself denouncing him. I cannot be engaging him in dialogue if I am engaged in destroying the means of his speech acts, and thus in destroying him or transforming him into something other than he is. If, in making myself other than a slave, I am making myself other than a thing, I am liable to find that this involves treating him as a thing, or at any rate a third person or *alter*.

The proposition 'the master must be the master if he is to cease being a master' is, I suppose, a dialectical tautology; but it becomes a good deal more than a tautology if the master–slave relationship, while real, is not the whole of the reality about us. That is, if the ruler is not entirely contained and imprisoned within this or any other categorization of the ruler–ruled relationship, he can act – which includes the performance of speech acts – outside that categorization. Moreover, unless he can wholly control the communications universe in which he acts, he will speak outside that role, and some of his words will reach the ruled in forms not wholly intended by the ruler or expected by the ruled. To these, the ruled will reply, and the context he sets up by doing so will modify the linguistic exchanges intended and expected to be otherwise. In proportion as this happens, we enter a situation of language power very different from the simple dialectic of the master–slave relationship. The master is no longer wholly a master, or the slave wholly a slave, since the master no longer enjoys unmitigated linguistic authority to define the slave; and on the other hand, the ex-slave has lost the absolute freedom to annihilate the master by defining him as a non-master (or *ci-devant*). The master has lost and gained; he is no longer imprisoned within an absolute and one-dimensional power; in admitting that he is not only a master, he has acquired additional freedom of action. He may well think the deal worth making, especially if he retains 99 per cent of the advantages of being a master. The ex-slave still has a long way to go. But from the moment the two of them accept mitigation of the master–slave relationship, the further reversal or transformation of their relationship begins to move from a pattern of dialectical negation towards one of Clausewitzian communication. They have strategies and counter-strategies for working on one another's wills; and when will is working on will by means of the sending of messages, they are in second-person communication.

There is theory which will deny this, on the grounds that the freedom of manoeuvre they have acquired is illusory; socially constricting forces are at work which will force them back into the relationship of master and slave. This may very well be; the prediction sets up a pattern of warnings which should receive serious attention. But the statement that it must be so – that I am imprisoned within a certain categorization because there is no alternative – begins to resemble the sort of holistic utterance I was taught to regard as non-refutable and non-investigatable. At best it is rhetoric, introductory to an investigatable statement; and operational and performative rhetoric can lead to methodological naivety. I recall picking up some Soviet-Marxist tract of the bad period and finding in the opening pages an assertion to the effect that bourgeois societies believed themselves to be founded on absolute and unchanging laws. Reflecting that this anyway was false, I turned to the last page of the book and found there was something about the eternally viable laws of Marxism-Leninism. The first fallacy probably had something to do with generating the second.

Those with a keen eye for ideology will have noticed that I am changing roles and speaking now as the recipient or target of the liberating statement. If someone insists that I am imprisoned within the structure of my own reifications and goes on saying so even when, after self-examination and reflection, I am convinced that I am not, we may reach a point where I am convinced that there is no way to persuade him that I am not; and about this point, I may begin wondering about the performative character and intent of his statements. Are they error, myth, or strategy? He may be prevented by some intellectual blockage from seeing that I am not imprisoned; he may be cheering himself with the illusion that I am imprisoned in the master–slave relationship and so possess greater power and less freedom to manage it than I believe; or he may be seeking, by means of performative statements, to imprison me in that relationship, and in the role of master, for reasons arising from his own notions of revolutionary strategy. We have begun talking about the politics of polarization. One-dimensional rulers have the choice of remaining the rulers they are or ceasing to be rulers at all. Sensible rulers try to avoid giving themselves that choice and may accept the alternative of becoming rulers who are also ruled, which is or may be to say, citizens in a polity. But the revolutionary strategist tries to thrust the one-dimensional choice upon them and to deny them the alternative. In the case I am supposing, he is to be found attempting to do that by means of performative speech acts.[4] He is either compelling recognition of the world as it really is or forcing the world into a one-dimensional shape for his own one-dimensional purposes. The chances that he is attempting the former increase in proportion as he has left room for deciding whether or not the world is as he says it is; room, that is, for recognizing the possibility that it may not be as he says it is; but performative statements – especially those which perform upon the hearer rather than the speaker – are extremely difficult to construct in a refutable form. If someone says – performatively – that I am what I am not, how am I to reply? If someone is performing speech acts whose effect, if unmitigated, would be to terminate communication between us, by what speech acts shall I mitigate his performance and keep him in communication against his intent?

The problem of the legitimacy of polarization raises the problem of distinguishing between true and bogus revolutions. If the ruler is really a slave-master or is deceived in thinking that he is not, it is hopeless to attempt mediation between master and slave; a false structure of two-way communication may have to be broken down. But the bogus revolution is found when the revolutionary in bad faith is attempting to impose one-dimensionality where this is not sufficiently imposed by factors outside his own speech acts. The distinction is highly recognizable in principle but very hard to draw in practice; especially if we phrase it as a distinction between absolute and relative, between situations where the partners really are as master and slave and situations where 'master and slave' represents part but not all of the truth about them. I may have unfairly suggested that this is as the distinction between ideal and actual, and that therefore purely revolutionary situations never exist, and revolutionary strategy is never justified, in real life; but this is not the contention I am arguing for. The message I am trying to convey is that there will be bogus revolutions as well as real ones, and situations in which it will be hard to decide whether we are playing bogus or for real. Enough of us have faced nasty little Antigones trying to make us behave like Creon for their own nefarious purposes to know what the bogus situation is like; and it is only one more step to the situation in which Antigone, with the utmost integrity, of course, is so

[4] The term 'performative' here is not used precisely as in Austin; I am arguing that either a true/false statement or an Austinian performative may act upon speaker, hearer or referent, and modify his circumstances – how to do things to people with words.

certain that we *are* Creon that we are beginning to have doubts ourselves and may react so energetically that we prove her right. If she is wrong and we are not Creon, we urgently need means of converting tragedy into comedy. There may be an unnecessary tragedy if we lack them, since tragedy is necessary only if she is right.

We inhabit an overcrowded, over-communicative, inter-subjective world in which people easily become convinced of each other's bad faith, and these suspicions are often justified and often self-fulfilling. There has come to be a politics of bad faith, consisting in the performance of speech acts in which I define you as acting in bad faith in such a way that your only means of being in good faith is to give me what I want (possibly your abdication or self-annihilation). If you are in bad faith, you deserve this treatment and cannot escape it; if not, you need means of replying to my statement, which it must be remembered is performative rather than descriptive. Because I disbelieve your good faith, I have placed you in the position of being in bad faith; I have performed an act of power designed to reduce your freedom of action. Your reply – which I am busy reducing your freedom to make – will have to be similarly performative, upon yourself and on me. But speech of this kind is both self-actualizing and escalatory. The trouble with escalation is both that it is counter-productive and that it makes an end of two-way communication. In a conversation where each of us is constantly moving into denying the legitimacy of the other's contributions, we have to test whether such denials must continue, whether the contest between us is dialectical or Clausewitzian, whether the escalatory tendency in our speech has to run its course. Come, let us delegitimize together. The crucial question will be whether it is possible for my speech acts performed upon you to permit, and continue permitting, a reply by you in terms of acts performed upon me; and so forth. If this is possible, the linguistic polity will have been preserved in the form of mutually perceived, inter-communicative strategies. Such seems to be the politics of the performative dialogue; we now need to look at theories whereby speech may be perceived as counter- and inter-performative.

All speech, we have premised, is performative in the sense that it does things to people. It redefines them in their own perceptions, in those of others and by restructuring the conceptual universes in which they are perceived. Given the premise of inter-subjectivity, it is important to realize, there can be no such thing as a purely self-defining speech act. A recent book about revolt bears the title *The Right to Say We*.[5] Now clearly I cannot

[5] R. Zorza, *The Right To Say We* (New York: Praeger, 1970).

say 'we' without redistributing a number of other human beings among the categories 'we', 'you' and 'they'. To do this to people can have very considerable consequences for them, and these I perform by an act of my own. Liberation even, that image of such potency in the contemporary sensibility, involves an act of power over others: a speech act by which I define myself is performed in another's universe and redefines him as well as me. Our language assigns us roles, either directly or indirectly; to reshape language so as to reshape myself is to reshape another's self, both by changing the ways in which I appear and perform in his universe and by changing the ways in which he can define himself. As our common universe becomes increasingly second-person and inter-subjective, it is increasingly hard for me to redefine myself without committing some direct (but, alas, not necessarily second-person) attack on his definition of himself. The problem is that of affording him the means of counter-performance.

Henry Kariel's[6] recent writings appear to me to travel some distance into this problem. He develops very ingeniously – from a standpoint which I take to be radical – the concept of play as a means of countering the repressive tendencies of languages. The prevailing language structure assigns to us universes in which we play roles; it does so without consulting us and in ways which we may very well find repressive. But on the margins and at the buried roots of language, there is a rich field of ambiguities, absurdities, and contradictions awaiting our exploitation. By speech acts, other acts of communication and by acts themselves considered as communications, we not merely expose these to the satiric eye but use them to liberate ourselves from the lifestyles imposed upon us. We act in ways consonant with language and yet unexpected; we reverse roles; we discover contradictions and negations; we set off resonances whose subversive tremors may be felt at the heart of the system; and we discover roles for ourselves in the teeth of the roles which language seeks to impose. This is the image of the clown as liberator; but there have been some remarkably sinister clowns in our time, and when the clown or the counter-culture becomes evil it is often because, in his enthusiasm for antinomian behaviour, he has forgotten the unilateral and unlimited acts of power which antinomian actions may become when they are performed in and upon the lives of others. The polis is not the circus; a higher level of audience participation is guaranteed. I think, however, that Kariel's thesis provides an effective defence against this danger, though at a higher price than he may be willing to pay.

[6] H. S. Kariel, *Open Systems: arenas for political action* (Itasca, IL: F. E. Peacock, 1969); 'Creating Political Reality', *American Political Science Review*, 64.4 (1970), pp. 1088–98.

His strategy is an obviously effective means of dealing with a language universe conceived of in alien, impersonal or third-person terms: as Other, as a system or power-structure in which I am not as free as I could be and other persons or groups, or impersonal institutions, are enabled by the language to impose roles and universes upon me. I therefore set out to shake up, send up and generally disconcert Them and It. Well and good; but the spectre of the clown as evil has to be invoked to raise the question of You. What am I doing to you and how may you respond? It is simply not enough that I invite, enjoin or oblige you to join my act and become We. You are inescapably the object of some of my acts, the subject of some of the changes I induce.

Kariel's concept of language, if I have not distorted it, is not unlike the one I have been using here. He recognizes both that it performs upon us by assigning us a distribution of authority and roles which go with that structure, and that it is a sedimentation of unintended as well as intended results and therefore always negatable, always the source of means of reversing the roles which it assigns. If it can always be screwed, it can always be penetrated; it consists of a tissue of closed contexts which can always in principle be rendered open. Unless – and this I find hard to reconcile with the concept of play or of language – some rigorous historical dialectic separates it absolutely into one dead crust and one living growth, the game can begin at any point and can be played. I am trying to play my way out of the role which language assigns me. This involves my assigning to you a role in the implementation of the language-structure – whether that of ruler or of mediator, it will necessarily be that of manipulator – which may well be objectively justified; and my further assigning you a new role, consequent on my change of role, which is far more the creation of my freedom. You need to respond, since you cannot afford to accept inertly the roles I have assigned you. Let us further suppose that you are – as, indeed, I have defined you – more interested than I am in maintaining the existing structure of role ascription; it will actually be harder for you if you are not as I have assumed; and let us finally suppose that I am seeking to pen you up in that role as a first step to making you surrender it. What do you do now?

If we are talking the same language, and I am merely exploiting its content unintended by you, either of us has the last word; there is not a last word. The game I am proposing is one that two can play. If I can discern unexpected possibilities in your language, you can discern others in mine; if I can perform in unexpected fashion the roles which language thrusts upon me, you can perform in ways I do not anticipate the roles which I am thrusting upon you. Let us certainly keep in mind here the differences between real and bogus revolutions; you may indeed be a ruler so far imprisoned in your role that you respond with precisely the degree of brutality I have expected of you. But it was of Brezhnev and Daley that Auden wrote, in *August 1968*: 'The ogre cannot master speech.' If you have not lost control of your own language, you can understand the games I am playing with it; and though I have seized the initiative and caught you off guard, it still gives you plenty of opportunity for counter-manoeuvre. And if you are in power, the language I am turning against you is still more your language than it is mine. By discerning a latent irony or absurdity in the role you have assigned me, I have reversed some language game and sought to imprison you in a role assigned to you; but there should still be opportunity for you to discover ambiguities in the language by which I do this and to manoeuvre between the role I seek to fix on you and the roles which language otherwise makes available to you. There is a complex of role-ambiguities out of which you may answer me and I you. Frictions are back in the medium, and the comedy of strategies is on.

Kariel's sense of the absurdities inherent in language, then, seems to involve only an impure dialectic and to be wholly compatible with intelligent conservatism. It was, after all, Michael Oakeshott who defined political conversation as 'pursuing the intimations of a tradition of behaviour', and pursuing the intimations is very much what the clown and the counter-clown are doing. That the ruler may be seen as comedian, not ogre, is apparent to anyone who has lived in England and seen the extent to which comedy is used as an instrument of rule and of ruling-class adaptiveness; it can easily be overstated, but it is there. We had better remind ourselves of the truism that the conservative may be as disrespectful of rigid structures of authority as any radical; he knows the advantages of freedom of manoeuvre and does not propose to be imprisoned by the system he desires to maintain – that is not what he is maintaining it for. He will therefore play politics as a game with zest and appreciation; nor need it be a very clean game. If Creon succeeds in treating the whole thing as a joke, what happens to Antigone, for whom it is no joke at all? In some versions of the tale, she manages to insist on death for them both rather than let this happen; but suppose Creon puts the choice before her in exactly those terms?[7] The weapon of death is still available, but it is used on others as well as on herself. If she wants an ending in terms of finite values – of comedy and

[7] A literary and political exercise: CREON: *All right, go ahead and bury him; I'll issue a statement and fix it up somehow.* Complete the play from this point.

polity – it is her business to outwit Creon, not outdo him in authenticity; she can leave him with the option of accepting the result.[8]

I am enlarging the truism that revolution is not a game for two players into the statement that the character of language as a two-way communication system is hard to reconcile with revolution as a one-way act of power. Therefore, the verbal strategy characteristic of the revolutionary is the reduction of You to a choice between We and Them, or even It. He justifies doing so on the grounds that They have for some time been saying You to him in such a way that They mean It when they say You. This may well be more or less true; it corresponds to recognizable experience; but it is difficult to eliminate the second person altogether from any shared language system. The unintended sediment sees to that. When rulers reduce men to things, or You to It, they do so by a kind of deliberate blindness, as when the Lord hardened Pharaoh's heart, but revolutionaries do it with their eyes open. Rulers do not much care about authenticity, but revolutionaries do; their search for it carries them to the point of saying We, but authenticity alone does not impel them to say You, and revolutions are notoriously bad at becoming polities or games for two players. The character of the language polity seems to indicate why this is so. Humpty Dumpty wanted power, but would matters have been any better if he had desired language that would have represented his intentions with absolute purity? We are humanized by language and by communication with one another in polity; but the medium, it seems, is necessarily impure.

[8] The comedic ending is, of course, compatible with Antigone's being wholly in earnest about her central value-judgment.

CHAPTER 4

Political ideas as historical events: political philosophers as historical actors

Speaking as a historian who regularly returns of his own free will to that strange series of caves inhabited by political philosophers and illuminated by not a few totally artificial suns, I am peculiarly conscious how easily one can be taken to say not only what one did not intend to say, but what one specifically and explicitly declared one's intention not to say. Let me start by recalling that First Law of interdisciplinary communication which runs: 'Nearly all methodological debate is useless, because nearly all methodological debate is reducible to the formula: You should not be doing your job; you should be doing mine.' I would like, as far as possible, to disclaim paradigmatic pretensions; I am moved by the passion of sympathy, not proprietorship, and it is my purpose to try to help, not to take over.

I have been asked to address myself to the question of how far the next generation of political philosophers, on receipt of suggestions that they should study the history of political philosophy, should become apprehensive lest their discipline become unduly pervaded by historicism.[1] I am not quite sure what they mean by this or what they are afraid of, and it is notoriously difficult to dispel the fear of threats which cannot be identified. It may help, however, if I begin negatively and destructively, by identifying several senses in which 'the history of political philosophy' need not and should not be taught to the next generation, because these senses of the term seem to me to lack sufficient precision of meaning. My hope that I shall not be charged with wanting it taught in these very senses rises briefly above its initially low level.

[Published in Melvin Richter (ed.), *Political Theory and Political Education* (Princeton University Press, 1980), pp. 139–58. An earlier version was delivered to the Conference for the Study of Political Thought, meeting at the Graduate Center of the City University of New York in April 1978.]

[1] [The conference, and the volume arising from it, addressed the question of what kind of education should be proposed for 'the next generation of political philosophers' (one has presumably appeared since the discussion was held). This paper was a reply to an address by the late Allan Bloom, entitled 'The Study of Texts', published in Richter, pp. 113–38.]

To begin with, then, I do not think that political philosophy possesses a unified and narratable history, or that the efforts of those who may disagree with me to prove otherwise are likely to provide legitimate paradigms for the coming *paideia*. I say this with some regret and even a sense of ingratitude, for the classical work of G. H. Sabine had an enormously illuminating and liberating effect upon me when I was an undergraduate of nineteen. But that was long ago and far away, and the next generation would not thank me for expecting them to start wherever I was then. I do not mean merely that nobody will ever again read the work of Sabine in the year 1943. His was, I now think, a survey volume of genius, and I still encourage undergraduates to read it – not least because survey volumes today seem to be written with the aim of avoiding genius at all costs. But, as I have argued at length elsewhere, any historian who tries to provide himself with a model of political philosophies as the products of historical processes is bound to ask the question whether what he is studying is in fact the record of a continuous activity with a history of its own. Breathe for one moment the words 'second order', and the possibility must arise that political philosophy is what happens when people reflect upon their political languages and that political languages are what social beings assemble from a multitude of sources to articulate and co-ordinate a multitude of activities. All this is simply too diverse and disorderly – being of the groundstuff of history itself – to have a single evolving pattern of history. The questions with which political philosophers come to deal may perhaps be perennial – I do not intend to deny this, though I do think we need critical means of determining when to say it and when not – but precisely when they are, they cannot be historical. There may indeed be a history made up of philosophers reading and responding to other philosophers – they are certainly to be observed doing this – but at the same time there is, far closer to the grassroots, a history of philosophers not being philosophers twenty-four hours a day and receiving information and inputs, both philosophical and non-philosophical, from beings inhabiting the same social and historical moments as those in which they happen to live. If political philosophy exists in the world of concrete history, it does not have a history altogether its own, and its attempts to provide itself with one are only a part of the story of what has happened. To descend from the question of kind to the question of degree, it may be added that political philosophy has probably been less successful at providing itself with an autonomous and continuous history than Christian dogma or scientific discovery; these, even the former, got further out of the marketplace (I use this last term in a Baconian rather than a Macphersonian sense).

What I have been saying depends upon a certain model of what political philosophy is, and how it is generated in society and history. About that model I may have occasion to say more, but my present point may be made without it, by suggesting that the notion that there is 'a' history of political philosophy disappears once we entertain the possibility that such philosophy may have been generated, and had a history, in more than one independently existing and unrelated civilization. In this debate we are not discussing (though the next generation very possibly may) the significance for us of political thought in the civilizations of Asia; but once we suppose that Wang Yang-ming may have been as important to the young Mao as Herbert Spencer, or that Augustan England and Tokugawa Japan may have arrived at interestingly comparable notions concerning the interrelations of land, commerce, war and virtue, we shall be forced to acknowledge that no single history of political thought or philosophy can possibly be written; for here are at least two such histories, which took shape and existed in complete separation from one another until the coming of the black ships. And each of these, I am prepared to argue, both can and must be further dissolved by criticism into an indefinite number of discrete historical phenomena, the discontinuities between which are at least of equal importance with the continuities.

It is the historical intelligence which is destructive of histories conceived as unities, just as it can discern that most of the historians described by Professor Bloom were very bad historians indeed. If the practising historian rejects the notion of writing an overall 'history of political philosophy' at a level higher than that of the textbook survey, he will *a fortiori* show even greater scepticism when faced by majestic schemes of general development through which political philosophy is supposed to have passed. He will not argue for exposing the coming generation to the view that political philosophy has passed from the city-state to the universal community to the nation-state, from feudal to bourgeois to socialist, from the ancient tradition of natural law to the modern heresy of natural right, or to any other of the intellectual hippogriffs still seen to lurch, entangled in their own coils, across the floor at political science conventions. These were at their simplest, models, and at their richest, myths: insights into and symbols of aspects of reality, like the hippogriff itself; it was only when they were imposed upon the historiography of the actual, of experience and event, that they ceased to be myths and became monsters instead. The historian is not in the monster-making business, so long as what one wants to know about political philosophy is simply what one wants to know about any other recorded human activity, namely what it was that happened and how.

None of the monsters I have mentioned was the work of a historian; all were the work of social philosophers of one kind and another, who thought they knew enough history for their purposes.

And it is here that we encounter the central problem of relating the discipline of history to the *paideia* of political philosophers. The historian's purpose may very well be somewhat critical and negative, and markedly non-imperialist. She may aver that she has no desire to convert political philosophers into historians – even historians of philosophy – and that she is offering only to teach them enough history to keep them out of Operation Frankenstein. But it is precisely on those interfaces where the practitioners of one discipline think they know all they need of another that Frankenstein is found begetting monsters in his sleep; and it is not enough to teach them their second discipline with negative and critical intentions, since the apparent humility of thinking they know all they need may well turn out to be the fatal step into hubris. On the other hand, it is futile to suppose that teaching the coming generation no history will prevent them supposing that they know some and engaging in a variety of pseudo-historical enterprises. Frankenstein did not die in the Arctic; he was picked up by a vessel of the Vanderdecken and Ahab Line and his monsters roam the world to this day. Nor, when the parable is applied to the case before us, could he altogether help acting as he did and does; the political philosopher of today is an intensely historical animal, conscious of inhabiting history even when she rejects it and bound to include historical statements among those which she makes and implies. I do not mean by this that every statement she makes must be a historical statement, but I do mean that if we do not want bad history as part of our political philosophy, we must do something to help the philosophers abstain from producing it.

But I have been urging that the attempt to provide political philosophy with a history will not be a sufficient means of reaching even this modest goal, and it is inherent in my argument that to think of history as an auxiliary or ancillary skill for the philosopher will not solve the problem of the interface, which is the problem of Frankenstein. We have to seek means of making the intensification of historical understanding part of the philosophical enterprise itself, without encouraging it to take over the enterprise as a whole. It has been suggested – and I think it can, within the proper limits, be maintained – that such a means can be looked for in the historical interpretation of texts, though this must be carried out by criticism and not by the Straussian philosopher's strange blend of innocence and esoteric initiation. Here, it is important to note, what is proposed is not that we should study the history of political philosophy, but that we should study political philosophy historically; a very different thing, and one which brings us much closer to the problem of historicism. I propose now to confront that problem head on, by considering why it is that to admit the notion of texts to the argument sentences the political philosopher to be an inhabitant of history, without sentencing him to think historically for more than part of his time.

To speak of texts is one way of admitting that the philosopher is not isolated from his own kind. He is aware of the utterances of other political philosophers, and indeed of other political beings of many kinds whose articulate speech acts constitute inputs to his consciousness. In saying what he says he responds to what he supposes them to have said, and the interpretation of other men's speech acts forms so large a part of his specialized activity that political philosophy has become a thing which he studies at least as much as a thing which he practises. It is possible to deplore this, or at least to set limits to its desirability; but it is a fact, and means must be found of coping with it as a fact. Because the philosopher spends much of his time responding to what others are supposed to have said, political philosophy may be spoken of as a 'conversation', a 'tradition', a 'dialogue' going on over time, and is a historical activity in the sense that it possesses a historical dimension.

Where there is conversation there are two speakers, and where there are two speakers neither has complete command over what is being said, even by himself. Let me hasten to add that there are limits to the extent to which political philosophy is a conversation even when there are two speakers. It may be supposed that whenever a political philosopher says anything, she is in part responding to something which she takes another to have said; but should Alter object, 'I didn't say that', or 'I didn't mean that', it would not be improper for Ego to retort, 'I don't care whether you did or not; all I wanted to say was that if such and such a proposition were to be enunciated, my comment would be such and such.' From that point on, Ego is emancipated from her conversation with Alter; the speech acts which she now performs, the language games into which she now enters, are contingent upon the obtaining of certain conditions which she may have specified quite correctly, and which do not in any event depend upon what Alter said or meant to say. Ego has entered into a hypothetical world of her own specification, self-legitimizing in the sense that the specifications she constructs may specify and include her reasons for constructing them; and the exercise may be a most valuable one for Ego herself and for anyone who may happen to be listening. Even Alter may learn something to his advantage from what must necessarily be something of a monologue on

Ego's part, and it is not inconceivable that the conversation which Ego broke off may at some time be resumed in a more beneficial form. It is the Socratic assumption that it always will be, though we do well to be sceptical of anyone's pretensions to play Socrates.

Now when philosophers say that they do not wish to be entrapped into historicism, they often mean, in part, that they wish to preserve the freedom to play Ego in the little monodrama I have just recounted; and this is indeed a freedom it is important to preserve. It was annoying for Alter that Ego gave him the alternatives of withdrawing from the conversation or remaining to listen to it as a monologue conducted by Ego within parameters she had constructed for herself; but Ego may have had something more important in mind than finding out what Alter wished to talk about and talking about that. She should be free to break off even the most bilateral of conversations, and what is more, she is free to do so. No non-coercive means of stopping philosophic disputants behaving like Ego has yet been found, and the commonest difficulty is the relatively trivial one of getting them to admit, even to themselves, that this is what they are doing. I have next to show in greater depth why it is that philosophers should and do have the freedom to operate upon the utterances of other philosophers, irrespective of their historical reality; but I aim also to show why it is that to do so will not always be an appropriate or even a possible strategy.

Ego behaved as she did because she sought the power and the freedom to determine what she was going to talk about. The affirmation, 'If so and so were said, then the reply would be such and such', carried with it the plain implication, 'And I don't want to discuss anything else.' The erection of a set of conditions – intellectually scrupulous though it may have been – was a power play, a bid to set the rules of the game to be played. Ego acted in this way, let us suppose, because she was aware of the muddle-ridden character of ordinary language, and knew how much of this confusion arose from its character as conversation, in which two or more persons are and have been talking at cross-purposes. She had reached a decision as to what it was she wanted to talk about, and she declared that decision; whereof she would not speak, thereof was she silent, and she compelled Alter to be silent also. Such, one might say, is language in its Hobbesian state of nature, except that the clarificatory monologue is the state towards which philosophers (Plato was not an exception) normally desire to lead all discourse; it is their means of escaping from the ordinariness of ordinary language, even if this is only escape into second-order talk about ordinary language. But it is perhaps a more common experience for us to find that we do not yet know what the muddles are, or even whether there are any in the part of the swamp we are traversing. The appropriate strategy now is not to terminate or explode the conversation, but to continue it. Ego and Alter must say to each other, 'Where shall we get to if we go on talking like this? We must go cautiously ahead and find out.' It may happen that their existing, ordinary, language turns out adequate to their purposes, and does not lead them into insoluble muddles. In that event, the distinction between first- and second-order language will, to some extent, fail to develop, but it does not seem on that account that the enterprise to which they committed themselves will prove to have been unphilosophical. If one side of the philosophical enterprise is to discover whereof one can speak, another is to discover what in the foggy blue morning – to quote the immortal Pogo – one has been talking about. If Ego and Alter succeed in carrying on conversation, each will be engaged in discovering what the other says and means to say, and – as an inescapable corollary – what he says and means to say himself.

It is the presence of what we mean by ordinary language that gives political philosophy its character as history. Strictly speaking, the language in which it is conducted is academic and extraordinary, and it might be better to call it a tradition of discourse. But it shares with ordinary language and other kinds of tradition the characteristic that it is a continuum of behaviour, compounded of material from many sources and available to many users in such a way that no one of them has unlimited power over it. Perhaps the key characteristic of tradition is that no single transmitter has complete knowledge or complete control of the messages he either receives or transmits; there is always an element of the implicit and perhaps the contradictory, which must escape his attention at any single moment of transmission. This does not deny his capacity to perform acts of unilateral clarification like Ego's; it merely provides the context in which such acts of self-liberation become necessary and possible. There must be a river before you can swim upstream; you cannot be purifying all the dialect all the time.

The theorem of linguistic continuity also presupposes the importance of Alter, as the most recent transmitter to whose use of language we respond in ways that must be dialectically related to it, but who was himself behaving in the same way towards some other transmitter before him. The chain of transmitters must formally be thought of as open-ended and immemorial; in the continuum of discourse called political philosophy it is, for complex and fascinating reasons, rendered visible and apparent over a time-span of up to two and a half thousand years, and can at any moment be short-circuited in such ways that we find ourselves responding with high immediacy to Alters who lived in Athens or the State of Lu as long ago as that. But if we are prepared to say that the relation between Ego and

Alter is a historical one, on the grounds that they occupy distinguishable moments in the same continuum or tradition of behaviour and respond to each other's attempts to use and modify it, then this relation must be a historical one, whether the distance separating them in time, space and context is very large or very small. It is the use of language – of language not perfectly controlled by its users – that constitutes the historicity of political philosophy, as of many another activity.

I hope I need not stress much further that to say this is not to fix a historicist straitjacket upon what Ego was doing when she exploded her conversation with Alter. She was at that point trying to establish the formal conditions under which language could be used to say certain things, and her assertion that she knew what could be done under specified conditions need in no way depend for its truth or falsity upon acts of historical knowledge. She established tests and appealed to criteria which were valid within the limits to which the conditions necessary for their validation could be made clear. To talk about the extent of this clarification was not simply to continue the tradition of discourse, or more sophisticatedly to discuss the conditions under which it was being continued. Nor was it immediately necessary to discuss the possibility that the language in use for purposes of specification contained unstated implications being borne along as part of the language continuum. The immediate necessity was to find out whether language was behaving as it had been said that it would behave, and only after that to begin considering why it was not so behaving; a question the answer to which might or might not have to do with the historicity of language. Ego would be on safe ground in affirming that the historicity of language did not immediately concern her, and that she hoped to establish conditions and a methodology under which it never would. It can be affirmed with equal force, however, that her enterprise was being undertaken at a certain historical moment and was helping to constitute that moment, but that, given the presumption of the language continuum, she should not hope to command everything that happened, or that she was doing, at that moment. Her experiment, considered as a speech act, would be heard by, and communicated to, people who were not committed to its original enterprise; her specification of conditions would be heard under conditions which it did not specify. The validity of the experiment would not be diminished when it was reabsorbed all the same. Ego need not worry about this; she should obey the First Law of Methodology and do her job; but her job would never be the whole of what she was doing.

Ego, then, has an unlimited right, but not an unlimited power, to set herself free from her interlocutor in a conversation or a tradition, or – what amounts to the same thing – from the uncontrolled historicity of her language. Let me now proceed to consider how this affects the problem of how far our understanding of other people's thought needs to be a historical understanding. I have already insisted that any linguistic relation between two persons can be thought of as a historical relation, and the fact that the historical distance between them may be as great as two and a half millennia only serves to highlight the problems of historicity which the relationship involves. We do in fact find ourselves in philosophical conversation with Plato, the author of the Book of Job, and Confucius, and while there are different ways of accounting for the fact, there is no need to defend or apologize for it. We may say that a great tradition, or a historical continuity, connects twentieth-century Westerners with ancient Greeks and Hebrews, and if it is harder to say this of ancient Chinese, we may plausibly predict of the next generation[2] either that they will have connected themselves with the grand continuity that descends from Confucians, Taoists and Legalists, or that they will have developed still further our interest in the varieties of historical experience that have produced and transmitted the ideas of Plato or of Han Fei Tzu. As for hard-nosed operationalist Ego, we have given her liberty to withdraw from the historical conversation whenever and in so far as she is able to, and we owe her no explanation of our reasons for remaining in it. She is not welcome to this congregation in the role of Lesser Inquisitor. Let her do her job, and we will listen to her.

We may say of our predecessors in the history of political philosophy that they are linked to us by tradition, by the continuity or the diversity of history, or by the fact that the questions they discussed were classical, perennial or timeless, and are still discussed by us. I myself do not particularly wish to say any of these things, though I am equally not concerned to deny any of them. It seems enough, and more important, to make the merely humanist point that when we are able to receive and decipher a transmission from any predecessor in our common enterprise, the reasons for receiving it are potentially so numerous and diverse that they do not need to be spelled out in advance. If the next generation plans to remain human at all – and, by the way, some of them don't – there is no human resource which they can afford to neglect.

But on the premise that we are using 'ordinary language', or a 'tradition of discourse', it must follow that Ego is receiving from her predecessors and interlocutors messages whose diversity is yet to be controlled and may never

[2] [A prediction, alas, falsified in the event.]

be brought under control altogether. Speech-acts and utterances in political philosophy, when viewed as historical phenomena, must be considered as multidimensional. There must be a diversity of contexts in which, a diversity of levels on which, they may be and have been interpreted; and the content of any given message can be exclusively specified only under conditions which are experimental rather than historical. It was the endeavour of Ego in the monodrama to substitute experiment for history, and she could enjoy only a specific and limited success in doing so. But while, at her end of the transmission, she is at liberty to reshape the message being received into the form in which she desires to receive and respond to it, there may be going on, elsewhere in the continuum – and she cannot altogether ignore that there may be going on – the effort to reconstitute the message as it may have been at the moment of emission, or at any intervening moment of transmission. The historian is bugging the time-stream and has interposed his own unscrambler. We cannot deny that he is there; we must find him his own job to do.

One thinks of the historian as endeavouring to discover Alter's original meaning and intention, and feeding statements concerning this into Ego's already overburdened sensorium. In point of fact, it seems unduly restrictive to think of him as overwhelmingly concerned with Alter's intended meaning, central as this may be to his problem. If political philosophy both emerges from and remains within a universe of ordinary speech, it is true of any statement – Ego's as well as Alter's – that it can be both made and understood in a number of contexts and on a number of levels. It is also true that the speaker's own problem may be to discover and determine his own intentions as to the context and level in and on which he desires to speak and be understood. We may go further. It is possible that his intention emerges as that of speaking and being understood in several contexts and on several levels; it is possible that the determination of his intention was never finally accomplished by him, and can never be finally accomplished by anyone else; and it is probable, rather than merely possible, that the meaning he intended his statements to bear was not identical with the meaning assigned to it by any one of the chain of transmitters – disciples, opponents, critics, scholars, historians – who may have conveyed the statement to Ego. The historian of ideas bedevils the philosopher, not merely by pointing out what some statement which the latter desires to use may have meant to the author from whom he receives it, but by pointing out the embarrassing richness of meanings which the statement may have and/or has borne to the author himself and to any other historical actor involved in its operations.

I have consistently depicted Ego as a highly analytical and operational sort of philosopher, who desires only to take up some speech act that has come to her attention and play language games with it. I have done this not in order to suggest that all philosophers are like this – though the type is common enough – but in order to widen the gap between Ego and Alter to the point where Ego may quite legitimately say that Alter's intentions are no concern of hers. In reality, of course, Ego may be a humanist, genuinely concerned to maintain and affirm the value of her dialogues with the dead; or she may be a historicist, convinced that Alter's thought, and her own, and the relations between them, can be understood only by reconstituting each in its own historicity. In such cases it really will matter to her that Alter's true name was Plato or Hobbes, and it really will matter that the utterance he desires to explore was one which Plato or Hobbes not only made, but intended to be understood in the sense which he desires to explore. But I have deliberately sought to define a situation in which Ego may detach Alter's utterance from Alter's intention so completely that it no longer matters to her who Alter was, in which case the most that can be said is that it might be best to stop using Alter's proper name. If you really do not care whether or not Plato said this, a name so potent is probably better omitted. Supposing a situation as extreme as this, however, what significance, if any, will still attach to the intervention of a historian between Ego and Alter?

Some might argue at this point that if Ego does not desire to use Alter's name, she had better not use his words either. Words, they might say, are phenomena so far historical that a complex speech act can never be finally divested of the meanings attached to it by the original utterance or accumulated in the process of transmission. Ego had better render Alter's speech into a notation of her own, if she really means to get away from Alter altogether and perform a speech act under conditions perfectly controlled. But I have premised that Ego's attempt to withdraw from the universe of ordinary speech into a laboratory universe of her own is always to be encouraged, but can never be more than provisionally successful; and what we have to do is consider the historian's intervention in the light of this supposition. It will mean that Ego may indeed rephrase Alter's speech to the point where Alter and his speech act disappear, but that outside the laboratory Alter and his speech will still be historically present and operative, and that the historian will be in there, scrambling and unscrambling, with them. What then is his value, or his nuisance value, to Ego?

In the first place it may be pointed out that historical criticism is a potent means of slaying monsters. 'Man's world', wrote Collingwood, 'is infested by sphinxes: demonic beings of mixed and monstrous nature which ask him riddles and eat him if he cannot answer them.'[3] And while some of these sphinxes are unfortunately real, others are phantasmata – monsters begotten in the sleep of reason – who will disappear if we point out not so much the right answer as the nonsensicality of the question. To point out that a given interpretation of an utterance could not have been its author's intention on grounds of historical anachronism may lead us to inquire into the reasons why such an interpretation should have been assigned to the utterance at any subsequent moment, including the present, at which, let us suppose, Ego is proposing to analyse the utterance as bearing that meaning. If she discovers, thanks to historical criticism, that there has never yet been any good reason for supposing that it meant that, she may well be moved to enquire once again what reason she has for so supposing. If she has a good reason – especially one non-historical in character – historical criticism will not invalidate it; on the contrary, it may reinforce it. But it will, somewhat indirectly, oblige her to restate this reason and gain added certainty that her sphinx is not a phantasma. So much for historical criticism in its negative form, when it leads to the conclusion, 'Hobbes did not mean what it suits you to suppose his words mean.' The next step is to ask the question, 'Why exactly does it suit you to suppose so?' But it is implicit in the assumption I have been making that historical criticism – or rather reconstruction – is less likely to operate negatively, excluding the meaning which Ego desires to impose on the words, than positively, drawing attention to the embarrassing richness of other meanings which they could have and have borne at one time and another. In this respect its value to Ego is surely that it vastly expands her consciousness of the variety of language games which she may play, while conveying a salutary reminder of the variety of language games which her readers may and will assume – whatever her declared intentions to the contrary – that she has been playing. We return to the point at which Ego's exit from the world of history into that of experiment is seen to be laudable but never complete, and it may be suggested that we have isolated some ways in which historical criticism can help provide dialogue between the historical and experimental modes of her activity.

In making what seem to me legitimate concessions to historicism, I have been trying to point out that the non-historical statement does not become the less non-historical when we discover that nevertheless it has a history and is in history. I have been implying that the specification of conditions of validation is sufficient to erect the laboratory and legitimize its experiments. Some may not find this satisfactory, but I will presume that the question is

[3] R. G. Collingwood, *The New Leviathan* (Oxford, 1947), p. 12.

likely to remain debatable and unresolved, at least to the point where we are not required to resolve it for the benefit of the coming generation (which is likely to reopen it, whatever we say). But a perfectly evident corollary is that Ego's choice of what experiments she will make, what meanings she will choose to impute to utterances, what laboratories she will build, takes place in the historical world and precedes her exit from it. To emphasize this is more important than to debate the completeness of her exit from its determining conditions. It is while she is still in the historical world, considering what non-historical operations she will perform upon it, that a critical knowledge of history seems most likely to discipline and reinforce her proceedings; and if we emphasize that her exit from history may not be complete and cannot be permanent, we do so in the hope of finding ourselves in alliance with her. But at the risk of over-combativeness, it is still necessary to point out that it is when Ego insists that her choice of an experiment is made in response not to happenings in the universe of ordinary language and a shared history, but solely and exclusively to happenings in the universe of experiment (if that has a history at all) that we must begin to see her activities as trivial, irresponsible and motivated consciously or unconsciously by an appalling thirst for power. Our universe is not to be transformed into a series of laboratory caves for Ego to reign over in the role of mad scientist. It is, once again, Oakeshott's antithesis between the self-made and self-worshipping rationalist and the inhabitant of a continuum of behaviour; or, as Burke once put it, there is no wickedness like the wickedness of this sort of metaphysician. Oedipus has become the Sphinx. There is, however, nothing about the experimental method which necessitates denying the character of history to the world as not included in the experiment of the moment; the First Law of Methodology remains intact, and the dialogue between Ego and Alter is interrupted but not abolished.

I have been concerned throughout to argue that if the political philosopher can be trained to see the utterances of others in their historicity – meaning simply to consider the wealth and diversity of what it was that was being said, felt, and thought, and of the ways in which it was possible for it to be said, felt, and thought – benefits of two kinds may be looked for. In the first place, the philosopher's capacity to receive and process information of different kinds will be vastly enlarged, while nothing seems to have diminished his capacity to screen out information which he desires to omit from consideration. In the second place, this training will enhance his capacity to view himself as a historical being and the acts of thought and speech which he performs as historical acts: to recognize, that is, that he is making choices and transmitting messages which are conditioned but which modify the structures that condition them, and that the historical world which he inhabits is shared with others and governed by the law of heterogeneity of ends, so that not all the consequences of his acts will be those he can foresee, intend or desire. Once again, we have not obliged him to think historically while he is constructing his thought-experiments, but we have trained him to resume thinking historically in proportion as the conditions specified in the experiment cease to obtain. Now these two sets of advantages can be thought of as operating in the world as it appears to a humanist, in which the resources of humanity are spread out over time, and dialogue, or relatively unmediated communication, between minds widely separated in history is a thing to be desired. The situation I have been describing is one in which the philosopher learns that he and his method share the world with other beings and other methods, some of which may be induced to counterpoint, limit and enrich the operations he practises. In the world thus described there is a plurality of powers and there are relations between these powers, and the political biases of my description may be said to be liberal. I do not reject this definition; I reject only that anti-liberal polemic which distorts the word 'liberal' by applying it to the world in which Ego operates unchecked. I have been trying to check her, and grant her a sufficient liberty.

But in essaying a humanist projection, I have also been seeking ways of making legitimate concessions to historicism. There is a historicist projection of the world in which the historicity of everything is at all points the condition of its being, and to which it would be highly relevant that the dialogue of Ego and Alter could be arranged so that each discovered her or his historicity. Now, at one level the objection to historicism is that it obliges us to think historically when we desire to think in other ways; at another, the objection is that it exposes us to rule by a new caste of philosopher-kings who claim to know more about our historicity than we do ourselves, and so much about everyone's historicity that they have power over it and them. For those of us who object as strenuously to Leninist philosopher-kings as we do to operationalist ones, and for the same reasons, I have emphasized the historical context of Ego's experiments in order to prevent her from becoming the latter kind of usurper (or Sphinx), and her freedom to perform experiments in history in order to defend her against the former kind. That is a modest, whiggish, commonsensical contribution to the debate between scientificist and historicist, a debate which I well know can be carried on at much higher levels of refinement and which looks like being so carried on by the next generation of political philosophers. Since I am a historian in an Anglo-American tradition which acknowledges its debt to humanism somewhat more freely than its debt to historicism, I have chosen to adopt a humanist approach to the borders of historicism, and to show how a historical sensitivity thus generated might be used to reach an accommodation with the reigning oligarchy of scientific experimentalists, and even to make them want one.

But the tradition from which I speak has enemies to the left, and a holistic or totalitarian historicism is notoriously one of them. Presuming as I do that the next generation will once again be exposed to seduction and abduction from that quarter – from bad Hegelianism, bad Marxism and worse Sartreanism[4] – I would lay a good deal of emphasis on the view that an essential ingredient of coping with the historicist is the ability to know your own history and to know and conduct yourself in it. Indeed, I will offer it as dogma that if the next generation of political philosophers is historically ignorant and historically incompetent, it will be hopelessly vulnerable to the holistic scientists of the right and the holistic historicists of the left, who are more than capable of combining against it. Frankenstein has many names and faces. But at the same time there is a legitimate and valuable historicism, as there are highly valuable forms of all three of the philosophies whose proper names I used a moment ago; and having spent my time in trying to show how much merit there is in viewing all kinds of political philosophy in their history, I should conclude by laying some emphasis on the prevalence of a political philosophy which is essentially a viewing of history. This stems from pre-modern roots, which are found wherever the tradition, or the republic, or the national state, or the revolution – all of which are modes of political association – is presented as having a history and facing problems of existence in it. It develops towards that modernity in which it is said that the political association is a historical animal and the individual's very consciousness of himself a historical consciousness, which determines the modes of his political and historical action. We may wish to repudiate this, for it has many grave inconveniences; but it does not appear that we can afford to neglect it. For one thing, it has developed a highly complex and subtle language, which is predominant outside our own tradition and wherever the angels are not Angles. We need to learn this language – I speak it very haltingly myself – and if we are not to be taken captive by it, we need one of our own, in which our awareness of our historicity is differently articulated. I have argued, then, both that the coming political philosophers will need to know how to think historically

[4] [The monsters of the twenty-first century will no doubt answer to other names.]

and that their thought will need a historicist dimension. In large measure I have argued this on adversary and disputatious grounds, but I would like to conclude by stressing my sense of the enrichment which such kinds of awareness may bring to our understanding of what the philosophical enterprise is, and which – even though they little note nor long remember what we say here – may help to rescue the next generation from the various forms of tyranny, technocracy and tedium which, as usual, threaten to afflict it.

CHAPTER 5

The reconstruction of discourse: towards the historiography of political thought

(1)

In this paper[1] I shall seek to give an account of how the historian sets about reconstituting political thought as discourse: that is, as a sequence of speech acts performed by agents within a context furnished ultimately by social practices and historical situations, but also – and in some ways more immediately – by the political languages by means of which the acts are to be performed. These acts are to be thought of as performed upon and modifying the status of (1) the hearers or readers to whom the speech is communicated, (2) the speaker or writer 'himself',[2] who is never unaffected by 'his' own act, and (3) the language-structure which is confirmed or modified by the act of speech and by the conditions in which it is performed. I shall defer, but I do not ignore, the question (4) of how the political and historical situation, or the political and social structure, may be said to be modified by the act of utterance performed in it. My immediate undertaking is to elaborate the concept of discourse as a series of acts performed in languages; and to carry this on, I must undertake some explanation of the notion of a 'political language'.

I am making it a cardinal assumption that the historian is concerned with the actions of agents other than 'himself'. Agents require, in order to be said to act at all, some scheme or structure of relationships in which their actions are performed. We may call this a context, and think of it as giving the action meaning and intelligibility; we may also, half-metaphorically, call this a space, in which other agents and patients, as well as the rules and conditions governing the action, are thought of as situated. A space

[Published in *MLN* (*Modern Language Notes*, Johns Hopkins University Press), 96 (1981), pp. 959–80.]

[1] Originally the second of three Christian Gauss Seminars in Criticism, presented at Princeton University in the spring semester of 1981.

[2] I use the masculine pronoun, placing it in quotation marks to remind myself and others that it could have been the feminine.

populated by a number of actors may be called a public space, and there are ways of intensifying the use of the word 'public' until it begins to do duty for the word 'political'. Language itself – the interchange of speech acts which the rules of the language seek to govern – may be thought of as entailing an act of power which the speaker performs upon the hearer; and there are other ways in which my utterances can be defined as acts of power, in the sense in which I impart to them an illocutionary force which others are not yet able to control. The verbs 'hear' and 'know' can be used to impart information in the imperative mood – 'Hear, O Israel', 'Know all men by these presents'; I command others to hear and to know what I am telling them. But as soon as another begins to hear my illocution, 'he' begins to understand, to interpret, to receive, to reject, to respond; illocution becomes perlocution and 'he' has begun to perform actions which I may not succeed in controlling, and which may succeed in modifying the perlocution performed by me; or rather, the act performed has begun to be the outcome of acts which speaker and hearer severally perform upon the locution and upon each other. At this point, speaker and hearer are in a relation closely analogous to that in which Aristotle situated any two citizens in a polis: that of ruling and being ruled. With speech as their medium, they are performing acts of power upon one another, but the acts of each have the effect of modifying the acts of the other, and it can even be argued that each is committed by the use of speech to a relation in which the other can rule 'him' as 'he' seeks to rule the other. There is therefore a point at which we may begin to think of speech itself as political; and it is also at this point that we begin to see how acts of speech may have a history. The next step in our analysis might be to search for the 'rules' which this way of 'ruling and being ruled' generates and according to which it is conducted.

I am approaching a 'politics of language' along a path signposted by the assumptions of classical individualism; and ever since the term 'liberalism' rather mysteriously became a dirty word,[3] there have been well-known and far from negligible objections to this approach. It may seem that I have been suggesting that speaker and hearer were created free and equal in some linguistic equivalent of the state of nature, where the one was as free to modify the acts of the other as the other was to perform acts upon 'him'. I do not, of course, mean to suggest any such thing. It is perfectly possible to conceive of universes in which the language in use by a given society, the assumptions and values which it contains, the rules by which it is conducted, appear to have been constructed by and for a class of rulers, and to have

[3] [Used in those days by the left, later by the right, always of the same people.]

been imposed by them upon a class of ruled – by masters upon slaves, let us say, or by men upon women – in ways which compel the latter to accept and operate the ideology of the former. What is much harder to conceive of is a universe in which the slaves or the women are not themselves language-users, or in which their masters do not require them to understand and reply to what is said to them; and it is known that the master–slave relation lends a peculiar poignancy (and the relation between sexes another), to the hearer's and interpreter's role in converting illocution into perlocution. It is difficult to construct a master–slave relation in which the slave does not use 'her' master's language to discomfit the latter and construct a world of 'her' own articulating. How far 'she' can go by means of counter-exploiting 'her' exploiter's language when 'she' begins to transform it or to invent a new one as an instrument in the transformation or invention of a new world of relationships, are questions it becomes necessary to discuss. I am seeking at the moment only to make it clear that they can be discussed within the paradigm of a world inhabited by language users; and I am doing so because it has become a shibboleth to assert that to study the history of language systems is to neglect the struggles between social groups that go on within the language systems.

(II)

It remains true, nonetheless, that languages are biased in favour of the ruling groups who more effectively develop and employ them. To understand how this comes about, we must pass from the individualist politics of the speech act to the generalized and segmented politics of the language system. We have so far defined the speech act as a relationship between two or more actors: the speaker and the hearer, the interpreter and the respondent; and we have thought of these persons as acting upon each other through the medium of speech communication (which implies that to understand, misunderstand, interpret or ignore my communication is a way of acting upon me). But there is a relation here between action and information. To send me any message at all is to act upon me; what information the message conveys, however, may make a considerable difference to the sort of act it is. It is notorious that the information contained in a given locution ('The ice is thin over there') is not necessarily sufficient to convey the illocution it is intended to perform ('Look out, you bloody fool!'). In this well-known instance, locution may be converted into illocution by the adoption of an urgent tone of voice, or (a more complex procedure) by the exploitation of several verbal and non-verbal conventions which convey the message 'I am the kind of functionary authorized to warn you when you are in danger by telling you that the ice is thin; therefore, I am warning you that you are in danger and telling you how.' Here the speaker, with benevolent yet political intent, has placed 'himself' in a role of authority, and the hearer in a role of responsibility: 'I have warned you; are you going to take any notice? If not, you are at fault as well as in danger.' It is not yet clear, and may never be, how far the speaker has succeeded in this.

In complex normative systems – and here I am venturing a little political theory – when facts, values and roles are intricately and ambiguously related, the conveying of information may have complex normative and political consequences. By informing or reminding the respondent of a given set of facts – or what are alleged to be so – I seek to oblige 'him' to act in relation to this series of facts rather than another, and to the series of values which a set of conventional norms ascribes to these facts; I oblige 'him' to act with reference to these norms, values and acts; and in doing so I may well ascribe a certain role to 'him' and a certain authority to myself; for the facts of which I remind 'him' constitute the situation in which I present us both as actors. I am liable to consult my own advantage in selecting the context in which I thus enjoin action, and I may be more advantageously placed than 'he' is, either by the structure of the context which I enjoin, or by the context in which I find myself able to enjoin it. I thus seek by my act of speech to modify 'his' situation and my own, and 'he' must seek to modify both situations by the character of the response 'he' makes to me. The very considerable resources of language are, I shall assume, available in some measure to the respondent as well as to the speaker. Since both are operating within a structure of norms and conventions, we may assume that there exist norms and conventions for engaging in this speech exchange; that is, there are available linguistic devices for selecting and conveying the information, and making it carry the implied norms, roles and ascriptions of authority which each speaker desires to enjoin on 'his' respondent. But once we assume that each respondent may be a speaker in 'his' turn, we have assumed that the linguistic device – the verbalized texture of facts, values, roles and so forth – is available and useful to both interlocutors in this dialogue. At this point both are agents, and it must follow that neither is simply a master or simply a slave; what is not clear is whether there are master–slave languages, in which neither master nor slave can define 'himself' as other than what 'he' is, or whether the master modifies the relationship, and permits the slave to act as other than a slave, by the mere act of engaging the slave in dialogue and permitting 'him' the use of language at all. I shall not explore this limiting case, though we ought not to forget its existence; I am at present concerned to report that the student of political discourse is generally engaged in the study of dialogues between speakers, hearers and respondents, each of whom is in some degree capable of exploiting the resources of language and performing acts of speech within the patterns imposed and permitted by the dialogue. These interlocutors, it must follow, are ruling and being ruled; but once again, we must not neglect the possibility that a community of rulers being ruled is, from the viewpoint of slaves or women, a community or class of rulers.

I have begun using the term 'languages' in the plural, and any one 'language' in this sense of the term is a linguistic device for selecting certain information, composed of facts and the normative consequences which these facts are supposed to entail, and enjoining these upon a respondent. It is presupposed that this 'language' will also be usable by the respondent, and will furnish 'him' with the resources for making statements other than those the first speaker desires 'him' to make; any 'available language', therefore, is available to more than one agent and facilitates the performance of more than one act. But our immediate concern is to pursue the character of these 'languages' and investigate the forms which they may take. I have defined them as selective, as devices for choosing and conveying certain information, and its normative and political consequences, rather than some other; and if there exist other linguistic devices, which choose and convey other information and its consequences, it follows that several such 'languages' may exist at one time, and may enter harmoniously or (more probably) dissonantly into the public discourse of a society. These 'languages' in the plural are not, then, 'language' in the abstract, or in the sense in which Greek or English is called a 'language'. Perhaps, it may be said, we should call them 'sub-languages', or by some less confusing name. I have heard it proposed to call them 'vocabularies', but to my ear that sounded somewhat too lexical; such a mode of speech is not a way of merely naming things, but of conveying and enjoining a selective view of political activity in general – a way of acting and of determining the actions of others. To call them 'rhetorics', or even 'idioms', would occasion me no trouble if others preferred it; but I have been using the term 'languages' for a long time, and it offers advantages which make me reluctant to give it up. It is convenient to be able to talk both of a 'politics of language' – which is what I have been discussing – and of a 'language of politics', reducible to a number of 'idioms' or 'sub-languages' which may co-exist, converge, diverge or conflict, and between which relations of translatability may or may not exist. All this the term 'languages' permits me to do, precisely because it slips easily from one level of meaning to another.

(III)

Long ago, on what must have been a day of mingled cloud and sunlight, I took to characterizing these entities as 'paradigms'. A good deal of trouble has followed from this artless initiative, and much of the ensuing discussion would not now be worth pursuing. It may be useful, however, if I indicate some ways of using that term[4] which I still find valuable as well as certain idiosyncrasies in my way of using it which I am ready to acknowledge. A paradigm, then, signifies in my usage a way of structuring a field of inquiry or other intellectual action which gives priority to certain organizations of the field and the activity while tending to screen out others; it encourages the presumption that we are situated in a certain reality and are called on to act, speak or think in certain ways, and not in others. It exerts authority, and it distributes authority so as to favour certain modes of action and those said to be engaged in them; it is intellectually and politically, and may be ethically or aesthetically, biased. It is historically conditioned, but tends to suppress awareness of the conditions governing its existence; when in the course of human events it comes to be replaced by a new paradigm, a new ordering of reality will be called for, which may or may not entail increases in awareness of the paradigm's historical conditionality. The process by which a paradigm disintegrates and comes to be replaced may be thought of as induced by acts of thought or speech, performed within the rules and subject to the authority which it permits, which either import elements of reality which it fails to order or expose previously unsuspected flaws in its ordering of reality.

It will be evident how many of these characteristics of the 'paradigm' I have employed in my characterization of the 'political language'; in particular, the account of how the paradigm disintegrates from within is crucial to my understanding of how the speech act, legitimized and rendered significant by the rules of the language game, is performed within it and nevertheless acts upon it so as to change what it permits to be said. Here is the relation of speech to language, text to context, central to my account of the history of political thought. Yet it is possible that I made needless trouble for others, if not for myself, by applying the notion of 'paradigm' so rigorously in a context of language and rhetoric. If rhetoric is 'normal

[4] There is an extensive literature on this subject, ranging from Thomas S. Kuhn's *The Structure of Scientific Revolutions* (Chicago, 1962, 1970) through Garry Gutting (ed.), *Paradigms and Revolutions* (Notre Dame, 1980); the latter has a bibliography. See also the present writer's *Politics, Language and Time: essays on political thought and history* (New York, 1971; Chicago, 1989) and John Higham and Paul K. Conkin (eds.), *New Directions in American Intellectual History* (Baltimore, 1979).

science', for example, the paradigm is the precondition of rhetoric and precedes it; there may be difficulties in depicting the paradigm as constantly active in speech and constantly affirmed and reaffirmed by it. Perhaps it is because I absorb paradigm into rhetoric that I find it easier to employ the word adjectivally or adverbially than as a noun; easier, that is, to say that this or that verbal convention functions 'paradigmatically' than to identify the 'paradigms' supposedly the scaffolding round which rhetoric is built. At this point the noun slips through my fingers, though I do not really mind so long as enough has stuck to them in adjectival or adverbial form.

It was a further difficulty that, in the early days of paradigm theory, the paradigm was held to define the community of its users as well as the field of activity in which they were engaged. The community engaged in a specific mode of inquiry was held to possess, and be possessed by, the paradigm currently defining their inquiry; it supplied them with their problems and their means of considering them solved; it legitimized their actions and distributed authority among them. If there should occur a 'scientific revolution' in which the paradigm was replaced by another, there would be a new definition of activity, authority and in the last analysis community itself; paradigm change must be in the fullest sense revolutionary. Such at least was what workers in my field understood was being affirmed elsewhere. Perhaps we were misinformed; it was apparent, at all events, that no such model could very well apply to a community – Oakeshott would have us call it a *societas* – where several paradigms were being rhetorically urged at the same time, and were in debate and interaction with one another. If the function of a paradigm was to preclude any consciousness of another paradigm, it could scarcely be used in argument and hardly even in rhetoric; its function was to remain unspoken, and indeed the history of what is not said or imagined is one of the most difficult aspects of the history of what is. But only at its outermost limits can the history of debate be written in terms of what is not debated, or the community of discussants be defined by its possession of a paradigm which decrees what shall not be discussed. It looked as if it was the spoken word which did most to allocate authority, and as if the unspoken word was only part – though an important part – of what legitimated it. In both the politics of language, and the languages of politics which composed the speech of political societies, speakers were to be seen enjoining paradigmatic structures upon hearers, respondents were to be observed modifying the same structures to suit themselves, and groups of speakers and respondents might be found energetically debating one structure against another, and even entering into second-order debate concerning their relative and comparative merits. The structures it has been so convenient to call paradigms were clearly not monolithically exclusive of one another, except in those limiting and possibly extrapolitical cases where debate and discourse simply did not occur; there could be debate within and also between such structures, and increasingly complex relations, of both dissonance and consonance, were being discovered between them. The term 'paradigm', then, must be either modified or abandoned; and it may be that no very final choice has been made. As for the structure of the *societas*, it began at this point to look pluralistic.

(IV)

The languages of politics, then, must be thought of as plural, flexible and non-final; each must permit of both responses and other speech acts which will modify it from within, and of various forms of interaction with other language-structures which will modify it from without. In setting up such a model for the use of historians, I have already ensured that there will be tension with philosophers; for these are languages of the cave and it is not enough for our purposes to clarify them. My next task must be to give instances of the kind of 'language' I am speaking about, and to clarify our understanding of how they are generated and used. In doing this, I shall to some extent speak from my own experience, which has been gained mainly in studying the political discourse of early-modern England; the risks of observer-distortion in making this selection are, I think, worth running. In my early work, then, I was concerned to uncover and explicate the language of the 'ancient constitution', which seemed to have been built up by applying the terminology and assumptions in use among common lawyers to the discussion of English property, government and history;[5] I found that Edmund Burke, looking back to the days of Sir Edward Coke, was moved to remark on the circumstance that the English had been in the habit of affirming their liberties in a language framed to articulate the inheritance of property.[6] The 'ancient constitution', and the verbal and mental prepossessions on which it rested, were seen to have been criticized and undermined by the doctrine of 'the feudal law', which was my shorthand for a critical reconstruction of the common law's terminology and history, carried out by methods of comparative philology. After nearly twenty-five years, the theses I advanced are at last being criticized by those who ask whether the language of the common law was really as self-sealing and self-activating as

[5] J. G. A. Pocock, *The Ancient Constitution and the Feudal Law* (Cambridge, 1957, 1987).
[6] J. G. A. Pocock, 'Burke and the Ancient Constitution: a problem in the history of ideas' (1960), reprinted in *Politics, Language and Time* (n. 4 above).

I suggested, and whether there was not a more intensive awareness of both Germanic philology and the vocabulary and assumptions of Roman civil law.[7] It is high time such questions were asked.

It was much in vogue, when I began working, to lay great emphasis on the Elizabethan and Jacobean obsession with 'the frame of order', and use of a language which elaborated the image of a universe of harmony, correspondence and degree. The pursuit of this theme seems to be suffering from a kind of exhaustion; it has not been very adequately explained why it flourished or why it declined, and we are all as tired of Shakespeare's Ulysses on the one hand as we are of John Donne's 'new Philosophy' on the other. In a different part of the field, there has been a massive exploration – I personally date it from William Haller's study of John Foxe[8] – into the language of the Elect Nation; the rhetoric which depicted English institutions, and later English revolutionary crises, as possessing typological, eschatological and millennial significance. A diversity of scholars – in particular William Lamont, Christopher Hill and Margaret Jacob[9] – have explored both how this language might be used to legitimate English institutions by heightening their religious importance, and how it might be employed in developing that antinomian and spiritual criticism of social institutions which we associate with the great explosion of sectarian radicalism in the years of the Interregnum. My own rather marginal contribution was an essay[10] pointing out that the third and fourth books of Hobbes's *Leviathan* are constructed around an eschatological framework, and that one half of this great classic of political philosophy has been systematically ignored because it isn't political philosophy.[11]

7 Kevin Sharpe, *Sir Robert Cotton, 1586–1631* (Oxford, 1980); Richard Tuck, *Natural Rights Theories: their origins and development* (Cambridge, 1980); Hans Pawlisch, 'Sir John Davies, the Ancient Constitution, and Civil Law', *Historical Journal*, 23.3 (1980), pp. 689–702; G. R. Elton, review of Arthur B. Ferguson's *Clio Unbound*, in *History and Theory*, 22.1 (1981), pp. 92–100. [I now of course add Hans Pawlisch, *Sir John Davies and the Conquest of Ireland: a study in legal imperialism* (Cambridge, 1985); Glenn Burgess, *The Politics of the Ancient Constitution* (Cambridge, 1992); and Alan Cromartie, *The Constitutionalist Revolution: an essay on the history of England, 1450–1642* (Cambridge, 2006).]

8 William Haller, *Foxe's Book of Martyrs and the Elect Nation* (New York, 1963).

9 William M. Lamont, *Marginal Prynne, 1600–60* (London, 1963); *Godly Rule: politics and religion, 1603–60* (London, 1969); *Richard Baxter and the Millennium* (London, 1980); Christopher Hill, *Antichrist in Seventeenth-Century England* (Oxford, 1971); *The World Turned Upside Down* (Oxford, 1973); Margaret C. Jacob, *The Newtonians and the English Revolution* (Ithaca, 1976). See also Paul Christianson, *Reformers and Babylon* (Toronto, 1978); Richard Bauckham, *Tudor Apocalypse: sixteenth-century apocalypticism, millenarianism, and the English Reformation* (Oxford, 1978); and Katherine Firth, *The Apocalyptic Tradition in Reformation Britain, 1530–1645* (New York, 1979).

10 J. G. A. Pocock, 'Time, History and Eschatology in the Thought of Thomas Hobbes', in *Politics, Language and Time*, pp. 148–201.

11 See now, however, Eldon Eisenach, *Two Worlds of Liberalism: religion and politics in Hobbes, Locke and Mill* (Chicago, 1981). [Much more has since been written on the religious content of Hobbes's thought.]

I have also been concerned with studying the role, in English, Scottish and American social criticism of the mid-seventeenth to late eighteenth centuries, of a language of civic humanism or classical republicanism derived from ancient and adapted from Renaissance humanist and Machiavellian sources.[12] This turns out to have furnished effective and widely adopted means of criticizing the reordering of society and government around commercial and cultural values which went on throughout the eighteenth century; and what is known as 'the republican synthesis' has turned out to be of such importance in our understanding of the Revolutionary and Federalist periods[13] that I have found myself, somewhat to my surprise, enrolled in the company of American historians and denounced as party to a conspiracy of American ideologues.[14] In work so far published, I have tended to stress the effectiveness of the republican and agrarian critique of commercial society; but, in company with others, have also been studying the rise of a rhetoric of politeness, manners, specialization of labour and the historical formation of personality, which was developed in part as a response to the republican critique and played a role of incalculable importance in the growth of modern historicism.[15] It lay at the back of the Scottish science of political economy, and we are now encouraged to consider how far it evolved with the changing vocabulary of civil and natural jurisprudence.

This partly autobiographical excursus is a means of reviewing a series of 'languages' which have over the last quarter-century become prominent as modes in which to study the history of early-modern Anglophone political discourse. Beginning with the already ancient and specialized vocabulary of the common law, each of the series has presented itself as a distinctive mode of utterance: a 'language' or 'rhetoric', therefore, possessing its own terminology, style and conventions, and revealing as we come to know it the implications and assumptions on which it rests and from which it regularly

[12] J. G. A. Pocock, *The Machiavellian Moment: Florentine political thought and the Atlantic republican tradition* (Princeton, 1975).

[13] See Higham and Conkin, *New Directions in American Intellectual History* (n. 4 above).

[14] Cesare Vasoli, '*The Machiavellian Moment:* a grand ideological synthesis', *Journal of Modern History* 49 (1977), pp. 661–70; J. G. A. Pocock, '*The Machiavellian Moment* Revisited: a study in history and ideology', *Journal of Modern History*, 53 (1981), pp. 49–72.

[15] J. G. A. Pocock, 'Between Machiavelli and Hume: Gibbon as civic humanist and philosophical historian', in G. W. Bowersock, John Clive and Stephen R. Graubard (eds.), *Edward Gibbon and the Decline and Fall of the Roman Empire* (Cambridge, MA, 1977); 'Gibbon's *Decline and Fall* and the World-View of the Late Enlightenment', *Eighteenth-Century Studies*, 10.3 (1977), pp. 287–303; 'The Mobility of Property and the Growth of Eighteenth-Century Sociology', in Anthony Parel and Thomas Flanagan (eds.), *Theories of Property: Aristotle to the present* (Waterloo, Ont., 1979). [The second and third republished in *Virtue, Commerce and History* (Cambridge, 1985). See further *Barbarism and Religion*, I and II (Cambridge, 1999).]

proceeds towards conclusions which are to some degree predetermined; though its claims to be called a 'language' are heightened when we find, as we frequently do, that it is possible to argue within it from opposed premises to diverse conclusions. Much of the historian's time is spent in becoming familiar with these rhetorics, or (I am tempted to say) learning these languages, so that 'he' can recognize one when it appears on the page before 'him' and can follow, and sometimes predict, where it will lead. 'He' may then have the experience – as I have had with Hobbes's *Leviathan*, and Hume's *History of England*, and Burke's *Reflections on the Revolution in France* – of reading a familiar text and suddenly noticing that it is in part conducted in an idiom, rhetoric or language which 'he' knows, and which will yield messages and patterns of meaning which may previously have been overlooked. This is how – to borrow an expression from a certain school of dogmatists among us – the historian 'learns to read'; and from the moment of such a recognition, 'he' becomes increasingly aware of the diversity of speech acts, or acts of signification and communication, which the author or the text may have performed, and which may constitute the historical events of which the text is the encapsulation.

Languages, rhetorics, idioms, paradigms, modes of utterance: I am not sure it matters terribly which of these terms we prefer, so long as our choice denotes a way of speaking and writing which is recognizable, internally consistent, capable of being 'learned', and sufficiently distinct from others like it to permit us to consider what happens when an expression or a problem migrates, or is translated, out of one such context into another. They seem to occur together, and it is obvious that they vary widely in character, origin and degree of organization. The language of theologians, for example, or of civilians, was an extremely complex technical speech, spoken by powerful and ancient professional corporations; each of them included questions of political authority and obedience, and of their epistemological foundations, in the wide range of matters with which they were held competent to deal. The language of the common law was spoken both by incorporated professionals and by a great many non-professional persons into whose culture it entered; and since it did not entail a formal theory of politics, its application to questions of law, constitutionality and government presented many idiosyncratic, and as it were metaphorical, features which helped to give it the enormous importance it possessed. The various humanist rhetorics of which I have spoken were not technical or professional in character – though they originated among, and were disseminated by, formal schools of grammar and rhetoric – so much as languages of culture, which were available to educated persons as means of discussing questions of morals and politics, and found their way into such persons' linguistic equipment along with other idioms arising from a diversity of sources. When we encounter – as we seem to do – a Machiavellian or a Hobbesian, a Burkean or a Benthamite language of politics, we may be dealing with the formidable cultural impact of a person of genius, though plainly more than the genius is required to explain the impact. And there is always the King James Bible. Such a term as 'language', then, has to be used on varying levels of precision, which is why it is convenient to have synonyms to fall back on. I will, however, propose a heuristic model in which a number of linguistic paradigms, idioms or what you will can be recognized as occurring together, so that they may be distinguished, and interacting with one another, so that a debate may be seen as conducted, or a complex text shown to have been written, in several idioms and on several levels of meaning at one and the same time. This will prove to be of fundamental importance to the understanding I shall also propose of the historical nature of the speech acts we encounter in the reconstitution of political discourse.

(v)

It is clear that I am not supposing a state of things in which each idiom or paradigm defines a community of persons who speak its terms and whose thinking is governed by its presuppositions. Such communities may indeed be found. When one is among scholastics or common lawyers or subscribers to a highly systematic body of doctrine, the language one hears or reads defines the company one is keeping; and there are of course occasions on which the language is unitary, monolithic and exclusive of all others. However, it is a presumption I do not discard that if it is to be a language at all, it must permit of the exchange of complex, non-identical and even contradictory statements; and though there are languages so densely authoritative that dissent and debate can occur only in heavily coded and Aesopian forms of 'secret writing', it is worth bearing in mind that any code must be addressed to a potential decoder, and must to that extent be public before it can be secret. There is a logographic necessity (to borrow terminology again)[16]

[16] On page 121 of Leo Strauss's *Thoughts on Machiavelli* (Chicago, 1958) we read of 'the perfect book or speech' which obeys 'the pure and merciless laws of what has been called logographic necessity'. It contains nothing that is accidental and we must therefore read it as written partly in code if its claims to perfection are to be upheld. In order to escape this version of the hermeneutic circle, we do not ask if the book is perfect, but whether it was written in code; one way to ask this question is to ask who knew the code.

that all secrets must be shared and all conspiracies open; on another level, rebellious ministers and disobedient sons apparently knew they were being exposed and censured by the *Spring and Autumn Annals*, and it may be a pity we do not have their similarly encoded replies (it would be like having Thrasymachus's version of the conversation at Cephalus's house).

But in the work I have been describing, I did not find it necessary to presume a world of hermetic communities, each sealed within its separate language. Such a world could certainly exist, but it would be organized differently from seventeenth-century England. Probably because I was dealing with an early-modern Western society in the first efflorescence of print culture, I tended to presuppose that a diversity of idioms (or whatever), some but not all stemming from the speech of specialized communities in the past and present of the culture, might converge in the writings of a single author – as Hobbes's vocabulary necessarily changes as he moves from considering the commonwealth to considering the Christian commonwealth – and would certainly merge before the eyes, and exist concurrently in the understanding, of whatever body of readers existed. Such a readership would in a sense be polyglot, but need not always be a privileged and leisured clerisy; the great explosion of unlicensed printing in Civil War London, of which George Thomason made himself the archivist, is a central if never quite repeated fact of English history. The model I present consists neither of a single and unitary community, nor of a number of segmented communities, of writers and readers, authors and respondents. It entails the problem – which on the whole I find an opportunity – that if we retain the concept 'paradigm' at all, we must modify it to allow for the possibility that a single community, and indeed a single author, may respond to a number of simultaneously active paradigms, overlapping and interacting, consonant and dissonant, requiring the actor to choose, but permitting him to combine, compare and criticize. From this it follows that my conception of a speech authority, and therefore of political authority, has tended to be pluralist and therefore liberal; and this is what some critics dislike. Methodologically speaking, all that I need claim is that I have been writing the history of debates conducted in a culture where paradigms and other speech-structures overlapped and interacted; where there could be debate, because there was communication, between different 'languages' and language-using groups and individuals. Post-liberal or anti-liberal intellectuals dislike being reminded of such situations; they think it more important to consider worlds of ideology and false consciousness, in which communication can take no form but that of the rulers deceiving both the ruled and themselves.

I have been moving beyond the term 'language' to give a central role to the term 'debate'; I have been proposing a model in which there are a number of 'languages', or whatever else we choose to call them, and within limits a number of language-using groups or communities, and 'debate' takes place among them. Debate in this sense may of course occur in purely oral form, though until very recently it could be recorded only in script or print; we have the case of the Putney Debates, where Ireton and Rainsborough are arguing not only about the issues that divide them, but about the terms in which they are to be discussed. Ireton objects to Rainsborough's use of a natural-law argument, and insists that property and franchise must be discussed in terms of the positive and historical law of England; and if we thought that Rainsborough did not quite understand Ireton's strategy, we should conclude that Ireton was exploiting his own superior sophistication in the playing of language games. This is the record of an oral encounter, but it is open to us to suggest that Ireton and Rainsborough were both literate inhabitants of an expanding print culture, and that the arguments on either side are arguments drawn from and recurring in books and pamphlets. The history of political thought is to a quite overwhelming degree the history of activities conducted in literate media. What went on in the millennia before literacy is difficult to recapture; what will go on in the era after literacy – with no communication that is not electronic and less certainty that messages will be recorded – is difficult to imagine; one supposes that political thought as I am describing it will be kept alive only in those academic communities which, like the monasteries before them, will keep reading alive as the necessary precondition of reflection.

But as long as our attention is focused upon print cultures, our conception of specialized sub-languages, and of specialized sub-communities employing them, must undergo a significant modification. We now encounter communities of disputants, typically made up of authors and respondents who are also authors, in the sense that their responses to the authors' acts of utterance have taken the form of further acts of utterance, performed in the same language-complex, and communicated in (as texts) and preserved by (as documents) the same written or printed media. This encounter both restricts and intensifies our understanding of the history of discourse. In the first place, it tends to restrict the 'history' of an utterance, an author, a text or a language, to the history of what was said or written and of what was said or written in reply, and so to the field of evidence defined by the records of acts of speech. We now find it easier to write the history of speech acts occurring in language-structures than to write the history of speech and language as occurring in larger contexts of social structure and action; and there arises the question of how the two structures are related to each other. It is necessary to demand that this relation be established, but it is a good deal easier to voice the demand than to satisfy it.

In compensation for this restriction, our capacity to understand the history of discourse, within the restricted field of the community of disputants, has now been enormously intensified by the access we have obtained to the realms of reflection and theory. We have now many series of acts of speech performed in response to other acts of speech, and performed within and upon the complex of language-structures whose history can now be written. For disputants not only perform actions; they perform language games which have discernible strategies and systems of reference, and they render these more visible by commenting upon their adversaries' playing of language games, and by reflecting upon the games they are playing themselves. Dispute and criticism may be both reflective and active: they inform concerning the players, their performances, the games they play and the universes the games are played in; and at the same time they perform acts by whose consequences the games, the actions, the players and the universes are in various ways modified. The community of disputants provides one among the agencies by which it is moved along; in each case an especially visible and informative one. The history of discourse is a selected and restricted history, but for this very reason it is one which can be written and from which we can attempt to move to the writing of others.

(VI)

The historian whose practice I am attempting to describe now regards texts and documents as media of political discourse, in which authors attempt to perform speech acts upon readers and universes, and respondents perform acts leading to dispute and reflection. This discourse is conducted in a context of shared languages, consisting of a variety of language games which arise over time; they are specialized to perform rhetorical and paradigmatic functions related to the conceptualization and conduct of politics; and they become media of both speech and dispute and are capable of being modified by the speech acts performed in them, as well as by whatever other formative agencies may enter into the constitution of language. In order to reconstitute discourse, then, our historian must set 'himself', at a minimum, the following targets: to discover the language or languages in which the text 'he' may be studying was written, and the parameters of discourse which these tended to impose upon its utterance; to ascertain the acts of utterance which the text or its author performed or sought to perform, and any points at which these came into tension or conflict with the parameters imposed by the languages; to ascertain any utterances which may have departed from or modified these parameters; to discover the language or languages in which respondents can be shown to have interpreted the text, and to inquire whether these were identical or non-identical with those contained in the text or intended by its author; and to ascertain whether this process of interpretation produced any of those tensions between intention, speech act and language which we may imagine as leading to modifications or innovations in political language and its usages.

Though this may sound a formidable programme, it is as I said minimal; and I should deserve to be in trouble if I had presented it as final or exhaustive. It is little more than a programme for a history of interpretation, such as is needed if we are to write the history of any continuous discursive activity, and has as yet made no innovative claims other than that there have existed at various times a diversity of specialized languages in which political discourse has been conducted and political 'thought' and 'theory' – whatever they may be – generated. Though somewhat technical in its vocabulary, it is relatively modest in its aims, and we shall find that it is capable of offending philosophers because it tends to break down intellectual systems into the performance of a diversity of speech acts, while at the same time offending historians because it tends to remain within communities of disputants and move only cautiously towards the question of how their speech acted and was acted upon in the larger contexts of social structure and historical change. We may also find that the practice I describe offends the more godlike readers of the text of history by obliging them to give priority to the actions of interpreters other than themselves. For the present, however, there are certain problems which our historian must confront in 'his' own practice, and of which I ought to say a little in conclusion.

This historian we are considering will spend much of 'his' time reconstituting the 'languages' in which political discourse has been conducted in the past; and it has become clear that the word 'languages' is being used to denote a variety of speech-forms, of varying degrees of specialization and therefore of specificity and explicitness. This is why, with deliberate lack of precision, I juxtaposed the terms 'languages', 'idioms', 'rhetorics' and 'paradigms'; it was as well not to be too precise at this stage of an empirical investigation; but it does follow that the historian must exercise self-discipline in claiming to have uncovered and reconstituted new modes of discourse or – heaven knows – new paradigms. Not all these speech-fabrics will have been equally explicit, or employed with equal self-consciousness; and the historian may therefore find 'himself' claiming to have reconstituted a mode of discourse of which its users were not conscious, and of whose existence 'he' may have little or no evidence beyond the convincingness of 'his' own reconstitution. At this point the gap yawns before 'him' which separates reconstitution from interpretation. 'He' must never forget that 'he' is less an interpreter than an archaeologist of interpretations performed by others; it is 'his' obligation to show that the interpretation was performed, that the language was spoken, that 'he' can produce examinable and in principle refutable evidence that these things happened; and the greater the range of the evidence 'he' can allege, the closer 'his' practice draws to that of a historian. If 'he' can show that 'his' mode of discourse was employed, 'his' language spoken, by more than one discussant of the time 'he' studies; that dialogue occurred in it; that there was controversy over, and modification in, the assumptions, terms and usages of which it consisted; that it approached or crossed the threshold of explicitness and critical self-consciousness; if 'he' can produce some Monsieur Jourdain of the past who will actually declare that such a language was being spoken; 'his' position is stronger than if 'he' can do none of these things and must fall back on the heuristic suggestion that if we suppose that such a language was being spoken, it will both facilitate our interpretation and enable us to perform hypotheses that may some day be used in testing the proposition that it really was. 'His' commitment to describe the actions of agents other than 'himself' has imported Ockham's razor into the programme; interpretations are not to be multiplied beyond what is verifiable. This is the more so because 'he' is dealing with discourse filled with criticism and reflection, which have a constant tendency to thrust speech towards the threshold of explication; what does not become explicit does not cease to be there, but it does not become easier to say that it is there. The interpreter of other people's consciousness does not have unlimited freedom to feed structures into it; Ockham was the author of the GIGO principle.

The historian is not impoverished by this requirement. Language is rich; the speech of politics is rendered richer by the multiplicity of its references, by its discussive and disputative character, by its intermediate status between rhetoric and reflection, practice and theory; even by its often questionable integrity, its biases and false consciousness. The speech of the past further enriches the historian by its remoteness from that of the present. It is a fact of this historian's experience that 'he' is constantly discovering new modes of discourse present in the texts and criticized in the debates of the past, and presenting 'him' with fresh knowledge about material which had seemed familiar. But once we admit that a famous and complex text may turn out to contain a wide range of 'languages' and be interpretable as performing a wide range of acts of utterance, the richness of our historical knowledge becomes a source of potential embarrassment. Take the richness first; we now know that the text performs many acts in many continuities of discourse; it follows that it has many histories, and has performed upon its respondents in many ways. Given that this richness was not only the product of its author's creative genius, but the product of historical conditionality, it will soon follow that the author did not predict, nor did the text control, the diversity of languages in which it could be read or of contexts in which it could be interpreted. Readers contemporary with the authorship may employ paradigms and priorities other than those the text enjoins: Machiavelli did not enter debate with scholastics, but scholastics read and interpreted him; Locke was indifferent to both ancient-constitution and neo-Harringtonian historiography, but these modes of argument were applied to questions which he considered. There are texts which outlive the author and the language-world which 'he' knew, so that the acts of utterance which they perform are translated into systems of discourse inconsonant with those in which they were performed by the author. The phenomenon of diachronous translation – as it may be termed – is one of the most recalcitrant for the historian to deal with; yet this is probably the point at which 'he' is most likely to feel justified in decomposing the texts into 'ideas' and claiming that 'ideas' have a 'history'.

But embarrassment arises once we claim that a text may be considered as a formal structure, on which an intellectual unity has been imposed by an act of its author, and that the imposition of this unity may – indeed must – be considered as an act carried out in history. It is easy to deconstruct these claims, resolving the text into a multitude of acts of utterance performed by its author and of interpretation performed by its readers, in language contexts not necessarily continuous or harmonious with one another; we find that the historical context is greatly enriched by carrying out such deconstruction. Yet an author may plan 'his' text as a formal structure, possessing its own architecture and coherence; and once the text has acquired material unity as a scroll, codex or book, it is possible to read it in such a way as to impute such a coherence to it irrespective of the author's intention or performance. There is in the 'great traditions' of political thought, or philosophy, a continuous activity of interpreters reading formal structure into texts, as well as an occasional activity of authors writing it into them. The former activity is going on about the historian as 'he' embarks upon 'his' enterprise with regard to any text, and 'he' must find 'himself' in dialogue and exchanging information with its practitioners. 'He' must indeed recognize that 'he' is in some measure a two-headed being, obliged to reconstitute even as 'he' deconstructs; the problem has been known to historical scholars since the days of Valla and Alciati.

The pluralist historian deals with this bifurcation by supposing that the ascription of formal unity to a text has been carried on by means of a language, or series of languages, specialized for the purpose; that this language activity has a history; that it offers 'him' one more context, neither less nor more significant than any of the others, in which the text may be shown to have possessed a history. But this does not quite free 'him' of the embarrassment occasioned by 'his' own capacity for critical discovery. As the historian reads the text, 'he' may find 'he' has thought of a way of giving it formal unity which does not seem to have occurred to any of 'his' predecessors within professional memory. This may have come about because 'he' has interpreted the text in the context of some historically existing language which has not been applied to it before, in which case both 'his' credentials and 'his' problems continue to be a historian's. But it is also possible that a new formal unity has been ascribed to the text by the application of canons not arrived at by the methods of historical discovery – for example by the conduct of the activity of political theorizing or philosophizing, whose history is at the same time being written.[17] The interpreter has now to show that non-historical thinking can be the means of supplying historical information, under pain of falling into that unacknowledged myth-making which supposes that history can be written (as distinct from being made) by persons not subject to the discipline of historiography.[18] 'He' will be tempted – and if not tempted, assailed – by the practice of ascribing to certain texts authority over history, so that every interpretation which can be performed on them becomes a statement of the author's historical action. 'We're only marching through history', says one of the Raiders of the Lost Ark;[19] 'that' – pointing to the Ark – 'is history'. If the historian wants to avoid the linked vulgarities of idolatry and blasphemy (into both of which

[17] Howard Warrender, 'Political Theory and Historiography: a reply to Professor Skinner on Hobbes', *The Historical Journal*, 22.4 (1979), pp. 931–40.

[18] For this see John G. Gunnell, *Political Theory: tradition and interpretation* (Boston, 1979); and 'Political Theory, Methodology and Myth', an exchange of essays between Gunnell and Pocock, *Annals of Scholarship*, 1.4 (1980), pp. 3–62.

[19] [I assume the name of this film is still familiar.]

the film so eagerly plunged), 'he' may save 'himself' through the presumption of otherness: that is through showing that the interpretation 'he' has just performed could have been, and preferably was, performed by some identifiable actor in history not 'himself' and living in a time other than 'his' own. To accept this discipline is to separate observer from actor, owl from eagle, that one of Odin's ravens who was always behind time from that other who always returned upon completion of the action.

CHAPTER 6

The concept of a language and the métier d'historien*: some considerations on practice*

What I shall attempt in this essay is an account of a practice and some of its entailments; and while one cannot verbalize a practice without offering a theory, it is my hope – seeing that we are all in some degree committed to a common practice – to stay as far as possible on this side of metatheory. I do not want to find myself affirming and defending a general theory of language and how it operates in politics or in history, still less to offer an account of my kind of historian as, himself, a historical actor or agent.[1] These are all real questions and from time to time they demand consideration; I propose, however, to let them arise, if they arise at all, out of the implications of what I shall be saying we as historians do. The *métier d'historien*, as I use the term, is primarily his craft or practice; his vocation and its significance, his experience of or action in history, are to me matters of self-discovery, to be met with in a time still to some extent our own. I shall hope, by proceeding in this way, to discover something about our shared and common discourse.

The word furnishes my starting point. The concept of a political language to me implies that what was formerly, and as a matter of convention still is, known as the history of political thought is now more accurately described as the history of political discourse. The actors in our history were of course thinking, and often thinking very hard; many of them belonged to clerisies or intelligentsias specially trained to think in various ways; but in order to give either them or their thought a history, we have to provide an activity or a continuity of action, made up of things being done and things happening,

[Published in Anthony Pagden (ed.), *The Languages of Political Theory in Early Modern Europe* (Cambridge University Press, 1987), pp. 19–38.]

[1] I am aware that pronouns in the English language are biased towards masculinity, and that no satisfactory usage yet exists for avoiding this bias. I say this in full consciousness of the presence of Judith Shklar, Caroline Robbins, Nannerl Keohane, Margaret Jacob, Joyce Appleby, Lois Schwoerer, Corinne Weston, and a great many more whose names command equality as their numbers defy condescension. [Katherine Clark, Janelle Greenberg, Kirstie McClure, Anne McLaren, Linda Levy Peck, Julia Rudolph, Hilda Smith, Patricia Springborg, Rachel Weil, Melinda Zook ... there is no need of a crack of doom.]

of actions and performances and the conditions under which these were enacted and performed; conditions, furthermore, which were directly or indirectly modified by the actions performed under them and upon them. We therefore suppose a field of study made up of acts of speech, whether oral, scribal or typographical, and of the conditions or contexts in which these acts were performed. And in moving next, in moving immediately, to the concept of language, we declare our belief that one of the primary contexts in which an act of utterance is performed is that furnished by the institutionalized mode of speech which makes it possible. For anything to be said or written or printed, there must be a language to say it in; the language determines what can be said in it, but is capable of being modified by what is said in it; there is a history formed by the interactions of *parole* and *langue*. We do not say that the language context is the only context which gives the speech act meaning and history, though we shall certainly be accused of having said that; we say only that it is a promising context with which to begin. What consequences we have drawn upon ourselves by choosing to begin here and not somewhere else we shall discover later on. Meanwhile, by insisting that thought must be uttered in order to have a history, and that such a history can be viewed as the interaction of speech act and language, we have taken the first and crucial step, though not the last – *le premier pas qui coûte* – towards constituting our history as a history of discourse.

The concept of language is both protean and subdivisible. We can use the word 'language' to refer to one of the great ethnically differentiated structures of human speech – English or Hopi or Chinese – though the historian of political discourse does not usually think of these as 'political languages' or as having a history created by the political acts of utterance performed in them. Perhaps we should pay more attention than we do to the fact, and its implications, that political discourse in early-modern Europe was multilingual. It is no uncommon thing to find a treatise on politics part in vernacular, part in Latin, part in Greek and part in Hebrew, and we might ask whether these languages were politically differentiated. We should also pay more attention than we have done to the phenomena of translation and ask whether the history of Hobbes's *Leviathan* in English is the same as its history in Latin; the answer will be both yes and no. But in general, languages ethnically differentiated are not the crucial categories in our study, and when we speak of 'languages of political thought' or 'languages of politics' we have in mind something else. We are concerned with idioms, rhetorics, specialized vocabularies and grammars, modes of discourse or ways of talking about politics which have been created and diffused, but, far more importantly, employed, in the political discourse of early-modern Europe. Let me pause to point out an obvious danger. We wish to study the languages in which utterances were performed, rather than the utterances which were performed in them; yet if we allow the boundaries between *parole* and *langue* to become too fluid, any utterance which long sustains an individual style may be mistaken for the language in which it was uttered. If we wish to posit a 'language', it should be possible in principle for two authors to perform in it; we are hoping to find language as context, not text.

When we speak of 'languages', therefore, we mean for the most part sub-languages: idioms, rhetorics, ways of talking about politics, distinguishable language games of which each may have its own vocabulary, rules, preconditions and implications, tone and style. An indefinite number of these may be found within a given language, and may consequently be found within a single monoglot text; for these ways of talking, while often profoundly at variance, do not typically succeed in excluding one another. While we may think of them as having the character of paradigms, in that they operate so as to structure thought and speech in certain ways and to preclude their being structured in others, we may not describe them as paradigms if the term implies that preclusion has been successfully effected. Once it became unclear whether 'paradigm' did or did not entail the latter assertion, the term became one that it was uneconomic to employ. Some languages succeed in driving out others; nevertheless political discourse is typically polyglot, the speech of Plato's cave or the Confusion of Tongues.

The historian of political discourse who is emerging from this account of his practice[2] spends his time learning the 'languages', idioms, rhetorics or paradigms in which such discourse has been conducted, and at the same time studying the acts of utterance which have been performed in these 'languages', or in language formed as a composite of them. It is extremely common, though it may not be necessary, to find that these acts in language have been organized into texts; nearly as common, though even less necessary, to find that these texts have authors, concerning whom information may or may not be available from sources limited or not limited to the texts. The historian may proceed from *langue* to *parole*, from learning the language to ascertaining the acts of utterance which have been performed 'in' them; after which he begins to inquire after the effects of

[2] From about this point for the next five or six paragraphs and at one or two other points in the text, I draw upon material prepared for seminars conducted in the Political Science Department of the University of California at San Diego, during the spring quarter of 1983. I wish to thank Tracy Strong, Charles Natanson and others for their comments and criticism.

these acts, generally on the circumstances and behaviour of other agents who used or were exposed to the use of the languages, and more specifically 'on' the languages 'in' which they were performed.

Certain consequences follow. First: the *histoire* he writes is heavily *événementielle*, because he is interested in acts performed and the contexts in and upon which they were performed. *Moyenne durée* enters with, but is not confined to, the language context; he is interested in *longue durée* only in so far as it gets verbalized, and thus enters the *moyenne durée*.

Second: the history he writes is heavily textual, a matter of written and printed utterance and response (most of the readers whom, as we shall see, he studies are known to him because they became authors in their turn). It is a history of discourse and performance rather than – though, as we shall see, it does not exclude – states of consciousness. He writes the history of *mentalités* only in so far as these are articulated in discourse, in the utterance and response of publicistic and polemic: i.e., at a level of relatively sophisticated behaviour and relatively dynamic change. The pursuit of *mentalités* (which is a noble chase) would take him deeper into *moyenne* and towards *longue durée*; there may be elements down there which do not surface into discourse at all; but the evidence which tells of their existence may be of a sort best studied by some other kind of practitioner. This historian is not ashamed to appeal to the division of labour.

Third: it is also a history of rhetoric rather than grammar, of the affective and effective content of speech rather than its structure. This is a statement of emphasis and priority; the historian may find himself dealing with grammar and structure, but he supposes there to be a depth at which structures are not cognized, employed in rhetoric or discussed in theory. At this depth there is *longue durée* but nothing more, and he does not go down there; not because he thinks it impossible, but because he thinks it is someone else's job. At depths where no self-propelling organisms swim, he is not sure there is any history, only bathyphysics; and he has his own fish to fry and his own tales to tell – equivalents in his universe to what Alcibiades did and suffered, to what one office boy told the other office boy.

This historian is in considerable measure an archaeologist; he is engaged in uncovering the presence of various language contexts in which discourse has from time to time been conducted. I report from my own experience – and I shall elaborate on the point later – that he grows accustomed to finding many layers of such contexts within the same text, and is constantly surprised and delighted by discovering languages grown familiar from other sources in familiar texts where their presence has been neglected. Such discoveries do not always heighten his regard for the ways in which texts have been read before him. He becomes aware of all the languages he discovers by an extensive reading of texts of all kinds, as a result of which he detects their presence and proceeds to 'learn' them as one 'learns' a language: i.e., by growing used to reading (but not speaking or writing) them, he comes to know[3] what things can be uttered in them and how these things are expressed. There are important problems in interpretation and historicity which arise at this point and will have to be considered; but the central concern of this volume requires that we address ourselves first to the question of how these languages, idioms or rhetorics may be specified as historical phenomena.

If I ask myself for examples of the kind of languages I have in mind, the first to occur to me – not as privileged or paradigmatic, but as typical – might be: the language of medieval scholastic, of Renaissance emblematic, of biblical exegesis, of common law, of civil law, of classical republicanism, of commonwealth radicalism; the list is biased by my own studies, but these move me at once to try and go beyond it. Of the items so far composing it, a number are of course highly institutional; they can be recognized at once as languages employed by specific communities in their professional discourse, as articulating their activities and the institutional practices in which they were engaged. It is important that early-modern political discourse was conducted so largely by churchmen and lawyers, and in the modes of discourse which these were in a position to impose upon others; for clerisies do not address themselves solely to their own members, but impose their esoteric languages upon a variety of laities and lay publics, sometimes to the latter's articulate displeasure. The creation and diffusion of languages, therefore, is in large measure a matter of clerical authority; the story of how literate professionals have become involved in directing the affairs of others and have obliged others to discourse in the languages which they have evolved; but at the same time, the story of how the laities have appropriated professional idioms to unprofessional purposes, have employed idioms from other sources in such a way as to modify their effects, or have developed rhetorics of hostility to the imposition of language upon them. Along this line we catch sight of the antinomian use of language: of the use by the ruled of the language of the rulers in such a way as to empty it of its meanings and reverse its effects. Appropriation and expropriation are important aspects of what we have to study; I say this because I am constantly accused of denying their importance by those for whom I can never make them important enough.

[3] [I must have had in mind – and might have done better to use – the Oakeshottian phrase 'gets to know'. See above, p. 4.]

It is important that the study of political language takes its departure from the languages of ruling groups, which articulate their concerns and are biased in their favour; but it is also important that the more institutionalized a language and the more public it becomes, the more it becomes available for the purposes of a diversity of utterants articulating a diversity of concerns. This diversification will originate within the ruling group, where there is commonly plenty of debate going on; but it may not remain confined within the original clerisy, profession or whatever it was. We may encounter cases where a language has been diffused beyond the original relationship of rulers to ruled by which it was created: where it is being uttered by other rulers to other subjects, by rulers uncertain whom they are ruling, by subjects uncertain by whom they are being ruled or on what authority, and even by revolutionaries using it in their efforts to throw off rule altogether. There are plenty of instances in early-modern Europe, even on the last supposition. The diffusion of a language may be a very different story from its creation.

The historian of political language will discover that language has a politics of its own; but to dwell upon this point, however important it may be, is to move away from the experience of the historian in discovering languages latent in the texts before him, which was what I set out to describe. Of the idioms emerging from the text, the historian has found that some are the languages of professional corporations articulating the practices which have made them powerful and their speech authoritative – and capable of being imposed on others – in society; but he will not find his experience arrested at that point. At a little distance from the case just supposed, for example, he may encounter the language of sacred or authoritative books – the Bible, the Organon, the Codex, the Talmud, the Koran, the Six Classics – and of those who employ it in their discourse. Should he be concerned with the language activity of incorporated or accredited professional exegetes, the case will not be much altered; but he may by degrees find himself dealing instead with a network or community of men of letters, whether professional or leisured, established or *arriviste*, who employ the languages of the professional corporations without necessarily belonging to them, and are capable, first, of adapting these idioms or rhetorics to the purposes of their own discourse; second, of generating and developing idioms and rhetorics of their own in the course of pursuing it. He will now find himself dealing with idioms generated less by professional practice than by the rhetoric of discourse: with modes of discourse formulated within the discussion of particular themes and problems, or with styles of discourse perpetuating the styles of powerful and idiosyncratic authors – a Burke or a Hegel, a

Leo Strauss or a Michael Oakeshott. Some of these authors will have been institutionalized as authorities serving the purposes of professional exegetes, others will not; and an author's historical significance is not measured only by his success in creating a mode of discourse – can we think of anyone after Hobbes who wrote in a Hobbesian idiom, especially in English? The point is that the historian is now dealing, not with the interlocking languages of a series of practising clerisies, but with a single though multiplex community of discourse, practising an activity which can only be characterized as rhetoric or literature; and that the language of political discourse, though we can still break it down into a multiplicity of sub-languages or idioms, must now be seen as capable of generating these idioms from within the activity of its own discourse, as well as borrowing from, or being intruded on by, idioms originating with other communities of discourse. At the beginning of the eighteenth century, journalism and belles-lettres, at its end classical economics, entered powerfully into the fabric of English political discourse; but at the same time there came into being the idiom of Burke and (far more deliberately created) the idiom of Bentham, both of which – but, if you prefer, far more obviously the former – may be said to have arisen as mutations within the changing patterns of political rhetoric or discourse.

The layers of language contexts which our historian-archaeologist brings to light are thus of a very heterogeneous character. Some are languages of professional practice, which have for some reason entered into the language of politics and become idioms in which it is conducted; others are idioms, rhetorical modes or styles, which are better thought of as originating within the discourse and rhetoric of politics, as the result of moves or performances carried out by authors and actors within it. To emphasize the former is to emphasize social structure, to stress that we are looking at speech articulated by churchmen, lawyers, humanists, professors, or perhaps the laities and occasionally the heresies defined by exclusion from one or other of these; to emphasize the latter is to emphasize discourse, to stress that we are looking at speech articulated by discursants acting within an ongoing activity of debate and discussion, rhetoric and theory, performing acts whose context is that of the discourse itself. What we mean by the creation and diffusion of political languages will vary as we adopt one or other of these highly legitimate perspectives; the social generation of languages entails one set of priorities, the rhetorical generation another. The historian-archaeologist, however, uncovering one layer after another of the languages which a text contains, finds himself obliged to adopt both; to him at least they are not categorically distinct.

We suppose these languages capable of being arranged along a scale which leads from the highly institutional and extraneous to the highly personal and idiosyncratic; though, as we shall see, these two poles are not mutually exclusive. As we near the latter pole, however, we encounter in an increasingly acute form the problem of what it is to speak of a language as an identifiable historical phenomenon. That is to say, the more we are dealing with individual styles of utterance, the creation of identifiable individuals in identifiable situations, the greater becomes the danger of confusing *parole* with *langue* and interpretation with identification. We ought not to say that we have found a new 'language', merely because we have found a highly individual style of utterance which bears its own implications and suggests its own practice; less still because we have merely found a new style in which we ourselves can read the utterances of discursants in the past and attribute modes and levels of meaning to them, for to do this is to reduce all history to a text which exists only as we can interpret it. The historian I am supposing aims to be certain, or as certain as he can be, that a 'language' or 'language context' which he claims to have discovered or uncovered existed *eigentlich*, prior to his discovery of it; he seeks means of showing that it was not merely his own invention, since he knows that *invenire* can mean both to find and to fabricate. This aim can be pursued in a number of ways.

The historian's confidence that a 'language' is not his own fabrication may increase: (a) as he can show that different authors carried out variant acts in the same language, responding to one another in it and employing it as a medium as well as a mode of discourse; (b) as he can show that they discussed one another's use of it, devised second-order languages for criticizing its use, and identified it verbally and explicitly as a language they were using (this may be called the Monsieur Jourdain test); (c) as he can predict the implications, intimations, paradigmatic effects, problematics, etc., which the use of a given language will have entailed in specific situations, and show his predictions to have been fulfilled or, more interestingly, falsified (this may be called the experimental test); (d) as he experiences surprise followed by pleasure at discovering a familiar language in places where he did not expect to find it (this may be called the serendipity test); (e) as he excludes from consideration languages not available to the authors under discussion (the anachronism test).

The historian learns a language in order to read it, not to write in it. His own writings will not be composed of pastiches of the various languages he has learned, like John Barth's *The Sotweed Factor*, but of languages of interpretation, which he has developed and learned to write, each designed to bring out and articulate, in a kind of paraphrase, the assumptions, intimations, etc., explicit and implicit in one or more of the languages he has learned to read. He is engaged in a kind of dialogue with Collingwood's famous formula: he may learn another's language in order to 'rethink his thoughts', but the language in which he expresses another's thoughts after rethinking them will be the historian's and not the other's. This leaves room for both critical and historical detachment; the historian's language contains his resources for affirming both that he is adequately interpreting another's *parole* and that this *parole* was in fact being conducted in the *langue*, or in the selection and combination of *langues*, to which the historian has assigned it. This is his answer to any extremisms he may encounter about the untranslatability or unreadability of texts; he claims ability to show in what a diversity of languages a text was being written and was subsequently being read, and to distinguish between these languages and those in which it was not and could not have been written or read at a specific time.

But all this implies his ability to re-institutionalize languages: to show that what may at first sight look like highly idiosyncratic modes of utterance were already, or became subsequently, known and recognized resources of the community of discourse, 'available languages' as the jargon has it, which were used and in some measure recognized as usable by more than one actor in that community. A language must be, as a style need not, a game recognized as open to more than one player. Once we acknowledge this, however, the distinction already drawn between the social and rhetorical creation and diffusion of languages becomes more than ever crucial. If we can show that a given language originated outside the universe of political discourse, in some social or professional practice, and then entered that universe in more or less specific circumstances, it is easier to say that it possessed an institutional character, and was available for the purposes of various actors in the language game, than it is when we see a language originating within that universe, in the speech acts and rhetorical moves and strategies of the game's players; for in the latter case we face the problem of showing how the actor's moves gave rise to language institutions, and there will always be those who emphasize the uniqueness of each move to the point where the institution it was performed in and helped to form disappears. It is now being questioned[4] – I think it ought to be questioned and I am not committed to any particular answer – whether the English

[4] A bibliography might be assembled on this point, drawn from the writings of Donald R. Kelley, G. R. Elton, Kevin Sharpe and others. I confine myself to citing Richard Tuck's *Natural Rights Theories: their origin and development* (Cambridge, 1980). [See above, p. 75n.]

'common-law mind' was in fact as monolithically insular as I suggested in *The Ancient Constitution and the Feudal Law*, published in 1957; but the effect of this criticism is to make the doctrine of the ancient constitution explicable as a good deal less of a *mentalité* and a good deal more of a move. If, as is now maintained, Englishmen of the seventeenth century were not so blinkered in their insularity as to be unaware that Roman and feudal law existed and might have enjoyed or still enjoy authority in England, then the proposition that they had never enjoyed it must have been less of an assumption and more of an assertion: an argument to which there might be a counter-argument, a paradigm to be established through the exclusion of its opposite. Sir Edward Coke, that great oracle of the law, would appear less the mouthpiece through which a *mentalité* articulated itself than a powerful advocate and successful pleader, employing speech, pen and print to induce his hearers and readers to adopt a position to which they were no doubt in many ways predisposed (it is not asserted that *mentalité* or ideology has no existence) but to which they knew but must deny that an alternative could be alleged. The speech act would become prominent in relation to the language situation.

A lot of evidence recently adduced is telling in favour of this revision, and I welcome it since I have no commitment to the *mentalité* type of explanation and am indeed inclined to see early-modern language situations as multilingual rather than monolithic. The problem of insularity aside, it is evident that a *mentalité* is too easily alleged if we think only of the normal operations of a language and not of the speech acts performed within and upon it; if we neglect *parole* in favour of *langue*. But somewhere in the debate over English historiography I catch sight of that powerful school of historians for whom there is no reality but that of high politics and all historical phenomena are reducible to the moves of insiders playing at the endless adventure of oligarchical government.[5] If they were right, there would only be *parole* and never *langue;* each move's success or failure would be determined within the *durée bien moyenne* of the current state of the game, never within the more durable contexts provided by social or linguistic structures. I am concerned to argue for a presentation of the history of discourse which situates it between *parole* and *langue*, between speech act and language context; and I am stimulated by the proposed revision of my interpretation of long ago because it sharpens the perspective

[5] 'The Endless Adventure' is the title of an early specimen (1912) of this genre by F. S. Oliver, concerned with English politics from Harley to Walpole. Post-Namierian practitioners include G. R. Elton (sometimes) and Maurice Cowling (rather more often). [It is now some time since the 'high politics' school was as powerful as suggested here.]

in which what I presented as a language can be seen in process of being modified and even established by the performance of speech acts.

But this returns us to the point at which the 'creation and diffusion of languages' must be seen as going on within the activity of discourse as well as in the interactions between discourse and other social phenomena. Our historian, engaged in identifying the language contexts in which speech acts are conducted, must be able to study the creation of languages anywhere in the social context and their diffusion into the activity of political discourse; but he must also be equipped with means of showing how the performance of speech acts not merely modifies language, but leads to the creation and diffusion of new languages in our sense of the term. There is the generation of languages by the activities, practices and contexts of society; there is the generation of languages by the interactions of *langue* and *parole* in an ongoing continuity of discourse. We may consider the latter as a special case of the former, but not as its epiphenomenon once we concede that language is a continuous activity which sets its own rules and even determines the ways in which these rules can be changed. It is our historian's *métier* to have learned a number of languages and established them as contexts in which acts of utterance are performed; he now needs ways of understanding how the acts modify the contexts they are performed in, and how some of these modifications lead to the creation and diffusion of new languages and new contexts. Furthermore, he is typically though not necessarily engaged in studying the history of a literature: that is, a form of discourse conducted through the production of written and printed texts, which it is his endeavour to explicate as events in that history; highly complex *paroles* or acts of utterance, intelligible in terms of the *langues* from which they were drawn, of their effects upon those *langues* and upon the worlds in which they were written and uttered. To see how *paroles* of this kind modify *langue*, and how in some cases they help create and diffuse new idioms of discourse, is an important part of his endeavour.

We last saw him in the role of archaeologist, uncovering languages or idioms of discourse as so many contextual layers, of which a text might be shown to be composed so that it performed in all of them concurrently. These idioms arose from a diversity of sources and might be derived from societies and moments in history no longer presently existing (it can be an important moment in the growth of historical self-knowledge when this is found to be the case). Each was specialized for the performance of acts and the conveyance of messages peculiar to itself; but competent disputants and rhetoricians were quite capable of mixing the layers, of weaving the idioms together in a single text and a single, but complex, continuity of discourse. When this has happened, the text must be seen as performing a number of utterances simultaneously, and the historian – ceasing at this point to be an archaeologist – must ask whether it performs a unified series of acts or a plural and heterogeneous series. In several perspectives, the historical among them, these are not mutually exclusive possibilities. We may, for example, think of the author, if a sufficiently dominant presence, as Penelope by day, weaving the idioms together in a single tapestry conveying a unified picture; but we will also do well to think of the text's readers (who need be nowhere near so sophisticated as the author) as Penelope by night, unpicking the design and reducing it to a selectivity of idioms and utterances. There are authors quite cunning enough to anticipate and exploit the diversity of reader response, but none, we suspect, who has ever anticipated all the responses which his text will elicit. Both the past and the future of a text viewed historically furnish us with grounds for emphasizing the diversity and heterogeneity of the utterances it may be performing or may turn out to have performed. To the political theorist, this means that the language of politics is inherently ambivalent; as William Connolly has put the matter,[6] it consists in the utterance of essentially disputed propositions. To the historian, it means that any text may be an actor in an indefinite series of linguistic processes, of interactions between utterance and context. It was wise of Quentin Skinner to employ an imperfect and continuous past tense when laying down that we must know what an author 'was doing' when he published a particular text;[7] for if what he 'was doing' includes and even privileges what he intended to perform, not only may his intentions and performances have been diverse and even divergent, but what he 'would turn out to have done' may prove almost exponentially distanced from any performance he intended. History consists largely of unintended performances, and the passage from intention to performance requires both the imperfect and the conditional perfect tense.

Our historian, ceasing altogether to be an archaeologist, seeks means of showing how *parole* acted upon *langue*. We suppose him capable of showing that any text was couched and performed in a diversity of idioms, each constituting a conventional mode of utterance and exerting a paradigmatic force. From this, and from his knowledge of the historical situations and contexts in which the author was situated and to which his utterance referred, he can render a specific account of a variety of speech acts

[6] William E. Connolly, *The Terms of Political Discourse*, 2nd edn (Princeton, 1983).

[7] Quentin Skinner, *The Foundations of Modern Political Thought*, I: *The Renaissance* (Cambridge, 1978), Introduction.

which text and author may have intended and/or performed. These acts, intended and performed in each of the text's several idioms or in all of them together, he proceeds to distinguish into the more routine – the utterance of conventions – and the more specific: the application of conventions.

When the conventions, paradigms and directives of which a political language may be thought of as composed are applied to and in political and historical circumstances other than those which it conventionally presupposes, two processes may be seen taking place. First, the new wine will be poured into the old bottles; the new circumstances, and the problems in thought and action which they generate, will be assimilated to those presupposed by the old conventions, so that the latter may continue to rule them: out of the old fields must the new corn come, as Sir Edward Coke – who understood this process well – liked to put it. The historian will find this process fascinating to watch, because it highlights the presuppositions of the old language, informs him as to what sort of universe its users were encouraged to presume they were living in, and enables him to form judgments regarding the historical situations in which it has been formed and was being used. He is not so rigorous a historicist as to presuppose that the attempt to pour new wine into old bottles is invariably a failure or productive of false consciousness; sometimes it is and sometimes it isn't, and some paradigms and languages display continuity in the midst of change over lengthy periods. But needless to say, there is a process in the contrary direction; the new circumstances generate tensions in the old conventions, language finds itself being used in new ways, changes occur in the language being used, and it is possible to imagine this process leading to the creation and diffusion of new languages – though exactly what this phrase would mean remains to be specified. Our historian will try to study the sequences in which such things may be seen happening, and there are two precepts which it may be worth inserting here.

One is that the creation of a new language may take place in the attempt to maintain the old language no less than in the attempt to change it; cases can be found in which a deliberate and conscious stress on change, process and modernity is among the strategies of those defending a traditional order, and it is in the logic of the concept of tradition that this should be so. The other is that, since the use of any language may be more or less widely diffused, the number of actors and the diversity of their acts involved in these processes can differ widely. Some language changes may appear as brought about by a concurrence or consensus of speech acts performed by so many actors, in so many language situations and with such diverse intentions, that it is easier to think of the changes in language as occasioned than as intended; as a product of the heterogeneity of ends rather than as the work of identifiable leading actors who can be shown performing innovations in *langue* by the utterance of aggregative or disaggregative *paroles* and imposing innovations and new language upon others. On the other hand, such conspicuous actors do seem to occur in history; they acquire, sometimes quite rapidly, the status of authorities who are to be followed or of adversaries who are to be rebutted; and it is not at all impossible to imagine some kinds of language change as brought about by the utterances performed by identifiable actors and the responses of others not less identifiable to them. Sometimes, it is true, this image proves to be historiographic illusion; we have been given to selecting noteworthy individuals and casting them in leading or representative roles which they did not always occupy; but if they were cast in such roles not by historians but by those whom historians study, the case is altered. Certainly we need means of asking whether Machiavelli or Hobbes or Locke played the role in history which has been conventionally assigned to him; but equally we need means of understanding how changes in political language may be seen as brought about by utterance and response performed by individual actors. We need both the morphology of *langue* and the dynamics of *parole*.

We think, then, of an individual who has something to say in and about a highly specific and in some ways unprecedented situation, but whose utterance is directed and constrained by the rules or conventions of the several languages available to him. The directives imposed by these languages are at variance with the impulses and constraints arising from the author's perceived predicament; and these of course arise in a variety of ways. There may be something in the situation, known or unknown or more or less known to the utterer, which is difficult to speak of in any of the conventional ways; or he may be in a casuistic or forensic dilemma, perhaps imposed upon him by the speech acts of some opponent in a dispute; or his reflection – possibly his profound and complex moral, epistemological or metaphysical reflection – on the predicament of himself and others in or as revealed by the immediate situation may have persuaded him that some trifling or drastic change in the conventions and presuppositions of language must be effected. We may think – it is important to be able to think – of his *parole* as a response to pressures imposed upon him by the *paroles* of others; but if we are to write history in terms of the interactions of *parole* and *langue*, it is important to see his *parole* as a response to the conventions of *langue* which he is using and of which he is more or less aware. The players perform speech acts according to the rules of the game; sometimes they discuss the rules of the game and develop second-order languages in which to do so; these have rules which may be subject to innovation, and a change in these rules may entail a change in the rules by which speech acts may be performed in the languages of the first order. A change in the rules of the language game brought about by some act of speech may be both prior and posterior to any effect which that act performs upon any player in the game; yet all acts are performed by players.

But we have not yet explained how such innovations may be effected, still less how they may end in the creation and diffusion of new languages. How an innovative speaker or author utters a *parole* which is new is clearly hard to categorize, not only because of the indeterminacy of the term 'new', but because of the tremendous flexibility of language itself. Quentin Skinner has accustomed us to speaking in terms of an author performing a 'move', and the number and variety of possible 'moves' is as rich as the resources of rhetoric itself; early-modern Europe was a highly rhetorical civilization. But such a 'move' was not only one made possible, however unexpected by an opponent, by the rules of some game; it may also, since we are in history, have been one which had the effect of altering the rules – whether like William Webb Ellis picking up the ball and running with it, or like Socrates and Thomas Hobbes suggesting that the game was being played according to the wrong rules. We may therefore define the verbal innovation as one which suggests, and according to its power imposes, some change in the rules or conventions of political language: it may propose an alteration in value signs, a treatment of that which was bad as now good or vice versa; or it may propose to remove the discussion of a term or problem from the language context, in which it has been conventionally discussed into some other context itself known but not hitherto considered appropriate to this discussion. Machiavelli's employment of the term *virtù* is an example of both kinds of 'move', and there are of course many other kinds. Let us note that such acts suggesting rule or paradigm innovation may be performed explicitly or implicitly, overtly or covertly, intentionally or unintentionally, and much depends upon *Rezeption* and reader response; the reader and interpreter may have the resources of rhetoric at his disposal too. Many an author has found himself a more radical innovator than, or even than, he intended to be or ever admitted he was.

How can such innovatory *paroles* give rise to the creation of new languages? A question we must discuss if we are prepared to consider the process originating with specific acts by specific individuals. There can be many ways of answering it. Let our author be perceived as having proposed some change in the rules of a language game; it may follow – given sufficient publicity – that the game is never the same again, because those who wish to maintain the old rules do so not by reiterating them as if the innovator had never existed, but by answering him and rebutting his proposals; and since those who answer an adversary must do so by accepting his language and presuppositions, even as a prelude to debating and denying their acceptability, a sufficiently resonant or scandalous innovator necessarily succeeds in imposing new language and new rules of the language game, though often in ways not congruent with his intention. Some great innovators, like Plato or Marx, create and diffuse new languages through their success in becoming authorities; others, like Machiavelli or Hobbes, through their success in becoming adversaries, to rebut whom new languages come into being. And such authors, it must be remembered, are innovators in the contextual field as well as the textual. They suggest new modes of discourse which are perceived as having innovatory implications in language contexts other than those they initially discoursed in; they are therefore read and responded to, and their *paroles* have consequences affecting *langue*, in contexts which need not have figured in their intentions. To disclaim an intention may not be to preclude an effect.

But I am speaking here of change in language: of the creation and diffusion of new language in the abstract and singular; and once we admit the term 'creation and diffusion of languages', the use of the plural, or the specific yet indefinite 'a language', obliges us to envisage a more concrete kind of phenomenon. Languages in this plural sense must be diffused as well as created; they must become available resources for the performance of speech acts other than those by which they were created, conventions themselves subject to innovation and change, *langues*, in short, rather than simple sequences of *paroles*. How a Machiavellian or anti-Machiavellian rhetoric became institutionalized in this sense, how it became an idiom or language available for the purposes of others besides Machiavelli and his immediate respondents (if he had any) is not an easy question to answer. There appear to be at least two ways of pursuing it. One is discursive: by 'learning a language', in the sense I sought to describe earlier, one learns to recognize it wherever it appears and to take note of its presence in a variety of texts and contexts, some of which may be very different from those in which we first saw it formulated. In this way, the historian may find himself studying the diffusion of a language throughout a widening and changing field of discourse, and reaches the point where it may be said that such a language is not merely the shared idiom of a series of disputants but an available resource diffused to the point where it was known to, and could enter the discourse of, persons engaged in discussions other than those for which it was originally intended. At this point the language has assumed a metaphoric as well as a paradigmatic role: what, it must be asked, were the effects of discussing a problem in language which originated elsewhere in social speech and suggested that it was a problem belonging to a certain family? The effects would be felt by the language as well as by the problem.

The advantage of studying diffusion and creation in this way is that it enables the historian to map the field of discourse and study action and change taking place upon it. The disadvantage is that it virtually confines him – though the field is so large that he need not sense the confinement – to the history of recorded discourse: to a history of texts and literature and intradisciplinary disputes, in which the response to an act of writing and publication is perceptible only when it is another act of writing and publication. It need not follow that the only actors in this story are publicists, though normally they will be; the languages he learns may turn up in private written discourse if any has survived – the public enters into the private – or in the written records of occasions of oral discourse in which early-modern English history, at any rate, is happily rich: parliamentary diaries, state trials, Putney debates. We are indebted to shorthand, it is worth recalling, as well as to moveable type. But the history of discourse among the literati – the history of text speaking to text – does not give us whatever history of *langue* and *parole* may have eventuated in the universe of orally transmitted language. Evidence about this is not easily come by, but it does exist; when the historian I am describing has any, he will ask such questions as how the discourse of orality may have interacted with that of typography, that of popular with that of clerical culture. If he remains a historian of literate discourse, he will concede that he is studying the speech of powerful and limited social groups; he will also claim that their discourse shows public speech in all its variability, changing under the pressures imposed by typography, controversy and high levels of self-consciousness. Within obvious limits, debate among the literati of the ruling order provides effective and illuminating criticism of that order's values, and he may elect to spend much of his time studying its history.

We begin to encounter here a further range of means for the study of the diffusion and institutionalization of languages: the study of the material and social structures through which they have been disseminated. Here such techniques as those of *l'histoire du livre* have much to offer. To know how many copies of the *Encyclopédie* were bought when, where and if we are lucky by whom, can be made to yield a great deal of information,[8] though it does not tell us whether, still less how, the purchasers read the book, or

[8] [The allusion is clearly to Robert Darnton's *The Business of Enlightenment* (Cambridge, MA, 1979).]

how they articulated their responses if they had any; it valuably reminds us that they may have bought the book with quite other ends in view. What such an approach does for the historian whose *métier* I have been describing is to heighten his awareness of the communicative spaces, fields and structures within which political languages were created and diffused. He needs, I am going to suggest, a much better geography of political speech in early-modern Europe: a sense of the territories and boundaries within which certain languages were distributed and certain paradigms authoritative, so that the public discourse of one *pays*, state or province might entail a grammar, metaphysics and ideology like or more probably unlike that entailed by another. Of course there is a double perspective here; there were two faces even to an English Janus; political culture was international as well as regional, and we must consider what happened when Grotius was read in London or Hobbes in Leiden, Locke in Naples or Montesquieu in Philadelphia. But such problems must be dealt with not only by reflecting on one culture's history as compared with another's, but by reflecting that political discourse takes place in a variety of communicative spaces and situations. Those who read *Leviathan* in London during the 1650s encountered it in the world of George Thomason, in the midst of a typographic and social explosion and a revolutionary crisis in speech and consciousness; those who read it in the Netherlands encountered it, for all we have yet heard to the contrary, in the different but by no means bland or neutral environment of university lecture halls where it was read and discussed in Latin (I simply do not know if there was a Dutch pamphlet discourse, as certainly there was an English, in which Hobbes played a part). This means no more than that *Leviathan* has many histories, and figures in the creation and diffusion of languages through many kinds of context.

The historian of the creation and diffusion of political languages is, as I have described him, a historian of the interactions of *parole* and *langue*; he is concerned with *parole* largely as it acts upon *langue*, as it acts to bring about changes in *langue* considered as an institutional structure of public speech available for the diverse and often conflicting purposes of many actors in a universe of discourse. This does not, and I think it never will, altogether satisfy those whose demand upon the historian of *parole* is that it shall be shown acting from, in and upon a highly specific situation composed of social relations and historical acts. But we must beware the fallacy of demanding the immediate where the mediate must suffice. Speech acts upon people; texts act upon readers; but this action is performed sometimes synchronously, through the fairly immediate responses of the hearers and readers, and sometimes diachronously, through the *parole*'s efficacy in bringing them to accept change in the usages, the rules and the perceived or implicit entailments of *langue.* In studying the creation and diffusion of languages, we are committed to processes which have to be viewed diachronously, however much they are made up of performances synchronously occurring. Languages are powerful mediatory structures, and to act in and upon them is to act upon people immediately perhaps, but by changing their means of mediation, which is often done indirectly and takes time. Certainly we must study changes in speech as they produce changes in practice, but there is always an interval in time sufficient to produce heterogeneity in effect.

CHAPTER 7

Texts as events: reflections on the history of political thought

The playwright Tom Stoppard was once heard to deliver a lecture entitled 'Theatre as Event or as Text?' He declared in its course that he wrote his plays to be performed by actors, and that when scholars discovered all manner of layers of meaning in the published texts, he felt as if his baggage was being unpacked by customs officials and he was saying, 'Well, I've got to admit it's there, but I don't remember packing it.' Fair enough. It is implicit in the act of publishing the text, however, that a play is performed more than once and that the text exists even when the play is not being performed. Furthermore, it is a basic rule of historical method that more meanings can be found in a text, or in any document, than the author intended to convey when he wrote it; and this is why (to pursue the dramatic analogy a little further) a play can always be performed one more time, enacting a different set of meanings than the time before.

So when Stoppard insists that it is rarely to the point to ask the author 'What does that mean?', an obvious corollary is that it is always possible for the actor performing or the critic reading the text to find meanings in it which the author did not know were there and which have not been enacted or discerned before. The text now becomes a matrix or holding pattern within which a series of widely differing events can and do occur. This is one of several reasons why authors, actors and critics usually hate one another heartily; but the author, who has created the text and made the events possible, is entitled to be surprised at – but not necessarily entitled to object to – any event that may be performed within it. There may be cases in which he can and must say, 'Look, that's really off-limits; with this text you just cannot do that'; but these are only limiting cases, and it is not clear that the author has a greater right to say that than any actor or critic may have.

[Published in Kevin Sharpe and Steven N. Zwicker (eds.), *Politics of Discourse: the literature and history of seventeenth-century England* (Berkeley and Los Angeles: University of California Press, 1987), pp. 21–34.]

I will now apply some of these reflections to the history of political thought. The phenomena we study under the name consist in the first place largely of texts – that is, of more or less coherent written or printed texts preserving their verbal content over long and unfinished periods of time – and many (though not all) of these texts are believed or known to have had authors about whom we know a lot or a little, as the case may be. Political thought is studied by scholars who practise various disciplines: critics, philosophers, theorists, historians, and so on. It is about historians that I want to write here, being one myself, but I need to say something about their relations with scholars practising other disciplines. I will be discussing these matters within the framework provided by the notions of text and event, though most of my emphasis falls on the suggestion that text and event for the historian are nearly the same thing: that the text is an event as well as a framework within which further events occur.

Quentin Skinner, in *The Foundations of Modern Political Thought*, lays down the premise that what is needed by historians is a history of political thought constructed on genuinely historical principles. He implies that histories of political thought are often constructed on principles that are not genuinely historical, and I return to that aspect of the question in my closing sentences. For the present let us consider what such a genuinely historical history must be. Let us propose – what may not be adequate for all purposes – that for the historian history consists of actions, events and processes. Events happen as the result of actions by persons; the actions are performed and the events happen in contexts that make them possible and (to the historian) intelligible; but they modify these contexts in ways that make other, differing actions and events possible and intelligible. This is part, though not all, of what is meant by processes. To French historians today, of course, this would sound like *histoire événementielle*; they would want to draw attention to the *longue durée*, to the type of infrastructure that makes events possible but changes so slowly that one must doubt whether it is modified by the events at all. The reply to this is that if one is writing a history of texts, one is writing a history of sophisticated verbal performances that are certainly events. To go deeper is to enter a history of languages and *mentalités* that do not consist of texts but into which texts – such as the Bible, the Koran, or the Six Classics – do seem to enter and produce profound modifications. To go yet deeper is to enter a world of grammars and deep structures and to encounter the question of whether such structures have a history or only a *longue durée*. And the true *longue durée* consists of material and geophysical conditions that may or may not pertain to the history of consciousness; even Marx could take it no deeper than the act of production. So let us return to that admittedly sophisticated and elitist world in which the actions of authors produce texts and modify the contexts and structures they do reach. This is the level at which a program in history and literature must desire to operate.

At this level a text can and must be seen as both an action and an event. To quote Skinner again, the first necessity in constructing a truly historical history of political thought is to equip ourselves with means of knowing what the author *was doing* when he wrote the text. This matter is not as simple as it may sound, however. To begin with, it does not reach that depth to which Stoppard was pointing when he said the author did not know himself what he was doing, and that when it was brought to his attention later he did not remember doing it or even recognize himself as having done it. Knowing is not doing, and to know what an actor (even oneself) was doing is not the same thing as doing it.

At this point it may be objected that the dramatist is writing a text for actors to perform, whereas the theorist may be writing a text for contemplatives to read. But this may not make much difference. I write long, complex theoretical treatises and histories, and my experience is exactly the same as Stoppard's when he claims that an author discovers what he is writing in the act of writing it and often does not know what he is writing until he sits down to write. As I wrote these sentences, I had only the vaguest notion what was coming next. The experience of authorship seems exactly the same in this respect in both cases, and I have always believed there is something naive and philistine in the distinction often made between 'creative' writing (which is always about images and fictions) and 'critical' writing (which is always about facts). Furthermore, I doubt how far one can really press the distinction between the actor performing and the reader reading. As students of literature, we are familiar with the idea that reading a text can be a complex action, and as students of history, we need – as I shall try to show – to think of the reader as an actor in the same historical sequence as the author.

So to *know* what the author was doing when he wrote the text is not to repeat the author's experience in *doing* it; it is to reconstitute the experience in terms designed to make it intelligible to the historian, and this is certainly not what the author was claiming to do. I have never met anyone who wrote in order to communicate with historians in the future, and I do not suppose I ever shall. As we reconstitute the author's actions, then, it is in order to watch him performing it, not to repeat the performance ourselves; we write about it in the third person, not the first, and perhaps this is what the distinction between creative and critical is really about. I could use words like *Entfremdung* and *alienation* at this point, but it would probably be better if I did not. Third-person reconstitution of the author's action, however, necessarily involves looking at it in ways and saying things about it that would not have, could not have, and did not need to become apparent to the author himself – finding things in his baggage, to use Tom Stoppard's imagery, which he did not put there or know he had. If we could read what historians will say about us, we would probably be even more astonished, though perhaps less outraged, than we are when we read reviews of the books we write; and that is saying a good deal, because the review is one starting point (only one) of the book's history.

We set out to reconstitute the author's performance, to study the text as event (something happening) and as action (something done); but third-person reconstitution is aimed at providing co-ordinates, at situating the action in the midst of conditions and circumstances that will help us understand, first, what the action in fact was and, second, why and how it was performed. The author may not have needed to know what these were, but we do. This is where the emphasis shifts from text to context, and also – again to use terminology borrowed from Skinner – from intention to illocution and perlocution. In both the first (Stoppard/author) and the third person (Skinner/historian), we know that the author did not begin by acquiring a set of intentions and proceed to acquire a set of words with which to carry them into effect. He found out what he meant to write only in the act of writing it. This places illocution at the centre of the picture and perlocution in the next frame. We study the text in order to see what it says, what effects the words constituting it actually carried out (or, if we are cautious, may have carried out); and this means that we know more about the intentions it did perform than about other intentions which it might have performed but did not.

If this were the whole of the story, however, it would follow that we knew the author only from the text. Often this is not the case; we know a lot more about the author from other texts he wrote, his correspondence, his friends' recollections, the police files on him – and from the knowledge we have as competent historians of the social and historical universe he inhabited, knowledge not identical with his own because we can obtain it only by reconstitution. All this information enables us to form hypotheses about (1) intentions and actions he may have performed without our noticing them at first reading; (2) intentions and actions he may have performed without noticing them himself; (3) intentions and actions he might have performed but did not; and (4) intentions and actions he could not possibly have performed or tried to perform, whatever our misguided colleagues may urge to the contrary.

Now we know that to situate the text (and the author) in a context is necessary in order to reconstitute the text as a historical event; and because we have a diversity of information concerning its (and his) universe, we face the problem of deciding how this context is to be constructed, how its component parts are to be selected from the diversity of historical information at our disposal. To historians of the school to which Skinner and I (among others) belong, it seems evident that the primary component of this context has to be language. There exists a language, or a complex of more than one language, with which things can be said or illocutionary acts performed, within which (it is the next step to add) they must be performed. The primary context within which the speaker or author and his speech or text are situated must be that of the language he speaks. Here, of course, an argument can develop. A Vulgar Marxist may appear and point out (rightly) that the language itself is formed within a context of social relations, so that (he adds wrongly) it is possible to know the context of social relations and infer the character of language from them. To study language as if it operated autonomously, the Marxist will say, is idealism or something nasty like that. The reply is that of course language takes shape from its social context, but we do know by now that it is not just a mirror. The trick is to see in what ways language indicates the context in which it is formed and in what ways it does not; what signs it contains that point directly at the phenomena of social relations, what signs that point at them indirectly, and what signs that point away from the phenomena of social relations as historians may perceive them. (The historian must now decide what to make of that.) To do all this, the language-oriented historian adds, one must infer the egg from the chicken; if one wants to know how language indicates society, one must look at the language and see how it works – what it told those who used it about their society and what it did not. And if one wants to know how a speaker's or author's illocutionary act was concerned with things going on in his society, one must go through this same mediatory structure: the language context. What will continue to part the language-oriented historian from the intelligent Marxist (the Vulgar Marxist having been left in his wallow) is that the latter will want to pursue the language–society relationship, whereas the former, for whom the relation between language and illocution comes first, will want to discuss the language as a historical phenomenon that operated autonomously enough to provide the primary (not the only) set of conditions within which the illocution was performed. The history of political thought becomes primarily, though not finally, a history of language games and their outcomes.

The historian's reconstitution of the context that makes the text, as action and event, intelligible now becomes a matter of reconstituting the languages in which certain illocutions – those defined as existing for the purposes of political thought – were carried out, and of discerning what the individual text, author or performance did with the opportunities offered and the constraints imposed by the languages available to it. A number of interesting problems arise here, some of them historical and some of them theoretical. To take the former first, what are these languages of which I speak in the plural, and how does one reconstitute them? About thirty years ago I wrote a book, *The Ancient Constitution and the Feudal Law*, which set something of a fashion for this sort of method, and I have been practising it ever since. In the early-modern period (1500–1800) it is especially useful to say that there was not just one specialized language of political thought – such as the idiom of Christianized Aristotelian philosophy, which many considered the paramount language for these purposes – but a number of them; and that these were located in and derived from the activities of a number of specialized professional groups: in England not only the still-scholastic academics who kept the medieval and Aristotelian idiom going but the common lawyers, the established clergy, the dissentient and radical Puritans, the specialists in classical rhetoric who Thomas Hobbes believed were largely to blame for the civil war, and so on. It was Edmund Burke, so far as I know, who was the first to point out the historical importance of the fact that the English talked about their liberties in the common-law language of real property. Historians of political thought, at least in the early-modern period, spend much of their time reconstructing these languages and reconstructing the performances of texts, by pointing out that they were performed in this or that language or combination of languages. Because this is still a fairly recently perfected archaeological technique, it is still common to find that one has made some exciting discovery in it; as that Thomas Hobbes was doing eschatology, John Locke natural jurisprudence, Edmund Burke common law or paper-money theory, and so on. And this may still be surface archaeology, not carried out by any sophisticated technique of excavation. The author's use of this or that language may not be indirect or concealed but perfectly explicit; it may simply have been neglected by scholars who have been trained to look only for forms of thought considered important for reasons sometimes not historical at all. The merit of the technique I am describing is that it obliges the scholar to ask what languages people in the past really spoke, and what forms of thought they considered important, and so to re-emphasize previously neglected answers to the Skinnerian question, 'What were they actually doing?'

'Languages' such as these are not, of course, 'languages' in the same sense as Latin or English, but specialized idioms existing in Latin or English and sometimes translatable from one to the other. It seems inadequate to call them 'vocabularies'; that term sounds rather too lexical. I am following Burke in calling them 'languages', but possibly they should be called 'idioms' or 'rhetorics' instead. Those I have described so far may be called 'institutional languages', meaning that they were the idioms used by powerful corporations of intellectual specialists: scholastics, rhetoricians, common lawyers, and so on. It is possible, however, to detect the presence of 'languages' by other means and see them as existing in other ways. In *The Machiavellian Moment*'s early chapters I tried a problem-situation approach. I asked, 'In what idioms did people deal with a certain intellectual problem: that of the sequence of events in secular time?' Here is the answer I came up with: 'in three idioms: those of custom, grace, and fortune'. Now there might be a rough-and-ready professional differentiation among these three: custom was a lawyer's word, grace a theologian's, fortune a rhetorician's. But that was not of much interest when I wanted to exhibit the presence of all three idioms in the writings of Machiavelli, who was neither a jurist nor a theologian but much closer to being a rhetorician – which is one reason why he does more with the concept of fortune than with the other two. What I was then in a position to suggest was that Machiavelli belonged to a culture limited to these three idioms for dealing with the problem, but that he selected and rearranged from the modes of speech available to him in such a way as to produce extraordinary changes in them.

But languages sought out by methods such as that tend to become increasingly implicit, and the historian faces increasingly severe problems in demonstrating that they were really there. An 'institutional' language is rendered much easier to detect by the existence and activities of the institution within which it is spoken; it will be relatively self-conscious, and there may even be a secondary literature about how it should be spoken. One that is implicitly present, as a kind of sub-language or idiom within generalized 'ordinary language', will be a good deal harder to verify. In *The Machiavellian Moment* I was obliged to show that idioms and modes of speech resting on custom, grace and fortune – which later helped to generate a rhetoric of virtue, corruption and commerce – could be detected in the writings of the people I had under study, and that they were employed consistently (i.e., consistently with the characteristics I had ascribed to them) and also consciously. One does this essentially by learning to speak the language in question and then showing that some author in history was speaking it also. Obviously, however, you must confront the query, 'How do you know you have not invented the language and read it into the text? If you are a historian, as distinct from some other sorts of reader, you are not allowed to do that.' Here you must produce the best available evidence for the autonomous existence of your language in history. The more authors you can show to have made use of it the better. If you can show them arguing with one another in it, so that it produces different results and grows and changes in the course of usage, better still; and if some Monsieur Jourdain should appear in your history who says, 'We seem to be talking in such and such an idiom, whose characteristics are such and such', and such as you have said they must have been, you get up and dance round the room. This does not happen very often, and sometimes you must face the fact that you are sitting on the fence that divides the historian from other kinds of readers, in which case you must be very careful what you say.

We have now moved from saying that texts are events to saying that languages are the matrices within which texts as events occur, and our history has become less a history of individual performances and acts of authorship than a history of languages, or (as David Hollinger has put it) one of continuities of discourse. We have reconstituted a context, or a series of contexts, in which the text as event may be rendered intelligible, thus permitting us to read a whole series of meanings into the text – as many as there are idioms or languages in which it may be seen as performing. A really complex text, occurring in a really complex historical situation, may be seen as performing polyvalently: not only will there be several continuities of discourse (another term is levels of meaning) within which it may be read and seen to have acted but it may be seen as performing all manner of cunning games as it moves from one level to another. No student of literature needs to be told what I mean here. If we have succeeded in demonstrating that the continuities of discourse were historically actual, that they were recourses of language available for use, and modified by use, over periods of historic time, then we have escaped the reproach that we are merely reading them into the record; that we are dishonest customs searchers planting in the baggage of Tom Stoppard's author the concealed goods we claim to have found there. All we are telling the author (should he be still alive to hear us) is that he was operating in more continuities of discourse than he knew at the time. And if he has told us that he did not know what continuities of discourse he was operating in, he has told us that he knew he did not know what we have just told him. He has, of course, also told us that he did not need to know at the time; that he did not need to know what he was doing – in Skinner's use of the phrase – in order to do it; that he did not need to go about like an Owl of Minerva looking over his shoulder. Well, we know that, because we are the Owls; but as soon as he has finished his act, he becomes one of us – like Monsieur Jourdain.

There seem to be two main senses in which texts are events and make history. One is that they are actions performed in language contexts that make them possible, that condition and constrain them but that they also modify. Texts, whether individually or cumulatively, act upon the languages in which they are performed: as they perform they inform, injecting new words, facts, perceptions, and rules of the game; and, whether gradually or catastrophically, the language matrix becomes modified by the acts performed in it. A text is an actor in its own history, and a polyvalent text acts in a multiplicity of concurrent histories. This is complex enough, but it is actually one of the easier shapes in which to conceive a history of public discourse. If I were ever to write a long-term history of political thought in Britain, it would probably be organized in terms of the rise, change and decline of the various idioms in which that activity from time to time has been conducted. This, however, would certainly be attacked as failing to do justice to the magnitude of the great masters and their masterpieces; and certainly Thomas Hobbes, say, and Jonathan Swift are bad men to reduce to the status of performers in any finite number of circus rings. You cannot write a history in terms of the great texts; but there is a sense in which the great texts are difficult to reduce to history. This is because they continue to be read and used by people who are not historians.

The second sense in which texts make history is that texts have readers and outlive their authors. The author, in creating the text, creates the matrix in which others will read and respond to it. Readers, however, are like the actors as well as the critics in the dramaturgical analogy with which I began – in fact, it seems important at this moment to call the reader an actor in the sense that he is one in a historical process. No text is ever read exactly as its author intended it should be read; there is a sense in which the reader re-enacts the text, and this never happens twice in exactly the same way. The dramatist aims principally at providing occasions for actors to re-enact what he gives them; but the people Malvolio calls politic authors aim immediately at affecting the consciousness of other actors in political society: they are engaged in rhetoric, which is traditionally the most political form of speech. The dramatist may pursue the same aims but in a form more complex than rhetoric. But the readers' consciousness is no less active than the author's; they respond to him – which is why the concept of 'influence' has fallen out of critical use – and they preserve the independent activity of their consciousness by reading him as they intend, which may or may not be how the author intended to be read. Students of literature know that text–reader relationships are complex and unpredictable affairs; students of 'the history of ideas' may need to be reminded that they are a very large part of what they are studying.

It may be said that reading is an act of translation: I translate your message into my understanding of it. But if I do so in ways that effect no modification of the language you used, there is no change in the matrix within which we both act. It is another matter if I effect such a modification by illocutionary performances of my own. All I may do in such a case, however, is to continue, without interrupting, the history of the language in which your text was written. It is another thing again if I read you so as to translate your text into terms of some other of the languages or idioms in which our society conducts its discourse – which, in the situation of polyvalence, will be going on all the time. True, some idioms are remarkably resistant to translation and use their impenetrability as a means of gaining ascendancy over other idioms. It was notoriously difficult to present the thought of common lawyers in any terms but those of the common law, and this was part of what Sir Edward Coke meant when he instructed the understandably annoyed James I in the nature of 'artificial reason'. But sometimes the act of translation is possible. Since reading Skinner's *Foundations* I have become increasingly interested in the relationship between a rhetorical and humanist language whose fundamental notion was *virtue* and a scholastic and juristic language whose fundamental notion was *right*. There is a sense in which the two were not inter-translatable; what was meant by virtue was not part of what was meant by right and vice versa, and therefore Francesco Guicciardini, who was a doctor of laws, never used juristic language when writing about the *vivere civile*. It seems to have been Spanish Jesuits who invented the idea that Machiavelli was the author of a doctrine of *ratio status* (about which he says nothing) by translating him into the idiom of natural law, which is founded on the idea of *recta ratio*. Unlike Leo Strauss and Harvey Mansfield in our own day, the Jesuits did not contend that Machiavelli ought to have been talking about natural law, that he had deliberately and of evil intent chosen not to talk about natural law, and that he was therefore talking about natural law most particularly when he was not. Because natural law was a preponderant idiom in the society which both Machiavelli and the Jesuits inhabited, the latter were not wrong in drawing attention to the illocutionary force his writings possessed when read by them; they were on questionable ground only in attributing to him the intention of performing that illocution. Here is an excellent illustration of the transformation of a text by reader translation and of the problems in historical reconstitution to which it may give rise. It was Leo Strauss who propounded something called 'the pure and merciless laws of logographic necessity', according to which there were texts that performed all the illocutions that could possibly be read into them and whose authors had intended to perform all of them. This suggests that Strauss was trying to explode the concepts of both translation and history.

The most interesting acts of translation are anachronistic. They are performed by readers who live in times during which the matrices, idioms and language games have been modified, so that texts that are still current and still acting as the matrices for action are no longer limited to the performance of the illocutions they performed at first publication, and perhaps are no longer capable of performing those illocutions. Because the printed word is rather durable, many texts outlive the modification of their initial contexts, as well as outliving their authors. Some of them acquire the sort of authority that leads individuals living in a series of modified contexts to recur to them, and these become the subjects of what are called traditions of interpretation, which are continuous histories of anachronistic – or, if you prefer, diachronic – translation. It may be that traditions operate according to predictable laws; I once tried to formulate some in an essay called 'Time, Institutions and Action'.[1] However that may be, we have here a most interesting category of texts surviving in language matrices that modify the actions performed with them but that they continue to modify through their surviving capacity to act in themselves as matrices for action.

Of some of these texts we say that they are classics; that is, that their traditions of interpretation have been prolonged into the present in which we ourselves live. How these classics are selected I will not attempt to discuss, except to say that the persistence of both original writing and textual archaeology ensures that texts newly written or newly recovered may become classics in relatively short time; examples could be given from several disciplines. When a text is being read, responded to and employed in various kinds of illocution, in any 'present', some of those making use of it will have the concerns of the historian; they will want to reconstitute the actions of its author (if any) and its readers at various moments in past time. Others will want to perform actions in the matrix it provides, which

[1] [Chapter 10 in this volume.]

will be actions performed in the present and which will not entail knowing what others were doing in the past or – if this were possible – knowing what one is doing oneself in the same way that one can know what another was doing by reconstituting his action. The reason why it is difficult to have historical knowledge of our own actions is that such knowledge is attained by reconstituting an action in a context designed to render it explicable, and it is very difficult to reconstitute an action in the moment of performing it for the first time. To be both playwright and actor is possible during the first run of the play; to be both playwright and critic is almost impossible (though if Stoppard did not want to expose himself to critics, he would not publish his plays). The respondent to a classic text who wants to use it in an original act of illocution is like the actor; the respondent who wants to perform the act of reconstituting another's illocution is more like the critic. Perhaps it is unfortunate that the word 'critic' is often used to define the former, whereas the word 'historian' is very justly used to define the latter.

The former category, when referring to those responding to political texts, commonly embraces political theorists and philosophers; when referring to those responding to texts of 'literature', it embraces critics of the kind who were once called New Critics. It should be obvious by now that the actions of philosophers and New Critics are wholly legitimate, that the actions of historians are wholly legitimate, and that the two kinds of legitimacy do not negate each other. Yet historians and non-historians frequently quarrel. I think it is unnecessary for them to do so, and being a historian myself I naturally think that historians are blameless (except when stupid) and quarrel with non-historians only when the latter are stupid enough to deny the legitimacy of what we are doing or think we are denying the legitimacy of what they are doing. If A wants to employ text Z in performing act P, and says 'Z means P', I know this is shorthand for 'Z enables me to perform P'. I do not say 'Z does not mean P'; still less 'If Z means P, then Z is wrong.' I may say, 'Nobody before A, to my knowledge – and this goes for the author of Z – has ever used Z to mean P', or I may say, 'That is very interesting; to hear that A finds P in Z suggests that others before A may have used Z to perform P, since A's action may be historically continuous or discontinuous with the actions of others before him.' Perhaps it would help A to know which it was; but it would not help A to perform the illocution P, only to know what kind of act it was when he performed it. Only if P was the kind of act that entailed making statements about the previous history of actions performed in the matrix Z provides could A's statement about the 'meaning' of Z be true or false from the historian's point of view.

The word *meaning* has now taken on more meanings than one. In listening to the discourse of students of political thought, I have found it a good rule of thumb that if someone says, 'Hobbes said . . . ', he means, 'Thomas Hobbes (1588–1679) said or meant to say . . . ' and is speaking as a historian. Whereas if he says, 'Hobbes says . . . ', he means, 'Hobbes means to me, or enables me to say . . . ' and is speaking as a theorist or philosopher. That is how it should be, in any case; unfortunately there is a historic present I find it hard to avoid myself. It is also clear that the status of the word 'Hobbes' varies from sentence to sentence. To change the scenario a little: in 1976 I attended two conferences marking the bicentennial of the death of Hume, and at each it was evident that for the philosophers present, to say 'Hume says' meant using the word 'Hume' as little more than a trigger that set in motion various language games they desired to play. They did not care or need to know about the historical David Hume who was born in 1711 and died in 1776 and performed many acts of various kinds between those dates. For the historians present, the word 'Hume' was a historical expression denoting the life and actions of that individual, and they used it only to introduce historical statements. The difference between the two usages was so absolute that it caused no confusion, only non-communication. Things might have been worse if it had been supposed either that the philosophers were talking history, or that the historians were negating the statements of the philosophers. Then there would arise a sort of historical fiction, a history of political thought constructed on non-historical grounds and claiming historical truth for non-historical reasons. All that the historian has to say to the philosopher, or to the New Critic, is that the latter's statements need not be history now but will be history in a few moments. The Owl of Minerva is never in the present, but its flight will return.

BIBLIOGRAPHY

The last decades have witnessed a dramatic expansion of literature on the methods of studying the history of political thought. Here follows a list of works[2] especially relevant to the contents of this essay.

Boucher, David, *Texts in Contexts: revisionist methods for studying the history of ideas* (Dordrecht: Martinus Nijhoff, 1985).

Condren, Conal, *The Status and Appraisal of Classic Texts: an essay on political theory, its inheritance, and the history of ideas* (Princeton: Princeton University Press, 1985).

[2] [Compiled in 1987.]

Dunn, John, *Political Obligation in Its Historical Context: essays in political theory* (Cambridge: Cambridge University Press, 1980).

Gunnell, John G., *Political Theory: tradition and interpretation* (Cambridge, MA: Winthrop Publishers, 1979).

Hollinger, David A., *In the American Province: studies in the history and historiography of ideas* (Bloomington: Indiana University Press, 1985).

King, Preston (ed.), *The History of Ideas: an introduction to method* (Totowa, NJ: Barnes and Noble, 1983).

Rorty, Richard, Schneewind, J. B., and Skinner, Quentin (eds.), *Philosophy in History: essays on the historiography of philosophy* (Cambridge: Cambridge University Press, 1984).

Intermezzo

CHAPTER 8

Quentin Skinner: the history of politics and the politics of history

It is no light task – I deliberately open in mandarin English – to discuss the work of a professional historian such as Quentin Skinner in a journal such as *Common Knowledge*. Historians inhabit the academy without serious discomfort and are professionalized as an association of practitioners of various highly specialized disciplines of inquiry. These do not much overlap, and the second-order conversation generated within each is concerned with what its practitioners already know to be going on among them. They have chosen, and to that extent formalized, their subject-matter, and though their methods of inquiry may be vehemently debated and rapidly changing, there remains an in-house expectation that they will continue in succession to their former state. Such professionals, in short, believe that they can challenge themselves without unpacking all their presuppositions. *Common Knowledge*, on the other hand, seems directed at, and even sometimes written by, intellectuals not necessarily identifiable with the academy – some of whom mistrust the idea of academic fields and question not just the possibility but the desirability of methodical scholarly inquiry.

Intellectuals of this latter kind, even when working on what they term historical projects, resemble philosophers and philosophers of history more than they resemble historians. They are interested in history less as a multiplicity of experiences, some of which may be reconstructed, than as a predicament; they ask what it is like to live in history, and what if anything can be said, or done, or said to be, in that condition. They are interested in themselves, they are questioning themselves; and that is philosophy. The historian, on the other hand, obstinately declares that there are ways of basing one's knowledge in one's own world so that it becomes a means of saying what others have been, done, suffered and said – a declaration that carries the ultimately, if mitigatedly, conservative implication that experience and action persist for long enough to be spoken about.

[Published in *Common Knowledge*, 10.3 (2004), pp. 532–50.]

(I)

Socrates and Thucydides were contemporaries. We have no idea whether they knew, or knew of, one another, but if they did it would be possible to fancy that they wisely kept out of each other's way. There is no reason to suppose, and good reason to deny, that philosophers have been much interested in the question central to historians – 'what has happened? what is it that has happened?' – or in the historian's discovery that this question can be answered by narrating and re-narrating the happening until we discuss the diversity of its meanings (I have just used a singularly dangerous word). The history of historiography can be presented as increasingly one of archaeology. As happenings recede in time, we acquire knowledge of the circumstances in which they happened, so that the narration of events becomes increasingly a narration of their contexts as supplying them with meanings (note the plural). This pursuit has never much interested the philosopher, who desires the meaning of anything to be supplied in the form of an answer to a question put by the philosopher. Inescapably, however, there are occasions on which the two pursuits overlap.

Quentin Skinner, the subject of this essay, quotes the English medievalist F. W. Maitland as remarking that until he was past thirty he read very few histories 'except histories of philosophy, which don't count'.[1] Skinner's life work has been – yet this statement is not complete – devoted to making them count again by representing philosophies as sequences of acts performed in history, necessarily raising the question whether narratives of these acts 'count' as history or as philosophy; and, if they count as both, how the two are related to each other. It has been a very English pursuit in both disciplines, and the present writer suspects that if Skinner's subject-matter has been Anglo-European, its practice has been Anglo-American. It is also important that when Skinner has written history of philosophy, he has approached it by way of the history of political argument, of which philosophy has been a component so dominant as sometimes to claim identity with it. He has spent his life trying to break down this claim, but nothing prevents its being reasserted.

(II)

Skinner's life history has been deeply English, because the norms it has transgressed have been those of the English academy. Nothing seems more

[1] Quentin Skinner, front matter to *Liberty before Liberalism* (Cambridge: Cambridge University Press, 1998).

improbable than that the Regius Professor of Modern History at Cambridge should be a historian of philosophy (given that by 'philosophy' is meant for the most part 'political theory', an activity that draws upon philosophy, contributes to it, and approaches its status) and that he should be himself a theorist of interest to philosophers. But that is what Skinner has been since he became Regius Professor after a term as professor of political science (an appointment at Cambridge within the history faculty). In both offices he has written history of political thought and argued that political theory and philosophy are to be understood as political speech acts performed in history. He is the accredited master of this historicization as performed in the English-speaking academy, but this does not mean that he has synthesized history and philosophy or reduced these disciplines to aspects of each other. It is nearer the truth to say that there has been a continuing *Fakultätenstreit*, in which the philosophers have responded to the proposition that philosophy must be understood historically by treating it as a philosophical proposition that is to be explored, criticized and defended by the practice of philosophy, not by the construction of histories. Of the two volumes so far devoted to examining Skinner's work and its reception, the editor of one, the Canadian James Tully, is indeed both historian and political philosopher, but the content of his volume consists of analytical scrutinies of Skinner's methodological positions.[2] The author of the other, the Finnish scholar Kari Palonen, declares himself unversed in the history of the period (AD 1300–1700) within which Skinner has operated but proceeds to portray him as political philosopher, philosopher of history, and actor in both politics and history.[3] It would seem that the disciplines remain distinct, as asking and seeking to answer different kinds of questions, and that the writing of history – the pursuit of 'what has happened?' – has not deterred philosophy from claiming to scrutinize all questions including its own. What then is to be said of Skinner's achievement?

(III)

How these things happened can be clarified by a historical narrative – one, however, in which the writer of this review is obliged to cast himself as

[2] James Tully (ed.), *Meaning and Context: Quentin Skinner and his critics* (Princeton, NJ: Princeton University Press, 1988).

[3] Kari Palonen, *Quentin Skinner: history, politics, rhetoric* (Cambridge: Polity, 2003). [See now Annabel Brett and James Tully (eds.), *Rethinking the Foundations of Modern Political Thought* (Cambridge University Press, 2006), which reflects upon Skinner's first published volume from the standpoint of history.]

among the actors. The protagonist is an extraordinary man, the late Peter Laslett, who as a Cambridge historian in the late 1940s produced an edition of the works of Sir Robert Filmer, famous as Locke's target, and began research on Locke's writing of his *Two Treatises of Government*, which had revolutionary consequences for the history of seventeenth-century political thought.[4] It emerged that Filmer's *Patriarcha* was written long before that author's other works (published between 1648 and Filmer's death in 1652) and that it remained unpublished, though not uncirculated, until published with them by a group of activists in 1679–80. What Filmer 'was doing' – to anticipate a phrase of Skinner's – when he wrote *Patriarcha*, perhaps in 1630, must therefore differ significantly from what those who re-published him were doing in 1679; and the meanings he had intended to convey at the later date were not necessarily – even if they were significantly – those read into his text half a century later. In the case of Locke, the lapse in time was much less but the change in interpretation more dramatic. Laslett demonstrated that the *Two Treatises of Government*, which were published after the English revolution of 1688–9, were not written to justify that event but were composed as early as 1681, when the Whig connexion with which Locke was associated was meditating an appeal to political violence whose consequences would have been very unlike the bloodless transfer of power in England some years later. Not only was there a difference between the intention of writing and the intention of publishing, like that in the case of Filmer; the whole relationship between Locke as political philosopher and Locke as actor in the history of his time had now to be re-examined. Laslett wrought a local revolution whose effects were felt for many years.

The present writer now interjects himself into the story.[5] Aware between 1949 and 1952 of what Laslett had done and was doing, I was led by my own researches to realize that the re-publication of Filmer in 1679 led to two bodies of controversial writing: one, in which Locke took part, in the field of jurisprudence, the theory of government, and what we call political philosophy; the other, in which he did not take part, in the field of English history, the antiquity of common law and parliament, and the interpretation of the Norman Conquest. I was able to show that, since Jacobean times at least, argument in this latter field had gone on and had been what I came to call a 'language' of political thought, in which

4 Robert Filmer, *Patriarcha and Other Political Works*, ed. Peter Laslett (Oxford: Blackwell, 1949); and John Locke, *Two Treatises of Government*, ed. and intro. Peter Laslett (1960; Cambridge: Cambridge University Press, 1988).

5 [See further J. G. A. Pocock, 'Present at the Creation: with Laslett to the lost worlds', *International Journal of Public Affairs* (Chiba University, Japan), 2 (2006), pp. 7–17.]

English and even European issues had been discussed in volume and depth equalling those of 'political theory' and 'philosophy', to which so much attention had so rightly been paid. To Laslett's revelation of the importance of the 'moments' of composition, publication and reception, I was now led to add the importance of a plurality of 'languages' in which 'political thought' had been conducted, and among which the canonically accepted language of 'political theory' or 'philosophy', enormous as was its intellectual importance, was not the only language.

My work on this theme, *The Ancient Constitution and the Feudal Law*, was published in 1957.[6] By that time Laslett's interests had moved into a new field. His work on Locke not yet completed, he had begun editing a series of volumes under the title *Philosophy, Politics, and Society*.[7] These were very much English works of their period; informed by linguistic analysis and logical positivism, they inquired into the meaningfulness, if any, of propositions with such rigour as to raise the question whether anything worth calling 'political philosophy' could be said to exist. Laslett in 1956 famously pronounced that 'for the moment anyhow' it was dead; though by 1962 in the same series, Isaiah Berlin was arguing that it must persist, precisely where political questions of great urgency arose that could not be dealt with by means of propositions that rigorous analysts would accept as meaningful.[8] This was a moment, not the first, in Berlin's own removal from analytical philosophy into what he termed 'the history of ideas'.[9] I mention this because, though my own involvement in philosophy has been (to say the most) casual, and 'history of ideas' is not a satisfactory term for what I do myself, I was in the same volume of *Philosophy, Politics, and Society* able to attempt a statement of my own methodology based on my distance from that series's highly non-historical content.[10] If there were so many means of validating a statement, I found myself thinking, and as many kinds of statements as there were ways of validating one, it must be that each kind of statement had a history of its own, perhaps as one of those 'languages of

[6] J. G. A. Pocock, *The Ancient Constitution and the Feudal Law: a study of English historical thought in the seventeenth century* (1957; Cambridge: Cambridge University Press, 1987).

[7] Peter Laslett (ed.), *Philosophy, Politics, and Society* (Oxford: Blackwell, 1956); Peter Laslett and W. G. Runciman (eds.), *Philosophy, Politics, and Society*, 2nd ser. (Oxford: Blackwell, 1962); Laslett and Runciman (eds.), *Philosophy, Politics, and Society*, 3rd ser. (Oxford: Blackwell, 1967); Laslett, Runciman, and Quentin Skinner (eds.), *Philosophy, Politics, and Society*, 4th ser. (Oxford: Blackwell, 1972).

[8] Isaiah Berlin, 'Does Political Theory Still Exist?', in Laslett and Runciman, *Philosophy, Politics, and Society*, 2nd ser., pp. 1–33.

[9] Michael Ignatieff, *Isaiah Berlin: a life* (New York: Metropolitan, 1998), pp. 81–91, 94–5, 130–1, 225–31.

[10] Chapter I in this volume.

political thought' I was already being led to postulate. If philosophers held most or all of them to be nonsensical – when did I first notice Thomas Hobbes's attack on 'the frequency of insignificant speech'? – that simply raised the question, of greater interest to a historian, of why intelligence in the past had ascribed meaning to them and what had been done with the meanings they had ascribed. The first historians of philosophy, I learnt from Donald Kelley forty years later, were those ancients and early moderns who styled themselves 'Eclectics'.[11]

The English philosophers prominent in the 1956 volume of *Philosophy, Politics, and Society* were the analysts T. D. Weldon and A. J. Ayer, concerned to reduce language to what, if anything, could be meaningfully said with it. By the time Skinner began his theoretical work, however, his attention had focused on those, J. L. Austin and above all Ludwig Wittgenstein, who were presenting language as performance and speech act; and it is largely as a philosopher of this persuasion that he is now presented by Palonen. Skinner's publications began to appear in Cambridge from 1964, and dealt at first with English argument in the seventeenth century: in particular with Hobbes, who had not been a central figure in my work, since his significance, which was great, did not lie in the patterns of discourse I had been following.[12] Together with Machiavelli, Hobbes has remained central in Skinner's constructions of the history of politics; but these have been in some ways preceded by his writings on methodology and the philosophy of speech acts.

In 1969, Skinner published an essay, 'Meaning and Understanding in the History of Ideas', which came to be the manifesto of an emerging method of interpreting the history of political thought.[13] He demonstrated that much of the received history of that activity suffered from a radical confusion between systematic theory (or 'philosophy') and history. The greater and lesser texts of the past were interpreted as attempts to formulate bodies of theory whose content had been determined in advance by extrahistorical understandings of what 'political theory' and 'history' should be and were. This confusion led to errors including anachronism (the attribution to a past author of concepts that could not have been available to him) and prolepsis (treating him as anticipating the formation of arguments in whose subsequent formation the role of his text, if any, had yet to be

[11] Donald R. Kelley, *The Descent of Ideas: the history of intellectual history* (Aldershot: Ashgate, 2002).

[12] A bibliography of Skinner's writings will be found in Palonen, *Quentin Skinner*, pp. 181–90.

[13] Quentin Skinner, 'Meaning and Understanding in the History of Ideas', *History and Theory*, 8.1 (1969), pp. 3–53. The essay was reprinted in Tully, *Meaning and Context*, and revised in Skinner, *Visions of Politics*, I: *Regarding Method* (Cambridge: Cambridge University Press, 2002).

historically demonstrated). After treating these fallacies with much well-deserved ridicule, Skinner contended that the publication of a text and the utterance of its argument must be treated as an act performed in history, and specifically in the context of some ongoing discourse. It was necessary, Skinner said, to know what the author 'was doing': what he intended to do (had meant) and what he had succeeded in doing (had meant to others). The act and its effect had been performed in a historical context, supplied in the first place by the language of discourse in which the author had written and been read; though the speech act might innovate within and upon that language and change it, the language would set limits to what the author might say, might intend to say and be understood to say. The language would further have been a means by which the author acquired and processed information about the historical, political and even material situation in which he lived and was acting; and though a great deal of 'political thought' had been second-order language – thought about the language in which politics was thought about – it was possible to enlarge the 'context' (from now on a key term for Skinner and his readers) beyond the language to its referents (though once the historian began using referents not fully articulated in the language, the danger of prolepsis, and perhaps its necessity, must return).

(IV)

This essay of 1969 had an immediate effect, particularly strong among anglophone students of political thought, though not confined to them.[14] There arose a usage that spoke of a 'Cambridge school' of practitioners of this discipline, consisting of Laslett, Skinner, myself and John Dunn (who came to follow a trajectory of his own). Though I have worked elsewhere, there has been a strong Cambridge connexion between the four of us and our associates and former students in several English-speaking cultures (Skinner's works have been translated into many languages, and mine into some). What we have all been doing is insisting that a certain branch of the study of politics be perceived as a history of activity and be conducted within the discipline of history. This programme may bifurcate. On the one hand, it is necessary to think about political speculation in its historicity and about what it is to think about political speculation in this

[14] For a comparison between anglophones and others, see Dario Castiglione and Iain J. Hampsher-Monk (eds.), *The History of Political Thought in National Context* (Cambridge: Cambridge University Press, 2001).

way. Here what we call 'philosophy' continues to be of relevance. Many of Skinner's writings have been engagements with analytical philosophy, asking questions that he proceeds to answer about what it is to speak of actions and intentions, meanings and contexts, in a philosophical context dominated by Austin, Wittgenstein and those who have responded to them. Skinner has collected and revised these writings in the first volume of the trilogy with which this review will now be increasingly concerned.[15] My own writings on methodology have been less ambitious (though possibly more rash) because I do not claim an engagement with philosophy (if Socrates will allow me to avoid one) and have sought only to find linguistic means of presenting an act of political theorizing as an act performed in history.[16]

Though historicity can be abstractly considered, it is also necessary to write histories in which past events and processes are reconstructed and narrated. Palonen has very honestly told us that he does not claim to consider the history of political thought in Western Europe between the thirteenth and seventeenth centuries, about which Skinner has been writing since his first essay on Hobbes. In 1978, Skinner published a two-volume work entitled *The Foundations of Modern Political Thought*, whose silver jubilee has lately been celebrated. The two volumes are respectively headed *The Renaissance* and *The Age of Reformation*, but the main title implies a process: in some way political thought has become 'modern', and the 'foundations' of this process were in some way laid. Since the central contention as regards method is still that we must seek to understand what authors 'were doing', we must establish limits on the extent to which these authors were engaged in the process of becoming modern and to which becoming modern should be regarded as the outcome of the process. Neither in 1978 nor at any moment since will Skinner be found lapsing carelessly back into the prolepsis against which he warned us in 1969. Nevertheless, *The Age of Reformation* ends with the generalization that political thought became 'modern' through a process by which 'the state' came to be seen as an impersonal structure and not merely an attribute of the ruler, and that there was an accompanying process by which 'philosophy' came to be primarily concerned with 'the state' and the problems it occasioned.[17] It is

[15] Skinner, *Visions of Politics*, I: *Regarding Method.*

[16] For comment, see Hampsher-Monk, 'Political Languages in Time: the work of J. G. A. Pocock', *British Journal of Political Science*, 14.1 (January 1984), pp. 89–116; Hampsher-Monk, 'The History of Political Thought and the Political History of Thought', in Castiglione and Hampsher-Monk, *History of Political Thought*, pp. 159–74. [Also, D. N. DeLuna (ed.), *The Political Imagination in History: essays concerning J. G. A. Pocock* (Baltimore: Owlworks, 2006).]

[17] Quentin Skinner, *The Foundations of Modern Political Thought*, II: *The Age of Reformation* (Cambridge: Cambridge University Press), p. 358.

not too much to say that these processes, and the generalization based on them, have continued to preoccupy Skinner in his subsequent writings.

It is, however, vital to stress that the volume headed *The Renaissance* is concerned with something discontinuous: the 'political thought' of the Italian city republics between *c.* 1250 and *c.* 1550, where the primary political association was not 'the state' but 'the republic', an association of citizens practising the political virtues. Here it is impossible to avoid a chronology of scholarship. Three years before Skinner's *Foundations*, I had published *The Machiavellian Moment*, a work concerned with the same phenomenon and its subsequent history.[18] We were in regular correspondence, and the title of my work was in fact suggested by Skinner. In 2003, when we were celebrating the jubilee of *Foundations*, there occurred a reissue of *The Machiavellian Moment*, and I further published a book called *The First Decline and Fall*, dealing with many of the same themes.[19] In 2002, to complete the sequence, Skinner published the three volumes of his revised essays, *Visions of Politics*. It is in this setting that I inquire what history of political thought Skinner has been writing, as distinct from inquiring what he has been doing in presenting political thought as action in history.

(V)

The first volume of Skinner's *Foundations*, several of his intermediate writings,[20] and the second volume of his collected essays are concerned, like my publications of 1975 and 2003, with that episode in West European history between the thirteenth and sixteenth centuries when the fall of the Hohenstaufen and the removal of the papacy from Rome left several Italian city republics free to articulate their view of politics in the midst of their own internal crises. The culmination, to which Machiavelli was a witness, was the conquest of Italy by the Spanish monarchy in alliance with the papacy and empire. This episode has been considered a moment in the birth of 'modernity' – a concept in which I am not much interested – because Machiavelli was at one time considered an intellectual founder of

[18] J. G. A. Pocock, *The Machiavellian Moment: Florentine political thought and the Atlantic republican tradition* (Princeton, NJ: Princeton University Press, 1975). The book was reissued in 2003.

[19] Pocock, *Machiavellian Moment*; J. G. A. Pocock, *Barbarism and Religion*, III: *The First Decline and Fall* (Cambridge: Cambridge University Press, 2003).

[20] Quentin Skinner, *Machiavelli*, rev. edn (1981; Oxford: Oxford University Press, 2000); Skinner, 'Machiavelli on the Maintenance of Liberty', in Philip Pettit (ed.), *Contemporary Political Theory* (New York: Macmillan, 1983). The essay was revised in Skinner, *Visions of Politics*, II: *Renaissance Virtues* (Cambridge: Cambridge University Press, 2002).

the modern state (which he was not). More recently, Hans Baron considered Florentine republicanism 'modern', since it broke with the 'medieval' preoccupation with empire and papacy, *imperium* and *sacerdotium*.[21] Skinner and I agree in regarding Italian republican theory in another light. He associates 'modernity', as I have said, with the growth of the impersonal territorial state, which must be associated in turn with the non-Italian phenomena of the wars of religion and the escape from them in the late seventeenth century. We further agree, however, that the Italians came to articulate a view of city life as natural to man, and man as a citizen by nature – a view that has to be related somehow to the growth of the state and the views of politics and humanity that went with it.

The second volume of Skinner's *Foundations* is concerned with religious division and the increasing problem of resistance to authority in the name of religious truth, with which neither 'ancient' nor 'Renaissance' theories of citizenship were acquainted; it is not too much to say that 'the state' is a consequence of this question. The volume does not extend as far as the advent of Hobbes, with whom Skinner's earliest writings were concerned, but since 1978 he has published one major work about him,[22] and the third volume of *Visions of Politics* collects and revises essays that have Hobbes as their central figure. *Visions* II and III are concerned, as *Foundations* I and II were not, with the contention that Hobbes was the first to attack the 'republican' view of politics and liberty on behalf of another view of the same concepts, brought into prominence by the need to resist the English Civil War, which was in some measure a war of religion. This historical narrative, in which there is a way of travelling 'from' Machiavelli 'to' Hobbes (and there were those in the seventeenth century who saw the two as in opposition), has now to be connected with an argument in the second half of the twentieth century between political philosophers expressing opposed concepts of liberty – concepts that may be connected with those expounded by Italians in the sixteenth century and Englishmen in the seventeenth. The problematic relationship between political philosophy and the history of political thought, which Skinner's earliest theoretical writings set out to dissolve, thus seems to be reborn. That Skinner knows the difference between normative and historical writing cannot possibly be doubted. The problem, I shall now argue, is how the narrative enterprise is to be narrated

[21] Hans Baron, *The Crisis of the Early Italian Renaissance: civic humanism and republican liberty in an age of classicism and tyranny*, 2 vols. (Princeton, NJ: Princeton University Press, 1955).

[22] Quentin Skinner, *Reason and Rhetoric in the Philosophy of Hobbes* (Cambridge: Cambridge University Press, 1996).

as conducted in history, and how far it has been conducted by a sequence of actors.

The principal 'philosopher' in the twentieth-century narrative was Isaiah Berlin, whose lecture 'Two Concepts of Liberty' distinguished between a 'positive' freedom to do or be something – the definition of which might restrict one's freedom to do or be something else – and a 'negative' freedom consisting in the simple absence of restraint or prohibition to perform actions that one might wish or choose to perform.[23] This distinction raised important philosophical problems – what had being free to do with being human? – in which Skinner has been interested as both philosopher and historian. (Berlin figures in Skinner's inaugural lecture as Regius Professor and in his Isaiah Berlin Lecture to the British Academy.[24]) Skinner has not been attempting to solve the problems raised by 'Two Concepts of Liberty', but he has been concerned to ask whether there can be found in history – especially in pre-modern or early-modern history – a continuity or process of debate between opposed historical concepts bearing a relation to Berlin's 'positive' and 'negative' liberty: whether some such opposition has played a role in a history of political thought considered as a *durée*. The same concern may be found in my own writings, and Skinner and I agree in a certain sympathy for the 'positive', or as will appear, 'republican' position.

The methodological problem before us both is that laid out in 'Meaning and Understanding'. Is it possible to assert a continuity of debate, extending across generations and centuries, without imposing a false pattern and engaging in a false prolepsis? To claim that it is possible, one must be able to demonstrate (1) the continuity of the languages in which the debate was conducted and (2) the connexions between the speech acts by whose performance it was conducted. This seems possible in principle; the question is how both Skinner and I have attempted to supply such narrative, and there are differences between the critical problem of whether we have succeeded and the historical problem of how we have tried.

Skinner is concerned with a historical moment, composed of speech acts visibly performed, when Hobbes affirmed that the citizens of Lucca were not free *from* the decisions of a sovereign authority in which they might take part. James Harrington replied that the citizens of Lucca were free *to* participate in decisions, to rule and be ruled, and that citizenship was

[23] Isaiah Berlin, *Four Essays on Liberty* (London: Oxford University Press, 1969).

[24] Skinner, *Liberty before Liberalism*; Skinner, 'A Third Concept of Liberty', *Proceedings of the British Academy*, 117 (2002), pp. 237–68.

what made men images of God.[25] What continuities of speech, thought and action, however, are we to see as preceding and following this moment? Here we find Skinner using in 1982, and reiterating in 2002, language that may startle his readers. He distinguishes between a 'roman' view of liberty as the attribute of a citizen engaged in decision and action, and a 'gothic' view of liberty as the attribute of a proprietor whose rights are protected by a law to which he may appeal but in making which he need have played no part. He says that Harrington had detected Hobbes as the first to set the latter against the former, and Skinner further says that the principal 'gothic' theorist of our own times has been the late John Rawls.[26] The reader must blink. How is so much to be asserted without prolepsis? How are the 'roman' and 'gothic' languages of liberty to be narrated as persisting in continuity from early to modern times? How are the many speech acts (each performed in its own context and having its own consequences) of which their transmission must have consisted to be narrated as connected with one another? I find that long ago, reviewing *Foundations* at its first appearance, I wrote that Skinner used microscope first and telescope second: how does he set one instrument at the service of the other?[27]

(VI)

I have myself attempted this sort of thing, and so affirm that it can be done. In *The Machiavellian Moment* and subsequent writings, I proposed that Harrington restated Machiavelli's account of Roman liberty as the attribute of citizens whose possession of arms was the precondition of their freedom to act and display civic 'virtue', and that Harrington situated this account in a historical narrative of the loss and recovery in European history of this precondition.[28] (In this reading, Harrington does not use the word 'gothic' to denote Hobbes's theory of liberty but to denote an imbalance of

[25] Thomas Hobbes, *Leviathan*, ed. Richard Tuck (1651; Cambridge: Cambridge University Press, 1991), ch. 21; James Harrington, *The Political Works of James Harrington*, ed. and intro. J. G. A. Pocock (Cambridge: Cambridge University Press, 1977), pp. 170–1; Arihiro Fukuda, *Sovereignty and the Sword: Harrington, Hobbes and mixed government in the English Civil Wars* (Oxford: Clarendon, 1977).

[26] Skinner, *Visions of Politics*, II: *Renaissance Virtues*, pp. 160–2, 178–80.

[27] J. G. A. Pocock, 'Reconstructing the Traditions: Quentin Skinner's historian's history of political thought', *Canadian Journal of Political and Social Theory*, 3 (1979), pp. 95–113, here p. 101; Palonen, *Quentin Skinner*, p. 67.

[28] J. G. A. Pocock, *Virtue, Commerce, and History* (Cambridge: Cambridge University Press, 1985); Pocock, 'Standing Army and Public Credit: the institutions of Leviathan', in Dale Hoak and Mordechai Feingold (eds.), *The World of William and Mary: Anglo-Dutch perspectives on the revolution of 1688–89* (Stanford, CA: Stanford University Press, 1996), pp. 87–103.

land, arms and freedom between a king and his barons.) From Harrington, the contemporary of Hobbes, I proceeded to a moment beginning about 1700, when the advent of systems of public finance permitting the state to maintain a professional army led to both a vast enhancement of sovereign power and an altogether new view of liberty as the freedom to engage in the multifarious social activities possible in a society rich enough to facilitate a consumer culture, while taking no more part in one's self-government than the empowerment of representatives to control the state by financing it. There arose a 'commercial humanism' that drew on conceptual sources both 'roman' and 'gothic'.

The defect of this commercial humanism was that it did not achieve, and perhaps actually discouraged, any vision of the individual as a self defined by engagement in civic action and decision. Hannah Arendt declares that in the eighteenth century society became more important than politics, and humans were seen as behaving rather than as acting.[29] There arose a 'republicanism' that celebrated 'ancient virtue' as an opposite to 'modern politeness' and sought to revalidate the citizen who acted in his own defence, bearing his own arms, owning his own property (real land or real wealth rather than the fictions of credit), and knowing who he was and what was his virtue. The 'gothic' warrior might be at least partly assimilated to the 'roman' citizen; the opposition came to be one between 'ancient' liberty and 'modern'. If the former could be easily dismissed as archaic and even barbaric, the latter could be challenged as a progress into a future of 'corruption', meaning dependence on a multitude of social forces that no one had made or could control. A pessimist historicism arose from the tensions between real and movable property; as society moved from ancient to modern, the multiplication of goods diversified the personality until it ceased to be real to itself. The process continues through 'modernity' into 'post-modernity'.

This is territory into which Skinner has not yet travelled, though there have been indications that he may carry his interpretations past the era of Hobbes. In exploring new territory, I have been attentive to language that deals less with the state than with civil society and that took the form not of formal political theory but of civil history and political economy.[30] The advent of such language, I have been saying, is central to the 'history of political thought' in eighteenth-century Western Europe; we are at a

[29] Hannah Arendt, *The Human Condition* (Chicago: University of Chicago Press, 1959), ch. 6.

[30] J. G. A. Pocock, *Barbarism and Religion*, II: *Narratives of Civil Government* (Cambridge: Cambridge University Press, 1999).

point where we must consider the diversity of 'languages' and its history. I have not made use of Skinner's 1978 generalization that 'modern' political thought is concerned with the increasing impersonality of the state – is he still operating within that paradigm? If so, he may not arrive at conclusions at variance with mine, but he may narrate different histories, co-existing and interacting with those I have been relating. We are in a history where, even within the same texts, many things not necessarily compatible may be found to be going on concurrently. There need hardly be a master narrative of modern history that excludes or absorbs all other interpretations.

Skinner could be carried back to a concern with the state by his preoccupation with the interactions between 'roman' and 'gothic' concepts of liberty appearing in history in ways illuminated by the analytical distinction between 'positive' liberty and 'negative'. In 'republican' thinking, liberty is the freedom of citizens to exercise and expand the 'virtues' inherent in them; in 'negative' or 'gothic' thinking, liberty is immunity from interference with their capacity to do or to be what they wish. In the latter case, liberty may be expressed in the form of 'rights', which are protected by the state but may have to be protected from it. Here is the classic conundrum of 'liberal' thinking, but it is a further question whether the enumeration of rights is a sufficient description of the human personality's engagement in politics. These problems have histories and appear in history. Skinner and I have been writing histories in which the debates between opposed conceptions of liberty have been constant because they were of concern to the actors in history. My pursuit of the eighteenth-century debate over 'liberty' in 'commercial' societies has enlarged my horizon to include society as well as state; it has also left me examining a historicist debate in which 'roman' and 'gothic' were to a large extent subsumed by 'ancient' and 'modern'. Because the tensions between real and movable property were at times acute in Anglo-British thinking, there were tensions between 'ancient' and 'modern' conceptions of both citizenship and liberty.[31] I gained much notoriety by contending in *The Machiavellian Moment* that these tensions were carried on into the foundation of the American republic.[32] Here, as elsewhere, many of my critics seem to me motivated not only by the desire to celebrate the triumph of 'modern' liberty over 'ancient' but by a desire to deny that there was ever an 'ancient' position to be contended with. At this point, if

[31] I use the term 'Anglo-British' to indicate that problems originating in England were debated in Scotland, where they helped produce what we know as the Scottish Enlightenment.

[32] This contention gave rise to a prolonged debate, now held to have run its course, though its effects have not disappeared.

I am right, the debate between us becomes normative and contemporary, even ideological.

Skinner is certainly not one of the critics of whom I complain. On the contrary, he has shown and declared a sustained interest in both the normative and the historical importance of 'roman' and 'republican' thinking and in the interactions between these two. On the normative front, he has joined with Philip Pettit and Maurizio Viroli in exploring the idea of a 'republicanism' that asserts a 'third concept of liberty' as freedom from domination of the individual by others, thus both solving some of the linguistic puzzles raised by Berlin and serving as a prerequisite of both 'roman' and 'liberal' concepts of liberty.[33] I am myself doubtful whether the 'third concept of liberty' is capable of being articulated in the same detail as the two others with which it is linked. Once the individual is freed from domination, he or she must decide how to articulate and develop that freedom, and various choices will be presented. On the historical front, Skinner's study of Hobbes's attitudes toward rhetoric (which Hobbes did not finally reject) treats the latter as a language of 'roman' citizenship.[34] Skinner has written further about Machiavelli and collected those essays in the second volume of *Visions of Politics*. In conjunction with Martin van Gelderen and the European Science Foundation, he has also helped produce a two-volume symposium, *Republicanism: a shared European heritage*.[35] These works have pointed away from the thesis of *The Machiavellian Moment* towards 'republicanisms' that differed from the Anglo-American in involving less tension between 'ancient' and 'modern'. Benjamin Constant's famous work was a response to Jacobinism, not to the commercialization of the state a hundred years earlier.[36] Skinner and van Gelderen present many essays that deal valuably with the encounter between republic and commerce; it may be their subtitle that accounts for the non-inclusion of any systematic treatment of the foundation of the American republic, surely a central episode in this history.

In his most recent work – some not yet published and some, it may be, not yet written – Skinner may be returning to English history of the

[33] Philip Pettit, *Republicanism: a theory of freedom and government* (Oxford: Oxford University Press, 1997); Maurizio Viroli, *Republicanism* (New York: Hill and Wang, 2002); Skinner, 'Third Concept'. See also Gisela Bock, Quentin Skinner, and Maurizio Viroli (eds.), *Machiavelli and Republicanism* (Cambridge: Cambridge University Press, 1990).

[34] Skinner, *Reason and Rhetoric.*

[35] Martin van Gelderen and Quentin Skinner (eds.), *Republicanism: a shared European heritage*, 2 vols. (Cambridge: Cambridge University Press, 2002).

[36] Benjamin Constant, *Political Writings*, ed. and trans. Biancamaria Fontana (Cambridge: Cambridge University Press, 1988).

early-modern period. He has begun emphasizing the role, in the English Civil War and Interregnum, of a 'third concept', whose language insisted to the point of paranoia that to be unprotected by the law or by the mechanisms of parliamentary representation and consent was to be in the condition of a slave.[37] This language can of course be found recurring – increasingly as a language of radical Whiggism – in 1688 and 1776, though by the latter date it could be and was pointed out that Americans knew things about slavery that revealed their speech as the rhetoric it was. The question whether the 'third concept' of liberty as non-domination can be the key to the relations between 'roman' and 'gothic' versions of liberty depends, in the last analysis, on whether the 'third concept' can be shown operating as a distinctive force; and the reader will have detected my suspicion that it cannot. The concept of non-domination appears too deeply involved in the post-Harringtonian debate over the history of property in Europe, which had the effect of converting 'roman' and 'gothic' into 'ancient' and 'modern'. On quite another front – not so far discussed in this review – it is a curious fact that, since the second volume of his *Foundations* long ago, Skinner has not written much about the encounter between civic authority and spiritual, fully as important to Hobbes and Harrington as that between 'roman' and 'gothic' concepts of liberty. Skinner has not set himself in the context of J. C. D. Clark's revolutionary – or rather counter-revolutionary – revelation that the nations composing Hanoverian Britain were ecclesiastical polities, where philosophy was as much concerned with the state, society and religion as with the state, society and the individual.[38] It is the diversity of languages, reflecting the diversity of problems, with which the historian of political discourse remains concerned.

(VII)

This study of Skinner's writings to 2003 has focused on history rather than philosophy; or, to put it more precisely, less on his speech acts in affirming the cognizability of speech acts, their meanings and contexts, than on his reconstructions of events and processes in the history he has studied. I have set historical narrative before history-as-philosophy. Political theory (which

37 Skinner, *Liberty before Liberalism*; Skinner, 'Third Concept'. See also his contributions to van Gelderen and Skinner, *Republicanism*.

38 J. C. D. Clark, *The Language of Liberty, 1660–1832: political discourse and social dynamics in the Anglo-American world* (Cambridge: Cambridge University Press, 1994); Clark, *English Society, 1660–1832: religion, ideology, and politics during the Ancien Régime*, 2nd edn (Cambridge: Cambridge University Press, 2000).

merges into philosophy) has not disappeared from the inquiry; I am left asking whether concern with distinctions like Berlin's between 'positive' and 'negative' liberty has focused Skinner's attention on processes in the history of political thought in which similar distinctions, continuously discussed, shaped that history. My question is not a criticism. It is perfectly possible that rigorous historical inquiry will reveal such processes going on (perhaps even into a historic present). I have offered to trace such myself, from a standpoint that did not, as far as I remember, originate from a concern with Berlin's memorable lecture. It might perhaps be argued that Skinner's methodology has focused on the performance of speech acts in a context and that more remains to be done on the method of studying the consequences of such acts (a) as the context changes and its languages co-exist with others, while (b) the acts are received, understood and contested by others whose intentions and contexts are decreasingly identical with the author's. I have a sense that I am breaking untrodden ground in emphasizing Skinner's narratives of process, but there is nothing here to modify or challenge his insistence that political discourse must be studied as action in history.

Attention should now be paid to those who advocate other approaches, which they defend against what they see as challenges by Skinner and others. There are still those who wish to employ past texts, and the systemized thought of past theorists and philosophers, in the construction and solution of problems they address in their present. It is interesting to enquire just why they need to make use of texts they must interpret to fit their own needs and assumptions, but the validity of the language games they are playing depends upon the operation to which they appeal and not upon their understanding of their own historicity. Philosophers have engaged in construction of historical fiction since the first Platonic (and perhaps Confucian) dialogues; and whether Socrates, Protagoras and Thrasymachus ever said the things they are made to say is irrelevant to the purposes for which they are made to say them. As history becomes better documented and more problematic, however, this distinction becomes harder to keep up; and the philosopher needs to be reminded both that he is writing historical fiction and that he is living and acting in a history not defined by his intentions. In the United States, infested by the disciples of Leo Strauss, the claims of philosophers to know what history is still need rebuttal.

The historical fictions constructed by philosophers may be a legitimate branch of what can be termed 'historiosophy', the attempt to make history a source of knowledge or wisdom. Historians resist this attempt, on the grounds that history consists of what can be shown or said to have happened and conveys no other message. The search for wisdom tempts the philosopher to rewrite history as the search for what he or she thinks wisdom is. There are those, however, who wish to summarize or rewrite history as the story of how something has happened or came to be the human situation – a situation they have noticed for themselves without historians' assistance. This kind of summary or revision of history is not at all illegitimate. As we have seen in the case of Berlin, it is possible that these abridgments or interpretations of history will draw to the attention of historians processes and their outcomes that the latter have not previously noticed. It is also possible that the formation of these perceptions of history will itself have a history, part of the subject-matter the historian studies. The history of political thought must consist, in large and significant measure, of actors doing things that historians of political thought insist that *they* should not do. The latter's work is to write the history of the former in terms other than those in which they would have written it themselves; it is good for each to be reminded of the other's presence.

'Historiography', if the term may be accepted, reaches a point where 'history' becomes itself an object of attention: the name of an abstractly or formally described condition in which humans may find themselves trying to exist and which is the object of philosophical as well as practical attention. Here the distinction between historiography and historicism emerges. To the former – practised by historians – 'history' is a name for events and processes that may be said to have happened and can be narrated and interpreted, possibly as still going on. To the latter – the preserve of philosophers of history – 'history' denotes a condition in which processes go on, and which may be discussed independently of the narrative of what these processes have been. In the revolutionary and post-revolutionary, colonial and post-colonial, conditions supplying the history of so much in the last hundred or so years, 'history' may become a name for a condition in which humans do not know and cannot manage or control the processes happening to them, and most of what they say about 'history' registers their alienation from it. When this happens, the claim that there is a historiography in which processes may be narrated in intelligible terms becomes tendentious; it challenges and is challenged; it may resent and be resented.

It is of course relevant that most of the work produced in Cambridge and by those associated with it has been concerned with history in the early-modern period, between the fifteenth century and the eighteenth, and with a history of political thought largely anglophone. I have observed that Skinner has not yet ventured far into the eighteenth century; I myself cease from inquiry about the year 1790. It was left to the 'Sussex school' of historians to carry the narrative through the nineteenth century into the first half of the twentieth.[39] It might be argued that the technique of situating the speech act in its linguistic context, and inquiring what came of its action there, is peculiarly suited to a neo-Latin culture in which discourse was the preserve of established clerisies operating stable and continuous languages, and has not yet been tested in the conditions progressively arising as clerisies are replaced by intelligentsias and political discourse becomes increasingly demotic and alienated. A Skinnerian approach to the modern and the post-modern has not yet been tried.

There is something to be said, however, about (and by) the politics of the historical profession and even about the unashamedly anglophone – I hope Europeans have abandoned the term 'Anglo-Saxon' – character of most of the historiography here studied. It is the business of professional historians to reduce history to narratability while insisting on the limits within which this can be done. Both reduction and limits are regarded with understandable suspicion by many outside the profession and especially by those who have lost both their belief and their interest in methodical scholarship. It is possible that all historical narrative, all written historiography, is by its nature conservative-liberal in its intention and effect; it insists that there are always more or less durable conditions in human life, always some possibility of changing them, always limitations to the extent to which this can be done, always unexpected outcomes of the attempt to do so. It is possible also that 'history' in this sense can be written only in political societies with the capacity to manage their history in the present and, as a necessary accompaniment, to review and renew it in the perceived past. These prerequisites are perhaps why 'the history of political thought', as both phenomenon and practice, has been overwhelmingly neo-Latin, West European, and North American, while 'the philosophy of history' has been by turns German, Central European, Russian and (perhaps) extra-European. Within this formulation – to narrow the focus again – a recent attempt to survey 'the history of political thought in national context' has revealed that the relations among history, politics, jurisprudence and philosophy differ so greatly from one Euro-American academy and culture to another that only

[39] Stefan Collini, Donald Winch and John Burrow, *That Noble Science of Politics: a study in nineteenth-century intellectual history* (Cambridge: Cambridge University Press, 1983); Stefan Collini, Richard Whatmore and Brian Young (eds.), *History, Religion and Culture: British intellectual history, 1750–1950* (Cambridge: Cambridge University Press, 2000). See also the bibliography they offer.

the broadest unities survive.[40] Our world is divided, in short, into those who claim to have, to know, to write and to change histories of their own making, and those who say that this is not their situation and they doubt how far it is that of those who claim it. If 'history' in the former sense cannot be imposed on those who do not have it, they cannot demand its abnegation by those who have grounds for claiming it. A debate between participation and alienation seems likely to continue.

[40] Castiglione and Hampsher-Monk, *History of Political Thought.* Here may be considered the relation between Cambridge contextualism and German *Begriffsgeschichte*; see Melvin Richter, *The History of Political and Social Concepts: a critical introduction* (New York: Oxford University Press, 1995).

PART II

History as political thought

CHAPTER 9

The origins of study of the past: a comparative approach

I. THE DIFFERENT FORMS OF HISTORIOGRAPHY

In this essay I shall attempt to consider how far the history of historiography can be treated as the history of the problems occasioned by men's awareness of the past in different societies, and of their attempts to deal with these problems. This kind of approach has not, so far as I know, been made before. That is to say, the history of historiography has not been approached as primarily a part of the history of social man's awareness of his past and his relations with it; and this is understandable enough, as the historical phenomena we call by the collective name of historiography have been by no means limited to the attempts made by historians and other thinkers to understand the past and its relationship to the present. The various 'historians' whom we denote by this term have in fact been engaged in a number of different, though sometimes interconnected, activities: there has been the activity of preparing a record or chronicle of contemporary events and transmitting it to posterity, perhaps for that posterity to continue and transmit in its turn; there has been the activity of describing a past which is of importance to posterity and showing how that importance is exerted; and there has been the activity of explaining phenomena in the present by relating them to a past of which knowledge may be already traditional, or may require to be enlarged or manufactured for the occasion. The second and third of these activities (which are closely connected) presuppose knowledge of a past which is in some way important to the present; and if the first does not presuppose such a knowledge, it will soon, in the course of transmission from one generation to another, create it. All aspects of historiography therefore involve awareness of a past, but the intellectual operations which they necessitate are not confined to solving

[Published in *Comparative Studies in Society and History*, 4.2 (1962), pp. 209–46. Reprinted in P. B. M. Blaas (ed.), *Geschiedenis als Wetenschap* (The Hague: Nijoff, 1980).]

problems connected with that past's true character. These operations, the social functions which they discharge and the emotions with which they become involved, in fact form an enormously complex and various field of study. No comprehensive history of historiography has been or perhaps could be written, and all writings which have been devoted to the subject have in fact been selective; the present essay will be no exception.

But it has happened that most approaches which have been made to this subject have been of two kinds, neither of which has been primarily concerned with the history of man's relations with his past. In the first place, Greco-Roman historiography, which has of course greatly influenced our understanding of the term, was – like the traditional historiography of other nations – primarily concerned with the construction and transmission to posterity of intelligible narratives of contemporary events, often in ways that sharply limited posterity's power to criticize or reinterpret the narratives thus inherited. One main stream in Western histories of historiography, therefore, has been the history of the development of the narrative as a literary form, an intellectual problem and a social instrument; and though this approach has had the effect of confining 'historiography' to mean 'what has been written by historians' – a definition by no means always satisfactory – the traditional or classical 'history' has of course played a significant role in all three of these aspects. But in the second place, we live still in the shadow of the historicist revolution of the eighteenth and nineteenth centuries, which transformed our awareness of society and culture into a historical awareness of an unprecedented kind; and this revolution was carried out by social philosophers rather than by 'historians' in the sense in which the word was normally used at the time, or even in some of those in which it is used today. The changes in thought which produced historicism owed little to the mental operations of contemporary 'historians' in the Greco-Roman sense, or to any tradition of thinking inherited from them. They appeared, both then and thereafter, to have been rather the effect of changes in legal, moral and social philosophy – particularly as the word 'philosophy' was then used – and it has ever since been found best to write the history of these changes as such. What then came into being was historical philosophy, or philosophy of history, and its history has been written as the effect of changes in thought at a philosophical level of generality and abstraction. This was of course an entirely satisfactory and rewarding interpretation. The effect of these two approaches in combination, however, has been to give the impression that the history of Western historiography consists of narrative plus philosophy – as if the writing of history had been in the hands of humanist 'historians' in the Greco-Roman tradition, until it was transformed by the activities of social philosophers; and the prehistory of the historicist revolution has been written mainly as the history of philosophy in so far as it prefigures the changes which produced historicism. I shall suggest that, where these have become the assumptions of historians, they can both be usefully criticized and modified.

What has been largely omitted from the established interpretation is the history of historiography in the sense in which the word is being used here. If we once study the history of men's awareness that they have pasts which are important in various ways to their presents, we discover that historiography produced by this awareness, not identical with that produced by the Greco-Roman tradition, was appearing in Western Europe before the historicist revolution; and we may be led at least to raise the question of historicism's indebtedness to thought produced in this way. Moreover, the study of awareness of the past, and of historiography as a product of this awareness, although it is like others a limited and selective approach to the subject, enables us to construct a new method of studying the history of historiography. This method emphasizes that historiography is a form of thought occasioned by awareness of society's structure and processes, and makes it possible to explain the character of different historiographies by relating them to the societies in which they emerged.

II. THE CONDITIONS UNDER WHICH A HISTORIAN OF THE PAST CAN EXIST

What follows next is offered as a model account of the conditions under which a historian may exist whose aim is to study the past and its relationship to the present. The first prerequisite, obviously, is that the historian must be aware of a past, and this presupposes the existence of a society. An isolated individual could remember no past other than his personal recollections; an isolated chain of transmitters of tradition could remember only the recollections of the transmitters. The word 'past' as historians use it connotes a state of affairs of some social complexity existing over a period long enough to make it intelligible, a period now gone by but remembered. To remember such a past, and to communicate it to a historian, there is required a human organization of such complexity and duration as to carry the normal implications of the term 'society', and it follows that the activity of remembering and preserving the past must be studied as a social activity. The meaning of this activity must be studied before we can study the meaning of the historian's behaviour; he will appear either as a social functionary, carrying out a task imposed on him by society, or as an intellectual, tending to exceed the limits of any imposed function and to engage in independent or divergent activity within the general structure of his society.

Awareness of a past, then, is a social awareness and can exist only as part of a generalized awareness of the structure and behaviour of a society. Almost any society preserves statements of some kind concerning events which occurred in a past time; its awareness of these events is its awareness of its past; and this awareness plays some part in its life in the present. Since all societies are organized consciously or unconsciously to ensure their own continuity, we may suppose that the preservation of statements about the past has in various ways the function of ensuring continuity, and that awareness of the past is in fact society's awareness of its continuity.[1] (Whether this takes the form of awareness of myths or of verifiable statements of fact does not concern us at this stage of the analysis.) Since a society's structure is perhaps the most important single element in its continuity, it is often the continuity of the structure that the past is designed to ensure, and awareness of the past is awareness of the past of the structure. 'Beyond the annual cycle', writes Evans-Pritchard of the Nuer, 'time-reckoning is a conceptualisation of the social structure, and the points of reference are a projection into the past of actual relations between groups of people. It is less a means of co-ordinating events than of co-ordinating relationships, and is therefore mainly a looking-backwards, since relationships must be explained in terms of the past.'[2] It follows that the past of which a society is aware, and the continuity which it feels it has with that past, will vary from society to society with the social structure and the kind of continuity which that requires. Englishmen, Sicilians and Nuer will not only have different pasts, but will recall different aspects of those pasts.

But awareness of the past within a particular society is not simple awareness of the continuity of a single structure. A society normally consists of a number of continuous activities and a number of continuous structures, and if the function of the past is to ensure continuity, it may be predicted that any society may have as many pasts as it has elements of continuity, and that different individuals may be aware of different pasts, varying as they are associated with different activities, structures or other elements of

[1] Cf. E. Shils, 'The Intellectuals and the Powers', *Comparative Studies in Society and History*, I.I (1958), p. 6: 'The population of every society, and above all those who exercise authority in it, need to have at least intermittently some sense of the stability, coherence and orderliness of their society; they need therefore a body of symbols, such as songs, histories, poems, biographies, and constitutions, etc., which diffuse a sense of affinity among the members of the society.'

[2] E. E. Evans-Pritchard, *The Nuer* (Oxford, 1940), p. 108; and generally, ch. 3, section II.

continuity. The member of a lineage is aware of the past of his lineage; he sees it as consisting of generations of ancestors (depending on how the rules of kinship are reckoned in his society), and its continuity in the past assures him of continuity of status in the present and the power to transmit status to others in the future. The member of a club is aware of the past of that club, as the continuous observance of certain rules which ensure the continuity of the club's structure in the present and for the future. At a higher level of complexity, the lawyer is aware of the past as a continuous sequence of normative decisions, each directing and authorizing its successor and so transmitting authority to him in the decision he is called upon to give; and it is plain that his image of the past and its continuity with the present will depend upon the ideas held in the prevailing legal system on how decisions are made and authorize one another. The pattern may be repeated indefinitely, for priests, ritualists, scholars, artists and even historians: for all, in short, who are specialized by association with one or more of the organized continuities existing within a society, to the point where they become aware of a continuity and the mode of its organization. Each has a particular image of the past, in the form of a projection into it of the continuity with which he is associated, and a particular conception of the way in which its continuity in the past authorizes or otherwise ensures its continuity in the present and future. We are now dealing with something more complex than a simple awareness of the past, and I shall occasionally use the word 'past-relationship' to express this specialized dependence of an organized group or activity within society on a past conceived in order to ensure its continuity.

A society, then, may have as many pasts, and modes of dependence on those pasts, as it has past-relationships, and it will be of importance to the analysis of historiography as the study of the past to bear in mind that society's awareness of its past is plural, not singular, and is socially conditioned in a variety of ways. There is no *a priori* reason why these different awarenesses should grow together into a single awareness. Certainly, one of the continuities of which a society is aware may be that of itself as an organized whole, and in such a case it may have an image of its collective past and descent therefrom to assist it in maintaining that continuity. But it does not follow that this awareness of a collective past and its history will swallow up the particular awarenesses which specialized groups and activities within society have of their particular continuities. Each continuity, that of society as a whole included, will be conceived in specialized terms, determined by the particular continuity that exists in the present and by the manner in which it is supposed to derive assurance of continuity from its past; and these terms will differ so widely that their integration will be intellectually very difficult, even when it has become socially possible and desirable. In seventeenth- and eighteenth-century England, 'the English history' meant the received canon of traditional narratives, and did not include the histories of the English law or church, which were written by lawyers and churchmen and conceived in quite different terms. In France at the same time, 'l'histoire française' (the article is significant) had a similar meaning.

In studying the growth of a particular society's historical awareness, therefore, we should begin by paying close attention to the activities and institutions in its present which give rise to awareness of a past, and to the modes of awareness which they produce; for it will be out of these past-relationships that the variety of historiography we are studying may be expected to arise. The degree to which a society's images of its past have assumed documentary or literary form, and the variety of such forms which they may have assumed, will obviously be matters of importance when it comes to the development of historiography. It will not be premature at this stage to define historiography as a complex series of relationships between members of a society in the present and the traditional and documentary evidences of its pasts, and to assert that these relationships cannot be confined to those which exist with its 'histories', in the limited sense of its inherited narratives of events in its past. It happened for local and particular reasons that the word 'history' was for a long time used in Western society in ways that virtually confined it to meaning (a) such an inherited narrative, and (b) an activity of writing or thinking about such narratives; but we shall be able to show that other documents concerning the past were being studied, and disciplines of doing so being developed, even while the word was being used in this limited sense, so that we cannot afford to confine the study of historiography to what was at a particular time recognized as such.

But the more we become acquainted with the field of past-relationships, the more clearly it appears that we must have an extensive and detailed knowledge of any such relationship or group of relationships before we can understand the historiography emerging out of it. It is already evident that a society may have, in theory, as many pasts and relationships with those pasts as it has elements of continuity, and that the image of the past may be established in any of a great variety of documentary or non-documentary forms. We have next to note that the image of a past, or a tradition or a document inherited from a past, may be employed in a society in ways admitting of a wide variety in the degree of institutionalization, and that both the form and content of the document, and ideas about the authority it has for the present and the continuity between the past it suggests and the present, will tend to vary accordingly. For example, there may be a song or epic which is recited from time to time, and helps to uphold the continuity of society by giving its hearers imaginative and emotional contact with society's past; but there are no specified occasions on which it is recited, no class of experts charged with expounding its relevance to the present, no recognized class of problems which it is peculiarly associated with solving, and no body of received ideas about what its relevance to the present may be. In such a case, if one existed, we should say that the degree of institutionalization was low or negligible; and it is theoretically plain that there would be few ideas or none about the continuity between the past suggested by the epic and the present. In contrast we may imagine the case of a record of some past decision, produced in a court of law. Here there is a highly institutionalized social context, in which alone the document may be produced and have meaning as a record; and there are precise and elaborate rules defining the occasions on which it may be produced, the persons qualified to produce it and the manner in which they may do so, the problems which it may assist in solving and the relevance it may have to their solution. The degree of institutionalization is high, and it is likely, though not certain, that there will be experts and concepts capable of expounding with a good deal of elaboration the continuity, both of recorded events and of transmitted authority, connecting the past suggested by the document with the present. Between these extremes there is room for a great range of variations, not only in the degree, but also in the kind, of institutionalization; since the latter too will depend upon the function which the tradition, document or other object is called on to discharge in the present. It may easily be seen that institutionalization will affect both the context of the document and the form in which it is preserved. The inherited narratives, or 'histories', preserved by a society, will have their place in this spectrum of varying institutionalization, and we may find room there also for those elements suggesting a past which have been preserved by a society but discharge no known function in the present, and about whose character, origins and descent no clear ideas exist. These, however, belong rather to the next stage in the development of this argument.

For at this point we face the problem of adding to the existence of a past-relationship the presence of a historian; and it might seem that we have built our model in such a way as to leave almost no room in which to do so. Either there exist specialized persons and institutionalized means by which the content of the document and its relationship to the present may be expounded, or there do not. If none exist, there can be no historian. But if such means do exist, the task of exposition will be carried out by whatever class of specialists is charged with maintaining the element of continuity which has given rise to the past-relationship – by lawyers, priests, grammarians or whatever it may be; and there will be no need of a historian. This analysis seems to have left the historian only his (here less probably her) traditional role as the preserver, continuator and expositor of society's inherited narratives: a specialized functionary like the Chinese *shih* or the 'historiographer royal' of an early-modern Western kingdom. But this is a very small part of what we mean by the term 'historian'. We mean a student not only of inherited narratives, but of the documents that reveal the character in the past of laws, churches, languages and other phenomena of social life seldom exhaustively described in those narratives; and we mean something more than the expositor of a traditional relationship with a past. We have in mind rather an autonomous way of thinking which criticizes traditions and images of continuity and provides instead accounts of the past, and its relationships with the present, built up according to methods of its own. The term 'autonomous' is not especially precise, and it would be easy at this point to lay down some criteria of autonomy and use them to measure how far various writers on the past may have progressed towards our ideal type of the historian. A more appropriate proceeding in the present instance, however, will be to define the historian in the simplest possible terms and expand our model by asking, at each new definition, what are the minimum conditions which must be met before the historian, as we have defined him, can exist. Accordingly, we may define the historian as one who expounds a relationship with the past in terms varying from those which are traditionally used for the purpose, and next ask how this can happen. Such a definition has the advantage that it enables us to treat the historian both as a student of the inherited narratives of society and as a student of language, institutions and other elements of social tradition.

For the existence of a historian as we have just defined him, it may next be suggested, it is necessary to suppose a problem; and this problem must arise somewhere in the relationship between him and the object suggesting a past. Certainly, one could imagine a very simple case: that of a historian – or the individual later to be specialized as one – contemplating an object suggesting the existence of a past and wondering what it is and how it came to be in her experience. Much historical thinking, it may well be, has its origin in just so uncomplicated a curiosity. But the more we examine such a case, the less simple it will appear. The object has been preserved and transmitted to the historian's attention by some social process; yet this process has failed to provide any ready-made or traditional explanation of the object's presence or significance. This means that no need of any explanation has hitherto been felt, that the object has been thought of as discharging no particular function, or none which requires exposition. Yet now the historian requires an explanation. Something has clearly changed in the social situation – we may locate the change as occurring inside the historian's own mind – and as a result, the historian is confronted with a problem: a question to which there exists no ready-made or traditional answer.

The position becomes more complex, though not fundamentally different, if we suppose that there has existed a traditional explanation of the past which the object suggests and the continuity between that past and the present, but that the historian has now become dissatisfied with that explanation and demands a different one. Here again, there has been change of some kind, which has confronted the historian with a problem; but on this occasion we can see that there are likely to be increasingly complicated repercussions upon the historian's relationships (a) with other members of society, and (b) with the concepts and ideas traditionally current in that society. In the first place, the historian's dissatisfaction either may or may not be shared by other individuals in society; the changes which produce the kind of thought we are studying may be described as taking place within a context either of an individual's (or specialized group's) intellectual life, or of the relations between humans in society and of the ideas used to expound and direct those relations; the historian may be considered either as an intellectual or as a social being; and of course, none of these emphases need altogether exclude its alternative. But the past-relationships of a society, used to ensure its continuity, are of concern to all its members, and the problems which produce historians and their distinctive explanations may very easily become, in one sense or another, political problems. At this point the historian's attitude towards the problem that confronts her becomes complicated by mixed motives; she may, for instance, desire to restore a past-relationship which others have challenged, but be unable to restore it in its traditional form. The character of what may be termed her problem-situation will affect the character of the explanation with which she seeks to replace the traditional one.

But we have not yet asked why, or when, the problem that confronts the historian is what we should call a historical problem, or the explanation she or he provides what we should call a historical explanation. An individual who observes phenomena from a past, or the phenomenon of a past, and desires to know what these phenomena were and how they have come to be part of his present, may perhaps be termed a historian without further ado (though even this might be misleading); but the greater the dependence of present society upon its pasts, the more complex the past-relationships arising and the problem-situations that may arise within them; and at this point the possibility must be faced that many types of explanation which replace the traditional expositions are not what can be termed historical explanations in any normal sense of the term. If a traditional relationship with the past has been ruptured, the first instinct of society's intellectuals may be to restore it, and this may be attempted by reshaping myth, by historization or by the construction of a new image of the past in terms of some new continuity of which society has become aware in the present. Furthermore, even if a society has been forced to see its past in terms so far unlike those in which it sees its present that it can no longer suppose that past capable of ensuring its continuity, or in any way directly relevant to the present, its intellectuals may still be able to conceive of a body of universal truths or laws, of which past and present (however dissimilar) are both seen as local and particular illustrations or applications. In a society habituated to conceiving of universal laws and traditionally well supplied with concepts of such laws, this may be the natural and established way of dealing with any problem in the relations of past and present that requires solution; medieval and post-medieval Western Europe furnishes many examples of this kind. But we should deny this the title of historical explanation and use some such term as 'rationalism' instead; and, with our eyes on the eighteenth and nineteenth centuries, we tend to conceive the rise of historiography as a progress from rationalism to historicism. It will be observed, however, that universal laws may be responses to a breakdown in traditional ways of expounding past-relationships, and cannot be regarded as independent of the growth of historiography, as we are here defining it. At this point we should repeat our technique of defining the 'historian' with slightly increased precision and asking what conditions must be satisfied before one can exist as so far defined.

We shall therefore try the effect of using a Rankean criterion and defining the historian as one who tries to describe the past 'as it really was' – i.e., instead of constructing it in the image of the present, or of some element of continuity in society's present, to make statements concerning it which are capable of independent verification and constitute, as far as they are thus verified, a coherent picture of society, or some element in society, as it existed at some time in the past. Since we are envisaging the historian as arising within the context of some assumed relevance of past to present, we should add to our definition that, having described the past state of things 'as it really was', he then deals with its relation to the present primarily by showing how 'it actually happened' that that state of things became another, existing at some subsequent time, and so by extension became the state of things existing at the present.

Compared to the great system-builders of historicism, this is a modest picture, and it may even turn out that the historian in this sense of the term could not have come into existence except as part of the advent of historicism. Nevertheless, it is recognizably a portrait of the modern historian as one spends the greater part of one's time, and the state of mind and society it involves is a complex one which could not exist without the satisfaction of a great many preconditions. The aim of this article is a historical investigation of how this type of historian came into being in certain times and places, and it is nearly time to abandon model-building for some historical case-studies; but a few points should be made first about the preconditions which this definition entails. First, it is necessary that evidence about the past should be available in such detail and organization as to make a measure of consistent and self-validating description possible; second, it is necessary that the problem-situation should have arisen in such a way as to compel recognition that the past cannot be studied in traditional terms or as a simple extension of present continuities; third, it is necessary that concepts should have been or become available to the historian in which one can describe, not only the past as it existed, but the process of its becoming the present.

In order to see how these conditions may be met, we now turn to some historical instances and problems. Such a process can take place only in the context of some particular society, its relationships with the past and the problems that arise within those relationships. The complexity and variety of a society's past-relationships, corresponding in principle to the whole of its organization for continuity, have been much emphasized, as has the suggestion that the problems which produce the historian can arise only as the result of change, occurring somewhere in the social complex and spreading its effects throughout the whole. Consequently it seems unsafe to attempt any typology of historical problem-situations, and preferable to deal with some concrete instances of how they have arisen, and the kind of thought they have generated, in the contexts of several particular societies. But these instances will be dealt with according to the principles of the model, and in developing the latter a mode of study has been outlined which may prove valuable in investigating the history of historiography. It may be defined as establishing, first, the past of which the historian was aware and the reasons which he (in a probably male-dominated culture) had for thinking it significant to the present; second, the circumstances in which he became dissatisfied with the traditional account of the past and its significance, and the problem-situation in which he found himself as a result; third, in the light of the foregoing, the reasons for which he did or did not build up an account of the past and its relation to the present such as we may term historical.

III. CASES: ATHENS, PRE-CH'IN CHINA, MEDIEVAL AND RENAISSANCE EUROPE

In the field of modern classical scholarship, a controversy has gone on which we may recognize as one concerning the character of the past, and the relationship with it, responsible for the birth of historiography in Athenian society. Wilamowitz believed[3] that the first histories of Attica were the work of the *exegetai*, a board of Athenian officials charged with expounding and maintaining the ritual law, and that the discharge of their task had necessitated their keeping a chronicle of events by which sacred observances might be dated, and making a further attempt to date events in the past. If his interpretation were accepted, it would seem that Attic society was connected with its past mainly though the continuity of its ritual behaviour, around which it organized its recollections of other past events; and it is widely held that the *pontifex* and the *shih*, the primary Roman and Chinese historians, began their activities in ways very like that which Wilamowitz attributed to the *exegetai*. But Jacoby has argued[4] that neither the degree of specialization of the *exegetai*, nor the character of their work, rendered the construction of a chronicle necessary or even intellectually possible. All they were required to do, he maintained, was to certify that certain acts were sacred and had been immemorially held to be so, and this was hardly compatible with any precise dating of the past. In our terminology, he was arguing that the past-relationship expounded on by the *exegetai* did not involve the sort of problems which would lead to the construction of a chronicle or chronology.

Local historiography in Attica, according to Jacoby, originated as a local variant of what he termed 'Greek great historiography',[5] itself the product of two phenomena: the existence of a coherent though not simple body of epics and tales, forming a mythical past broadly common to all the

[3] U. von Wilamowitz-Moellendorf, *Aristoteles und Athen*, I (1893), pp. 260–90. [I suspect I was indebted to Jacoby for this reference.]

[4] F. Jacoby, *Atthis: the local chronicles of ancient Athens* (Oxford, 1949).

[5] Ibid, pp. 199ff. and 218ff.

Greek peoples, and the rise of Ionian rationalism which necessitated the reconstruction of this epos in terms more acceptable to the new standards of credibility. As political and cultural self-consciousness increased, each city desired to relate itself to this restated pan-Hellenic past and equipped itself with a body of more or less rationalized myths whereby the figures of the epos were given local habitations and adventures. Furthermore, whenever it was desired to equip local institutions, etc., with a past, these would be related to the local variant of 'great historiography' rather than to any past which was simply the expression of their own continuity. This thesis may be seen to present several features of our model. The relevant past-relationship is that formed by the body of epics and tales; the problem, arising within that relationship and compelling its restatement, is occasioned by the advent of Ionian philosophy. Thereafter there arise, in the life of each city, factors which impel it, first, to relate its collective identity to the past expressed in 'great historiography', and second, to historize its particular institutions by providing them with a past in the same way. [Such a 'past', it is clear, was imagined but scarcely remembered.]

But this seems to imply that the rationalized epos of 'great historiography' formed the only link with the past around which a historiography could grow and take shape, and that the various organized activities of Athens (and, by implication, other Greek cities) did not provide bodies of material about their pasts, modes of dependence on those pasts, or problems arising out of that dependence, sufficient to necessitate any specialized forms of thought about the past and its relation with the present. When it became necessary to equip religious or political institutions with pasts, this had to be done either by pure historization or by relating them to the Hellenic myths; they were not already equipped with traditional or documentary pasts which were the records of their own continuity. To go so far may be to oversimplify both the situation at Athens and the contentions of scholars like Jacoby; but the image we normally have of the polis suggests an intense concentration of social activities in the hands of a small citizen body and a corresponding lack of specialized sub-groups, and it is at least conceivable that such a society might lack specialized custodians of specialized relationships with different pasts. If such an interpretation could be maintained, it might help us to understand what is surely the most arresting fact about Athenian historiography when compared with that of the modern West – that it is not, in any significant degree, written about the past or the product of a concern with the past of organized society as explaining or justifying its present.[6]

[6] For this see M. I. Finley, *The Greek Historians* (London, 1959), introduction.

We should in effect be suggesting that Greek society lacked sufficient organized past-relationships to make such historiography necessary or possible.

A concern with the past grows out of a sense of continuity with the past, and though it is difficult to imagine any organized society altogether lacking such a sense, we have emphasized earlier that there may be wide differences in the extent to which a society's awareness of continuity is organized or institutionalized. If the Athenian polis had no bodies of specialists who preserved records and documents of the past and explained how they regulated and justified conduct in the present, or if this kind of activity existed but was underdeveloped, then we can understand why the polis did not construct its history as a complex of organized activities. It could happen also that the sense of social continuity was on the one hand strong enough to lead to the belief that the past was necessary to validate the present, but on the other insufficiently institutionalized to allow of the different elements of social structure preserving their own pasts and validating their own presents – they would not be what in early-modern England were called 'courts of record'. At the beginning of the fourth century, Athenians engaged in a controversy over the character of their 'ancestral constitution';[7] attempts were made to discover what this had been and show why it should or should not be preserved or revived; and here we seem to have a genuine case of concern with the past of an institution as giving authority in the present, and of the sort of situation in which historical criticism can arise. But it is still possible for scholars to doubt how far a work like Aristotle's *Athenian Constitution*, connected with this controversy, is a piece of true historiography, in the sense of an attempt to interpret and explain the evidences of a past, and how far it is rather historization, in the sense of a series of orderly pictures of events in the past, constructed simply to fit Aristotle's interpretation of the different elements in the existing constitution. Since our ideas about the past cannot but be affected by our ideas about the present, no 'historiography' can be altogether free of 'historization'; but the more we use the latter term, the more we imply that the past of the thing historized must be constructed either by simple extrapolation of its present characteristics, or by connecting those characteristics with a past known from other sources – which is to say that it lacks a past of its own with which its relations can be discussed. If it is true that the Athenian constitution could be provided with a past only by inventing origins for its

[7] K. von Fritz and E. Kapp, *Aristotle's Constitution of Athens and Related Texts* (New York, 1950), introduction; A. Fuks, *The Ancestral Constitution: four studies in Athenian party politics at the end of the fifth century B.C.* (London, 1953).

various components, or by ascribing their origins to figures in the national myth, then it must have lacked records of its own past and a class of experts who habitually consulted such records.

If this lack of an organized past were general – if it extended beyond the constitutional to the legal and the religious, and the other activities which might have preserved and consulted records – then we can see why the Athenian polis did not engage in study of its own past as an organized society, and indeed why Athenian historiography did not evolve into a study of the past at all. When its historians came to believe that no history could be written unless based on interviews with eye-witnesses of the events described, it was not merely that records of past events and modes of critically interpreting them did not exist; when Thucydides treated of events in the past only to demonstrate that they were less in magnitude than those of the present, it was not merely that the Greek world-picture was hostile to a developmental view of reality. Greek society, on this interpretation, simply lacked the sense of organized dependence on the past, and the means of studying and interpreting this dependence, which can come only in a society where there are a number of developed and probably institutionalized past-relationships. With its remoter past the Greek world was connected only by the single thread of 'great historiography', the interpretation of epics and myths; consequently there was nothing to be done with myths but to rationalize them, no alternative context in which to view them, and the rationalization of myths is not a technique which can give any picture of the society in which they took shape. Snorri Sturluson, contemplating the Norse myths about 1200, asked[8] the much more fruitful question: 'What manner of men believed these tales and why?', but he had the advantage of knowing that whereas he was a Christian, the makers of the myths were heathens, the working of whose minds must be explained to a Christian public, and he had a patriotic motive for doing so. He therefore set out to reconstruct the mind of early Norse heathenism, and made a very creditable attempt. But in general this method of interpreting myths did not gain ground in European scholarship until the early eighteenth century, and euhemerization and other attempts at retelling them in a rational form[9]

[8] In his prologue to the Prose Edda; see Jean I. Young, *The Prose Edda of Snorri Sturluson* (Cambridge, 1954), pp. 23–5. E.g.: 'Mountains and boulders they associated with the teeth and bones of living creatures, and so they looked on earth as in some way a living being with a life of its own. They knew it was inconceivably ancient as years go, and by nature powerful; it gave birth to all living things and owned all that died, and for that reason they gave it a name and reckoned their descent from it.'

[9] Chronology, the attempt first to rationalize mythical happenings and then to date them, provides in works like Isaac Newton's *The Chronology of Ancient Kingdoms Amended* (London, 1728) a classic instance of the sterility of this form of interpretation. [Much subsequent scholarship has corrected this judgment.]

persisted until much later; so long did the effects of the Greek poverty in past-relationships endure.

If we now turn to the picture of pre-Ch'in China conveyed – at any rate to the non-sinologist[10] – by the works of the philosophers of that period, there is suggested a society whose thought was dominated by one set of highly institutionalized past-relationships, those of the *li* or traditional rituals. These were conceived of as inherited from an ancestral past through a chain of transmitters, and their antiquity as authorizing their continuation in the present. Culture-heroes – the Former Kings – embodied that past and its ultimate authority; but the image of history formed by thinkers in this society must have been based very largely on the continuous observance of the *li* and belief in their continuous transmission. Sayings attributed to Confucius suggest a concept of the *li* as having a continuous history, marked by some breaks and changes, imperfectly recalled and recorded, but capable of being inferred, and even predicted, from an assumption of general continuity.

I can describe the civilisation of the Hsia dynasty, but the descendant state of Ch'i cannot render adequate corroboration. I can describe the civilisation of the Yin dynasty, but the descendant state of Sung cannot render adequate corroboration. And all because of the deficiency of their records and wise men. Were these sufficient then I could corroborate my views.[11]

Asked by Tzu Chang if the shape of the government of China ten generations hence could be known, Confucius replied:

Yes, the Yin dynasty, in the formulation of its system of ritual, borrowed from that of the Hsia dynasty, and one can work out what additions were made, and where any part was rejected. Similarly, Chou borrowed from the ritual system of Yin, and again, it is possible to discover what was added, and what was rejected. Hence, whatever the date, be it even a hundred generations hence, one can know by inference the corpus of ritual of the royal line which succeeds to Chou.[12]

In both these passages, Confucius is expressing an unquestioning confidence in the continuity of observance of the *li* – especially in the latter, where he assumes that it will be maintained into the future – and we may therefore suppose that his concept of history was formed very largely by

[10] I have been constrained to take the following translations more or less at their face value. They appear to display a series of attitudes of mind consonant with the theme of this article.

[11] Fung Yu-lan, *A History of Chinese Philosophy*, trans. D. Bodde, 2 vols. (Peiping and London, 1937), I, p. 55.

[12] S. Kaizuka, *Confucius* (London, 1956), p. 112; cf. James R. Ware, *The Sayings of Confucius* (New York, 1955), p. 28.

his observance and acceptance of that continuity. But it is also implied in the former passage that records exist, inherited from the past, whereby this presumption of continuity may be confirmed, and the question is being faced whether continuity may be presupposed where records are lacking. English common lawyers in the seventeenth century may be found confronting a similar problem and giving a similar affirmative answer;[13] and in such circumstances it is plain that the sense of continuity with the past has as yet encountered no challenge and presented no serious problem. In theory, there are two ways in which an established sense of continuity may be disrupted: the past may be found to possess characteristics incompatible with its continuity with the present, or a challenge may arise to the maintenance of the element of continuity in the present, necessitating a new approach to or assessment of the past. The former can happen only where there are highly developed techniques of consulting and expounding the past; the latter is not so stringently limited by this condition. On a limited acquaintance with ancient Chinese thinking, there would appear to be evidences of the former rather than the latter.

Taoist and Legalist thinkers are credited with the first attempts to maintain that since social conditions in the past were qualitatively different from those of the present, the *li* which were an appropriate guide to conduct them are not so now:

Our time and that of the Former Kings are as different as land from water; the Empire of Chou over which they ruled and this land of Lu are as different as boat from chariot. Your Master tries to treat the Lu of today as though it were the Chou of long ago. This is like pushing a boat over dry land.[14]

In reply, Hsun Tzu, the reintegrator of Confucianism, is to be found denying that 'ancient and present times are different in nature' and arguing, first, that the way of the Former Kings may be known by studying the way of Chou, which was near to it in time; second, that

the Sage measures things by himself. Hence by himself he measures other men; by his own feelings he measures their feelings; by his class he measures other classes; by his doctrines he measures their merit; by the Way he can completely comprehend things. Past and present are the same. Things that are the same in kind, though extended over a long period, continue to have the self-same principles.[15]

[13] E.g., Sir Edward Coke, *Eighth Reports*, ed. J. H. Thomas and J. F. Fraser (London, 1826), preface, pp. iii–xxiii. [Coke did not offer to predict the future state of the common law.]

[14] A. Waley, *Three Ways of Thought in Ancient China* (London, 1939), pp. 37–8.

[15] Fung, *History of Chinese Philosophy*, I, pp. 282–4; cf. H. H. Dubs (trans.), *The Works of Hsüntze* (London, 1928), pp. 72–5. [I do not know what Fung or Bodde meant by 'class'.]

In this sequence of doctrines, we seem to have a succession of ideas that will be repeated at other times and places. First, a set of institutions existing in the past is described as authorizing the maintenance of the same institutions in the present; next, historical criticism gives rise to the idea that the institutions of the past are appropriate only in the circumstances of the past, which no longer obtain in the present; third, the authority of antiquity is restored, but on grounds which no longer vest authority in antiquity as such, being those of universal and timeless validity. We appear to have moved from tradition to reason, but if the critical effort of the second stage is maintained, historiography will co-exist with reason. From the point of view of the present inquiry, the crucial question is that of the processes which led to the conclusion that past and present differed in nature. But here a doubt arises: was this piece of apparent historical reconstruction the result of a study of the Chou past, conducted in such detail as to lead to the conclusion that it was inimitable, or was it the result of something else – perhaps a Taoist metaphysical conviction of the transitory nature of reality, from which it was simply inferred that what things were now they could not have been then? This might be philosophy of history, but could not be historiography; and unless the rejection of tradition is founded on the intensive study of the past *an sich*, it is unlikely to leave behind it an activity of exploring the past and reconstructing its connexions with the present. The writer of this article is unaware whether historiography in this sense developed in ancient China out of study of the relationship with the *li* established with Chou and pre-Chou times; but it can happen that a strong sense of institutional dependence on the past leads to the paradoxical discovery that the past is *sui generis* and cannot be imitated. Some well-documented instances exist to which we now turn.

The civilization of Western Europe, towards the end of its medieval period, was particularly rich in past-relationships – meaning by that documents and institutions inherited from a past state of society and used to regulate conduct in the present, and concepts of the authority which they enjoyed. These documents and institutions were predominantly inherited from Greco-Roman civilization, though Hebrew and Germanic elements were also important. A profound sense of continuity existed with all of these pasts, expressed in the various concepts of how they exercised authority over the present; but at the same time each past was felt to be cut off and alienated from the present by the intervening fact of the Christian revelation. There was consequently as profound a sense of discontinuity as of continuity, and many important writings were undertaken on the theme of reconciliation. These did not, in the medieval period, take the form of historiography as the term is being used here, but the unique development of historiography in just that sense, which occurred in the West following the humanist Renaissance, may be connected with the unique wealth of relationships between Latin Christendom and pasts of which it could not regard itself as the simple continuation. By way of contrast, we may note that Hellenic historians were unaware of any organized civilization from which their own was descended, while Chou and the times before Chou were to ancient Chinese the direct ancestral continuation of their own society. We therefore proceed to examine some of the ways in which Latin Christendom was conceived as related to the Greco-Roman world through the elements surviving from that world which it used to organize its own society, and to show how these relationships become problematical at the Renaissance.

The narrative works of Greek and Roman historians, though they became of surpassing importance to humanist scholars, were of no institutional significance in medieval society. Far greater roles were played by the Latin language and by the Roman laws in their Byzantine codifications, both of which were continuously studied and applied to solving the multitudinous problems of medieval society and culture; we may state at this point that philology and jurisprudence, far more than the imitation of Livy, furnished at the Renaissance the origins of modern historical awareness. But if we now ask in what ways Latin grammar and Roman law were held to have authority over medieval life, we do not find simple statements of traditional continuity. To confine ourselves from this point to the field of law, though doctrines did exist whereby the authority of emperor, senate or people could be represented as still alive and validating law, something more was needed to retain for a largely pagan law its place in a Christian society. Mediating concepts had to be found and, especially in the most sophisticated phase of post-glossatorial jurisprudence, these were drawn from the vocabulary of scholastic rationalism. Universal principles of reason and morality were alleged, by whose aid the essential doctrines of jurisprudence could be distilled from Roman practice and rephrased in forms suited to medieval conditions. The example of Hsun Tzu has already shown that the use of universal principles may be an efficacious means of bridging the gap between past and present where a simple statement of direct continuity does not suffice; and carried to extremes, it involves denial that such a gap exists at all. In a scholastic age, moreover, when principles of this order were employed in the solving of all types of theoretical problem, their use in the field of jurisprudence may well have been automatic and unthinking; and tradition and reason may have seen to it that hardly any sense of a difference between past and present emerged into consciousness.

But on another level, the continuity of medieval jurisprudence with its past lay in the fact that interpretation and adaptation of Roman law had gone on uninterruptedly since the twelfth century. To the extent that glosses and commentaries upon glosses replaced the original texts as the sources of authority and the objects of study, Roman law tended to become a tradition in continuous adaptation; and in such traditions the most recent expression of authority, and its continuity with those preceding it, may come to be of more importance than the original form of the law (or other authoritative document), which may cease to matter or even disappear. But wherever it survives, or even can be imagined, there is the possibility of a fundamentalist revolt, a demand for return to the original sources. Such revolts, at once radical and reactionary, involve the repudiation of tradition; they raise the problems of how the original form of authority may be known, and what relation (other than traditional) it may bear to the present. That is why they may be important to the study of historiography.

Such a fundamentalist revolt may be detected in the impact of humanism on civilian jurisprudence, as well (no doubt) as in other fields of the humanist Renaissance. Equipped with scholarly techniques which made possible direct study of the source material to a degree not previously attempted, the humanists decried the medieval traditions of adaptation and generalization, and aimed instead to recover the exact meaning of the original sources so that they could be put, immediately and directly, into use.[16] To us their thinking appears both historical and unhistorical: the former, because they were undertaking to reconstruct the meanings which documents had possessed for those who had framed and used them; the latter, because in their belief that a document's original meaning could be directly applied, once found, to modern conditions, we recognize the humanist ideal of imitation, which we consider to have delayed the emergence of historical understanding till the late eighteenth century. The reality, however, is even more complex. The effort at historical reconstruction was undertaken only in consequence of the unhistorical ideal of imitation, which we may describe, in our terminology, as involving the rupture of a traditional relationship with a past and the substitution of a new one. Moreover, it

[16] J. Declareuil, *Histoire générale du droit français* (Paris, 1925); H. D. Hazeltine, 'The Renaissance', in *Cambridge Legal Essays* (Cambridge, 1926); L. Delaruelle, *Guillaume Budé (1468–1540) – les origines, les débuts, les idées maîtresses* (Paris, 1907); P. E. Viard, *André Alciat* (Paris, 1926); M. P. Gilmore, *Argument from Roman Law* (Cambridge, MA, 1941); J. G. A. Pocock, *The Ancient Constitution and the Feudal Law* (Cambridge, 1957), ch. 1.

is evident that the ideal of imitation can be longer and more successfully maintained in the case of something easily viewed in abstraction from its social environment – plastic and literary art-forms, moral standards, model political systems, idealized individual acts – than in the case of a working set of legal institutions, involved so intimately and in so many ways with the detailed functionings of society. While, therefore, the ideal of imitation lasted, in fields like the former, until it came under fire from the thinkers of the Enlightenment,[17] humanism in the field of law can be shown to have entered by about 1560 on the crisis of discovery that the past was too well known to be any longer imitable.

The techniques of the legal humanists were predominantly philological; drawing on their knowledge of the vocabulary of classical literature in general, they sought to establish the exact meaning which each word in the texts of the law had borne in the minds of its original users. Inevitably, therefore, they built up an enormously detailed picture of the usages, institutions and ideas of late-Roman society, organized around the law which had been a code of regulation of that society; and this picture they employed to interpret the texts of the law and equip them with their original meanings. They were, in fact, reconstructing Roman law by reconstructing its historical and social context; and the more successfully this enterprise was carried through, the clearer it became that the context in which alone Roman law was intelligible differed so widely from that in which its interpreters lived that direct application and imitation were not, in fact, possible. At this point the paths of the scholar and the practical lawyer began to diverge. It has been shown in a study of André Alciat (b. 1492) how,[18] after establishing the original meaning of a text, he proceeded to consider how it might be employed by the modern lawyer – a course which led him to adopt techniques of interpretation not much unlike those of the Bartolists against whom he was rebelling. But the school around Jacques Cujas acquired a reputation for an interest in the past which excluded all concern with the affairs of the present. Cujas appears to have been angry when it was suggested that Roman law had no contemporary value, but the story that he was asked for his views on a current problem and replied merely 'Quid hoc ad edictum praetoris?' is important, even if apocryphal, because it shows that the idea of historical study carried on without any reference to the present was becoming increasingly intelligible. The widening gap between

[17] P. Hasard, *La Crise de la conscience européenne* (Paris, 1935), ch. 2: 'De l'ancien au moderne'. [See further Joseph M. Levine, *The Battle of the Books: history and literature in the Augustan age* (Ithaca, NY, 1991).]

[18] Viard, *André Alciat*, pp. 132–64.

past and present, scholar and practitioner, was emphasized with deliberate iconoclasm in François Hotman's *Anti-Tribonian* (1567).[19]

Hotman composed his book in mockery of the 'grammarians', as he called the school of Cujas, but his attack is based on a complete acceptance of their methods. He concedes that they have shown that Roman law can be understood only after detailed reconstruction of the late-Roman world, but concludes that for this very reason it has neither meaning nor value in sixteenth-century France. He lays down as a principle, what the proceedings of the humanists had implied, that law must be appropriate to the circumstances and character of the people among whom it is to be employed, but insists 'que l'estat de la Republique Romaine est fort different de celuy de France'.[20] Moreover, since it is known that the Byzantine codes represent a conflation from various earlier law-books, it follows that they do not contain the organized body of law that prevailed at any moment or period in Roman history, and Hotman infers both that they are useless as law – since they have now doubly failed to pass the text of relevance to an actual society – and that they cannot even, as some have argued, be employed in the interpretation of late-Roman historians. Their study is on all counts a waste of time, and all the 'grammarians' have achieved is to condemn themselves by proving this.[21]

It might seem then, that the end-product of legal humanism was the discovery of a past without relevance to the present, and the relegation of Roman law to that past. But Hotman's situation was less simple than this. The law he had proved useless was nonetheless in use over wide areas – both in courts, as an instrument of actual jurisprudence, and in law-schools as a means of education – and he had to propose substitutes for it in both roles. His suggestions are illuminating. French courts, he considered, would find French customary law of far greater use; having grown up with the people and being expressive of their distinctive character and circumstances, it must always pass the test of social relevance, and not being reduced to a written form, it could not grow out of date or be relegated to the past by philological criticism.[22] Very remotely, the shadow of Vico falls across Hotman's pages: the French know their own law best because they have made it and it suits them; and in their customary law they find a tradition, and a direct relation with the past, which the civil law has proved not to provide. As for law

[19] Pocock, *Ancient Constitution and the Feudal Law*, pp. 11–14. [See further Donald R. Kelley, *The Foundations of Modern Historical Scholarship* (New York, 1970).]

[20] '. . . et neantmoins ne se peut apprendre par les liures de Iustinian'. Title of ch. 3 in the Paris edition of 1603.

[21] Ibid., pp. 13–15, 18, 20–1, 35–6, 86–7.

[22] Ibid., pp. 36–7, 101–2, 137–8.

as a means of education, Hotman proposed that from the great codes of law known to scholarship, a selection be made of the essential principles of jurisprudence. These could be used in the training of young lawyers, and might, ideally, equip them with so perfect a grasp of equity that they might sit like St Louis beneath his oak, and render judgments on all cases without the intervention of law-books or legal technicalities.[23] Hotman omitted Roman law from his list of codes from which this selection might be made, but gave no real reason why it should not be laid under contribution as well; and it is plain that once it was used in this way, a return would have been made to the techniques of the Bartolists, with their universal principles valid in both past and present. Such a neo-Bartolism was in fact springing up as Hotman wrote, in the works of François Baudouin, Jean Bodin and the *mos italicus* school of the later sixteenth century.[24] Since European jurisprudence could not do without Roman law, the present could not do without its Roman past and, denied its hitherto accepted continuity with it, found like Hsun Tzu an answer in asserting rational principles which made past and present one. It seems that an appeal to universals may regularly be made where continuous traditions break down; but, since in this case the methods of scholastic jurisprudence could be revived, the neo-Bartolists were rather restoring a tradition than finding an alternative.

But it would be too simple to conclude merely that the dominant rationalism of medieval Europe had submerged an attempt to develop the insights of historical thought. In neo-Bartolist rationalism and its successors, there may indeed be discerned an intention of re-unifying a past and present which philological criticism had threatened to drive apart; but as long as the techniques of that criticism existed, they could be practised, the minutiae of the past could be searched out and the attempt could be made to reconstruct the law in its Roman setting. Historical reconstruction did not cease in the face of the neo-Bartolist revival; it merely became an intellectual effort distinct from, though capable of being confused with, that of the jurisconsult proper. To Hotman as to Alciat, it was one thing to show what the law had been, another to show how this knowledge might help establish law in the present, and even neo-Bartolism was in a sense a comment upon a past-relationship. Historical thought in the full sense did not perhaps emerge; to a late legal humanist like Nicolas Peiresc the

[23] Ibid., p. 140.

[24] Baudouin, *De institutione historiæ universæ et ejus cum jurisprudentia conjunctione* (1561); Bodin, *Methodus ad facilem historiarum cognitionem* (1566).

effort to reconstruct the law in its original form, the humanist attempt to discover models for imitation and the rationalist search for the universal principles of jurisprudence were all one,[25] and we miss the truly historicist conviction that the justification of Roman law in the present lies in the constant adaptations and restatements which have kept it alive and relevant to present needs. But just such a doctrine could, as we shall see, arise from the ideas about continuity which the past induced by other systems of law; and nothing in the *mos italicus* or the concept of natural law prevented a civilian asking the question how, if Roman law was no longer what it had been for Romans, it had become what it now was for Europeans. The Englishman Arthur Duck and the Neapolitan Pietro Giannone both[26] paid attention to this problem, though no full-scale history of Roman law seems to have emerged in this period. The question 'How did the past become the present?' is not necessarily incompatible with the search for universal laws underlying both; each phenomenon may arise in response to the same challenge when traditional continuities break down; but there may be a difference between the specialized scholar who asks the former question, and the guardian of a traditional past-relationship who seeks to restore it by the latter means. Cujas figures in the first role, any partisan of the *mos italicus* in the second, and Hotman in both.

The most remarkable historical work undertaken by the legal humanists lies, however, in the more specialized field of feudal law. The *Corpus Juris Civilis* contained a number of imperial constitutions on this theme, as well as the *Libri Feudorum*, a Lombard work of the twelfth century which gave an account of the law of feudal inheritance and a history of the *feudum*'s progress from precarious to perpetual tenure.[27] Before 1520, Claude de

[25] See Pierre Gassendi, *Life of Peireskius*, Eng. trans. W. Rand (London, 1657), pp. 200–2: 'For he studied the Lawes, after the liberal method of *Cujacius*, which tends to illustrate the said Lawes from the Fountains themselves, and fundamental Maxims of Equity and Right, rather than from the Rivulets of the Doctors or Lawyers. And this it was, that chiefly made him affect the study of Antiquity; because it gave him great light therein . . . And what I said occasionally touching his study of Antiquity, comprehends principally Universal History, which he had so printed in his mind and memory, that a man would have thought he had lived in all places and times. For he held it evermore as a Maxime, that History did serve exceedingly, not only to give light to the study of the Law, but to the ordering of a man's life, and the possessing of his mind, with a rare and ingenuous delectation. For he counted it in some sort, more effectual than Philosophy, because she instructs men indeed with words, but History inflames them with examples; and makes in some sort, that we ought not to think much of our short life, making the same partaker of things and times that are past.' [For Peiresc as much more than a student of laws, see Peter Miller, *Peiresc's Europe: learning and virtue in the seventeenth century* (New Haven, 2000).]

[26] Duck, *De Usu et Auctoritate Juris Civilis Romani in Dominiis Principum Christianorum* (1653), criticized in Giannone's introduction to his *Istoria Civile del Regno di Napoli* (1723).

[27] Pocock, *Ancient Constitution and the Feudal Law*, ch. 3.

Seyssel was subjecting feudal law to a purely scholastic analysis,[28] but the humanists employed upon it their techniques of philological reconstruction; they attempted to establish the meanings which its Latin vocabulary would have borne in Roman usage, and thus to equate its institutions with those of Rome and to find there its origins. We can read[29] how they tried to make *feudum* a variant of *foedus* or of *fides*, and to find in *cliens* and *patronus* the true image of vassal and seigneur. But there were insuperable difficulties and, besides, an increasing suggestion that the language, the institutions and consequently the origins of feudal law were German rather than Roman, to be understood by study not of Roman agrarian law, but of the war-bands described by Caesar and Tacitus. There arose, in the mid-sixteenth century, 'Romanist' and 'Germanist' schools of feudal history; but it is noteworthy how much each school conceded to the views of the other. If Cujas thought that the different types of feudatory had each his parallel in some late-Roman type of agrarian tenant, he added that all must have been both barbarized in their vocabulary and militarized in their character as a result of the Germanic invasions; and if Hotman (some years after writing *Anti-Tribonian*) held that the Roman colonate explained the origins of serfdom but not of vassalage, and that the vassal's obligations to his lord were paralleled only in those of the war-companion to his chief, he instantly conceded that no trace could be found of the war-band's having been based on a relationship in land-tenure. Each school conceded that feudal origins must be sought in some blend of Roman and Germanic institutions taking place after the invasions, and European scholarship was left for three centuries to contemplate the chief and his companions dividing out conquered lands among themselves, and becoming transformed into lord and vassals in the process.

Whatever may be thought of it, this was a true historical explanation, of some subtlety in its handling of diverse institutions; and we may suggest here that it arose, not merely as a by-product of the humanist attempt at a reconstruction of Rome, but from the fact that feudal law figured in more than one legal system and so could not be explained in terms of the simple continuity of any of them. Because it was no true part of the Roman system, it could not be Romanized by Cujas, cast out by *Anti-Tribonian* and restored

[28] Seyssel, *Speculum Feudorum* (Basle, 1566), pp. 12–16. Seyssel died in 1520 and this work belongs to an early stage of his career.

[29] The main sources for humanist study of feudal law are Cujas, *Opera quæ de iure fecit*, II (Paris, 1637), and Hotman, *De feudis commentario tripertita* (Lyons, 1573), 'Disputatio de feudis', which contains (ch. 2) an analysis of the opinions of other scholars 'de feudorum origine it instituto'. See also Pocock, *Ancient Constitution and the Feudal Law*, ch. 3.

by the neo-Bartolists; but on the other hand, though Hotman's emphasis on the German origins of the *feudum*, like his interest in the Frankish origin of French institutions, may be connected with the fact that he had studied the *coutumes* at Paris, he could not explain the *Libri Feudorum* simply as showing the antiquity of French custom. If Roman law connected Western Europe with a classical past, feudal customs connected it with a German and barbaric one; and because the feudal element in the civil law seemed to figure in both traditions and to belong to both pasts, it was explained in terms of a complex blending between the two. Plurality of tradition, we may generalize, can both necessitate and render possible advanced historical explanations; if a phenomenon appears to be related to two pasts, it cannot be explained in terms of continuity with either of them, but if both appear to have contributed to making it what it is, it will be possible to suppose a process whereby the two entered into combination. Where two bodies of law give awareness of two past societies, complex patterns of institutional and even social historiography may emerge.

IV. LAW AND HISTORIOGRAPHY IN EARLY-MODERN ENGLAND, SCOTLAND, NAPLES, IRELAND, FRANCE

We may, at this point, turn from the awareness of the past provided by Roman law to see how some Western nations were at this time connected with their pasts by their systems of law, and what problems in historiography arose.

In the case of England at the beginning of the early-modern period, it may be broadly stated that a single body of law, the common law, determined the national awareness of institutional continuity. This was the only secular law in force in all parts of England, and all the institutions of government, in varying ways, could be seen as based upon it and presupposing its presence. Since the common law was held to be a customary law, all these institutions, consequently, were regarded, about 1600, as having the character of immemorial usage. It was an essential property of custom that it should be considered immemorial, for if the beginnings of a law could be dated to a specific time, its origin would no longer be in usage but in the authority of whatever will could be shown to have sanctioned its beginnings at that time. On the assumption that the law and constitution were customary, therefore, they were regarded as having existed without fundamental change since a time earlier than the earliest historical records, and historians were warned to defer to the authority of lawyers in this matter. In particular, it had to be maintained that the law and constitution had undergone no material alteration at the Norman Conquest, and indeed that William I's accession was not a conquest but had come about within the existing law.[30]

Belief in an 'ancient constitution' became one of the most potent of English myths until at least the end of the eighteenth century. Since the common law unified so much in English social behaviour, it unified Englishmen's thoughts about the past, and gave them a set of beliefs about their national history more satisfying, because more relevant to their present social structure, than anything they derived from the chronicles of earlier kings, and more unquestioningly accepted even than the myths of the original independence of the Anglican Church. English historical thought did not become unified, however, till after the period studied. Milton's *History of Britain*[31] is a different kind of book from its near-contemporary, Nathaniel Bacon's *Historical Discourse of the Uniformity of the Government of England* (1647); chronicle and record connected readers with different pasts and gave them different ideas of historical continuity. But it was the historiography based on records which was politically significant 'contemporary history', because it involved the character and authority of contemporary institutions. Throughout the seventeenth and eighteenth centuries, every major piece of either historical or political thinking involved, if it did not consist in, the adoption of an attitude towards the 'ancient constitution'.

Since hardly any serious attempt had yet been made to construct an absolutist version of history based on acceptance of the Conquest as the origin of the royal power,[32] the first real challenge to the doctrine of immemorial law came from the Army and London radicals of 1647.[33] The 'ancient constitution' was a doctrine of profound conservatism; it was the existing laws that were said to be good because they were immemorial, and their goodness was demonstrated by the purely traditionalist argument of inferring it from the uninterrupted antiquity of their usage. So deep-seated was the habit of appealing to the past that when the Leveller radicals desired to argue that existing laws were bad, they said in effect what Mo Tzu is reported[34] to have said to the Confucian traditionalists of his time, 'Your antiquity

[30] For analysis see Pocock, *Ancient Constitution and the Feudal Law*, chs. 3 and 4. [For subsequent commentary on this thesis, see most recently Alan Cromartie, *The Constitutionalist Revolution: an essay on the history of England, 1450–1642* (Cambridge, 2006), pp. 189–200.]

[31] Published 1669, but written earlier.

[32] But cf. Hill, *Puritanism and Revolution* (London, 1958), pp. 50–63.

[33] Ibid., pp. 71–89; A. S. P. Woodhouse, *Puritanism and Liberty* (London, 1950), *passim*; J. Frank, *The Levellers* (Cambridge, MA, 1955); Pocock, *Ancient Constitution and the Feudal Law*, pp. 125–7.

[34] Fung, *History of Chinese Philosophy*, 1, p. 78.

does not go back far enough', and constructed the myth of a set of liberties more universal than those now obtaining, which had been enjoyed in an Anglo-Saxon golden age and lost at the Conquest, on which act of usurpation the existing and unjust laws were founded. To these primeval liberties there must now be return. Leveller fundamentalism, however, did not lead to a recrudescence of historical study (which was already in a flourishing condition); it was not founded on a reinterpretation of the documents of a past, but merely on a vehement conviction that what ought to be had once been. Contemporaries observed, besides, that when Levellers were asked why the alleged ancient liberties were just, or why they should be restored, the answer, which could not be given in terms of existing law or even historical continuity, came in the form of an appeal to 'reason' or 'nature' which might annihilate the appeal to the past which the Levellers were themselves making. Once again – though this time in a radical, not a conservative form – a tradition of continuity, once broken, had to be restored by means of a rationalism which rendered the past unnecessary. Yet the Levellers were not blind to the need to explain how the 'just' past had become the 'unjust' present; their emphasis on the Conquest shows this. Normative rationalism and historical explanation are not simple incompatibles; they provide the answers to different questions, which become distinct when a traditional means of justifying the present is ruptured.

It was in the first place disinterested scholarship, rather than partisan fundamentalism, which provided the key to historical criticism of the doctrine of immemorial law. Elizabethan and Jacobean learning noted the many similarities between early English law and language and those of the Germanic invaders of Western Europe, and Sir Henry Spelman (1562–1641) set about a vast comparative reconstruction of the institutional vocabularies of the barbaric kingdoms.[35] His role may be compared to that of the 'grammarians' of legal humanism, and whatever his intentions, the results of his work were as subversive of tradition as theirs had been. He showed not merely that early English law was Germanic, and therefore not immemorial but post-Roman, but that a great part of it was feudal – and feudal in such a state of development that it could be no older than the Norman Conquest. English law, he concluded, was a composite of Anglo-Saxon, feudal, civilian and canonist elements, and there was need of a historian to analyse it into its components. This being done, he wrote, the scholar would be 'come to the lists of the modern common law, and I dare venture

[35] *Archaeologus* (London, 1626); *Glossarium Archaiologium* (London, 1664; posthumous). Pocock, *Ancient Constitution and the Feudal Law*, ch. 5.

no further',[36] but analysis must be followed by synthesis, and there would have had to be a history of how the elements had been combined – a history of the common law quite other than common lawyers were in the habit of writing. Spelman had provided English law with what it had hitherto lacked: the complexity of tradition that necessitates historical explanations.

No such history of English law had, however, been written by the late eighteenth century. Spelman left his work unfinished, but noted in the last year of his life[37] that this method might be used to demonstrate that the House of Commons was not immemorial, and so to check its pretensions. This cue was taken up between 1675 and 1685 by Dr Robert Brady, as part of the controversy over the Bill of Exclusion and Filmer's patriarchal writings.[38] Brady was among the highest of Caroline Tories, and his attack on the Commons' antiquity was certainly intended to subject their authority to that of the Crown. He did not, however, base the royal power unequivocally on the Conquest, and when he argued that feudal land-tenure had been imported by the Normans and that the laws and councils of England thereafter must be interpreted in a strictly feudal sense, the weight of his attack was directed against the politically disastrous consequences of anachronistic thinking. With Brady's pleas of 1684 for the understanding of early constitutional history in its own legal and agrarian setting,[39] English historiography attained the same realization of the importance of the temporal context as had been reached by Hotman more than a century earlier. The history of how England had ceased to be a feudal kingdom, however, was beyond Brady's powers.[40]

Neither historical criticism nor Lockean rationalism brought about more than a modification of 'ancient constitution' thought during the eighteenth century. Emphasis on custom and the immemorial seems to have slackened, but there remained a steady beat of orthodox insistence on the antiquity of a constitution which differed from its predecessor in seventeenth-century thought only in the greater certainty which was now felt that it possessed

[36] E. Gibson (ed.), *Reliquiæ Spelmannianæ* (London, 1698), pp. 127–32.

[37] If the unfinished treatise 'Of Parliaments' (*Reliquiæ*, pp. 57–65) was composed in 1641; Pocock, *Ancient Constitution and the Feudal Law*, pp. 120–2.

[38] Pocock, *Ancient Constitution and the Feudal Law*, ch. 8.

[39] 'Epistle to the Candid Reader', in Brady, *Introduction to the Old English History* (1684): '. . . but as to the Matter here treated of, whoever reads our Old Historians and hath not a true Understanding and Apprehension of it, neither can he truly, and as he ought, understand them, nor will he ever be able to arrive at the Knowledge of our Ancient Government, or of what Import and Signification the Men were that lived under it according to their Several Denominations; of what Power, and Interest they that contended with our Ancient Kings about Liberty, and Relaxation of the Government, nor indeed what truly the Liberties were they contended for.'

[40] Pocock, *Ancient Constitution and the Feudal Law*, pp. 218–27.

'principles' or a 'spirit' which could be apprehended and explained. There was, then, an increased rationalization of tradition – carried out by means which owed as much to Polybius, Machiavelli and Harrington as to Locke or, later, Montesquieu[41] – but this did not prevent the typical English (and perhaps American) political thought of the century being as firmly centred on antiquity as on nature. French enlightenment, Benthamite utilitarianism, Scottish sociology and the beginnings of authentic historicism worked on this thought, no doubt, in many ways, but in 1790 many of the phenomena of Leveller anti-Normanism were being repeated in Paine's writings; and almost all of the 'opposition' ideologies of the period involved a species of fundamentalism. The constitution was endowed with a set of original principles from which it was said to have declined as the result of corruption and to which it must now be restored.[42] To the questions 'Why were these principles good and by what right may we restore them?' an answer could be found in whatever exercise of reason was supposed to have detected them; but to the question 'How did the decline or corruption which has brought us to our present state come about?' some kind of historical reply must be given, and these differed widely in character. Pamphleteers preferred to write dramatically of the machinations of wicked ministers; deists ascribed all to the clergy; but more serious writers attempted the establishment of deeper causes, looking back to Polybius and the cycle of governments, or forward via Montesquieu to the Scottish endeavour to discern stages in the progress of society. Not all sought to ascribe historical change to the operation of universal causes; there were those who generalized instead about the course of European history as they knew it. Fletcher of Saltoun, in 1698, explained the decline of 'gothic' free government by the revival of learning and of trade, the use of gunpowder and the rise of standing armies,[43] and his scheme does not differ very greatly from those of Robertson or even Macaulay.[44]

[41] Caroline Robbins, *The Eighteenth-Century Commonwealthman* (Cambridge, MA, 1959).

[42] See writers as diverse as Bolingbroke, *Dissertation upon Parties* (1734), and Major Cartwright, *Take Your Choice* (1776), and *The English Constitution Produced and Illustrated* (1823). For refutations see, e.g., Josiah Tucker, *A Treatise Concerning Civil Government* (1781) and Burke, *Reflections on the Revolution in France* (1790). For modern treatments, Hill, *Puritanism and Revolution*, ch. 3, 'The Norman Yoke', and H. Butterfield, *George III, Lord North and the People* (London, 1949), pp. 337–52.

[43] *A Discourse of Government with Relation to Militias* (Edinburgh, 1698). I am indebted to Professor Robbins for drawing my attention to this work.

[44] William Robertson, *A View of the Progress of Society in Europe from the Subversion of the Roman Empire to the Beginning of the Sixteenth Century*, in *Works*, III (London, 1824), pp. 9–316. It will be seen that the historical framework in which Macaulay sets his account of seventeenth-century England is the typically eighteenth-century one of the subversion of feudal government by the rise of standing armies; e.g., *History of England*, ch. 1.

Historical explanation, then, yet again accompanied the rationalization of tradition, but the past-relationship that was the source of tradition remained operative in English thought. In his *Reflections on the Revolution in France* (1790), Burke consciously described and appealed to what he considered the oldest orthodoxy in English politics, the 'principle of reference to antiquity' which consisted in seeing in the law and constitution the operations of immemorial custom.[45] As had several times been pointed out in the previous century, if English institutions were customary, they were rooted in nothing but usage and prescription. If an institution was accepted by the common law, this was recognition that it had on innumerable occasions been tested and approved by experience, but no more than this could be known of it. Reason could not wholly explain, nor could historical inquiry wholly reconstruct, the circumstances in which or the reasons for which it had been found satisfactory, but there existed a presumption in its favour which outweighed anything which 'speculative philosophy' might find to say either for or against it. Burke can be found saying all this – casting aside, be it noted, much of the progress which the eighteenth century had made in reconstructing the history of laws and states of society – but it had been said before him in the writings of common lawyers; and in view of the plainness of his allusions to the immemorial character of the constitution and to the established English habit of appealing to ancient standing law, it seems that Burke was not responding to the first stirrings of a new historicist outlook so much as reaffirming a purely English traditionalism, a conception of the past's continuity with and authority in the present shaped by the ubiquity of a customary law. The Burke who wrote in England was not the Burke imagined by his readers in contemporary Germany.

In the late eighteenth century, then, the English (but not Scottish) awareness of the past was still very largely traditional rather than historical. The traditional belief in the continuity of institutions had not yet encountered problems which compelled its critical restatement – indeed it is still not altogether clear just when or why this finally came about – and both the late development of institutional historiography and the pragmatic traditionalism of English conservative thought[46] can be explained by reference to

[45] For a detailed analysis of Burke's affinities with seventeenth-century thought, especially that of Sir Matthew Hale (d. 1675), see J. G. A. Pocock, 'Burke and the Ancient Constitution: a problem in the history of ideas', *Historical Journal*, 3.2 (Cambridge, 1960), pp. 125–43.

[46] 'They beyond the seas are not only diligent but very curious in this kind; but we are all for profit and *Lucrando pane*, taking what we find at Market, without enquiring whence it came.' Spelman (perhaps as early as 1614), in *Reliquiæ Spelmannianæ*, pp. 98–9.

the fact that post-medieval England possessed one unifying system of law which, being customary, relied for authority on the presumption of its own continuity. The mere affirmation of continuity can produce only traditionalism; historical explanation can arise only where there is some awareness of discontinuity; and this could be imposed upon English thought only by a demonstration that at some time a large body of alien institutions had been brought into the kingdom, so that subsequent happenings must be explained in terms of their interaction with older institutions of a different character. This would be a demonstration of what I have called plurality of tradition; and we may now proceed to examine what happened when a legal structure imposed this plurality, and its problems, at the beginnings of historical thought.

In sixteenth-century Scotland, for example, there was no indigenously evolved body of common law, and lawyers were accustomed to study the civil law, often at French universities, in search of maxims and doctrines which could be applied to Scottish tenures and customs. One Scotsman, Thomas Craig of Riccarton, studied under François Baudouin at the time when French scholars were engrossed in the problems of the *Libri Feudorum*;[47] and in *Jus Feudale* (1603) he recalled his discovery that the characteristics of Lombard feudal law recurred in the land law of both Scotland and England, so that it was necessary to suppose the growth and distribution of a body of feudal institutions common to all Western Europe. He wrote in his old age, forty years after his studies at Paris but twenty-three years before Spelman published similar conclusions concerning English law; and had Scots lawyers been as accustomed as English to explain their law purely by reference to the records of its former continuity, Craig's discovery might have been as long delayed as Spelman's. But because Scots law was not self-sufficient, but required regular borrowings from civil law, Scottish students were exposed to the legal-humanist spirit of historical reconstruction and discovered that their law was part of the general phenomenon of European law, and that it could only be understood by supposing it part of the history of that law. Plurality of tradition was partly the discovery of scholars, partly inherent in the situation of Scotland; and one may wonder how far the efflorescence of Scottish historical sociology in the eighteenth century was the consequence of Scotland's lack of self-sufficient institutional traditions.

A far more elaborate example of the historical explanation that is necessitated when the phenomenon to be studied cannot be related purely to

47 *Dictionary of National Biography*, article 'Craig, Thomas'; see generally Pocock, *Ancient Constitution and the Feudal Law*, pp. 79–90.

its own past may be found in Giannone's *Istoria Civile del Regno di Napoli* (1723). Giannone wrote to vindicate the secular rights of the kingdom against papal intrusions; but where English apologetics in the like case began with the assertion that England had always been an 'empire' possessed of a purely native jurisdiction sufficient for all purposes, Giannone's preface defines an almost antithetical situation. If Naples had been an island in the midst of the ocean, he says,[48] there would have been nothing to record of its civil history but the laws which its princes had from time to time enacted; but the laws actually in force are a patchwork of elements – Roman, Byzantine, Norman, Suabian, Spanish – each of which belonged to an alien system and was imported into Naples, where it received modifications. The history of the kingdom is therefore intelligible only if we study, first, the major legal systems of Europe and, second, the changes they have undergone in response to local conditions. Similarly the papal claims to jurisdiction in the kingdom necessitate a history of the temporal power – like Marsilius and Hobbes, Giannone studies its history because he does not accept the orthodox accounts of its foundation – and of its establishment in Naples. There is no Neapolitan 'ancient constitution' for Giannone (though in Sicily, 'an island in the midst of the ocean', one was believed in[49]); far from thinking that Neapolitan law rests on the record of its own continuity, he maintains that it is derived from so many sources that only a history of Naples as part of the history of Europe can make it intelligible. But where English writers insisted that the unique traditional continuity of their law rendered it proof against papal claims, Giannone achieves the same result by insisting on the unique historical complexity of the law of Naples. In both arguments the unique development of national law is made part of the case for sovereignty; but the English contention rests on an appeal to tradition, Giannone's on the concept of history.

Scotland and Naples furnish cases of historical thought arising from plurality of tradition, when the present has to be explained by reference to a past other than the nation's own. What happens when a society's present compels two different conceptions of continuity with the past is further illustrated by material from Ireland and France. James I's Attorney-General for Ireland, the judge and poet Sir John Davies, wrote *A Discovery of the true causes why Ireland was never subdued until His Majesty's happy Reign* and

[48] *Istoria Civile*, I: 'Introduzione'. [See further J. G. A. Pocock, *Barbarism and Religion*, II: *Narratives of Civil Government* (Cambridge, 1999), pp. 29–41.]

[49] The development of Sicilian historical thought is studied in R. Romeo, *Il Risorgimento in Sicilia* (Bari, 1950).

published it in 1612.[50] It had been decided to assimilate the Irish to English habits and obedience by transforming Gaelic methods of holding land to English tenures at common law, and Davies was engaged in this work. He therefore believed that the warlike instability of Irish clan society was due to its lack of fixed laws of tenure and succession, and wrote a history of medieval Ireland in these terms. What lends his thought real distinction, however, is his treatment of the Anglo-Irish: he argues that the medieval settlers, isolated on a stationary frontier and unprotected by royal courts, found it easier to attract Irish tenants than English; they thus assumed the relationships of Irish chiefs to their followers and became, in habits, speech and dress, Irish themselves. Davies saw Irish history in terms of the effects upon social behaviour of different systems of land tenure, and could not have done this if he had not had two such systems to observe and compare. When he wrote of purely English history, however, he gave a classic statement of the theory of immemorial custom; his Irish experience did not compel him to revise his ideas of English law.

The situation of France with regard to the institutional past might serve as a convenient antithesis to that of England. Instead of a single body of customary law in all parts of the kingdom, there were several distinct bodies of *coutumes* obtaining in different regions, and in the south the civil *droit écrit* which was not, at least in theory, a customary law at all. Since there were several laws, there were several modes of continuity with the past, and since French past-relationships were plural, they presented problems. When the national institutions were considered as a whole, they could not be imagined, like those of England, as forming a single body of law or a single continuous structure; if they had a single history, it could not be readily extrapolated from their workings – as the notion of immemorial custom was from the normal assumptions of the English courts – but had to be discovered or reconstructed. We therefore find that the idea of an ancient constitution was harder to maintain in France, and that critical historiography developed sooner, than in England.

The idea that all laws are formed out of the immemorial customs of the people was not unknown in late-medieval France; it obtained in all medieval thought where customary law was to be found. Claude de Seyssel's *Grande Monarchie de France* (1519) is mentioned by many historians[51] as containing an authoritative statement of this view of the French constitution. But at

[50] Pocock, *Ancient Constitution and the Feudal Law*, pp. 59–63.

[51] E.g., W. F. Church, *Constitutional Thought in Sixteenth-Century France* (Cambridge, MA, 1941); J. H. M. Salmon, *The French Religious Wars in English Political Thought* (Oxford, 1959); A. Lemaire, *Les Lois fondamentales de la monarchie française d'après les théoriciens de l'ancien régime* (Paris, 1907).

the same time it is observable that Seyssel comments, as on a thing remarkable, on the fact that French institutions have survived unchanged since their beginnings under Pharamond or Clovis.[52] He asks how this can have happened in a world where all things are unstable and subject to fortune, and has recourse to a Polybian theory of mixed government to explain it. In 1596, we find the much more 'modern' Étienne Pasquier asking the same question,[53] and concluding that neither good fortune nor good counsel is a sufficient answer of itself; he chooses to emphasize rather the astuteness with which successive French kings have embraced opportunities, sent by fortune, of extending the jurisdiction of their courts and officials. But neither Sir John Fortescue nor Sir Edward Coke found anything to marvel at in the immemorial antiquity of English institutions, or thought it required historical explanation. For them it merely proved that English laws had been found perfectly satisfactory by long and continued experience,[54] and they took this view because they thought of all English law as custom, which was perennially being subjected to the test of experience. Seyssel and Pasquier lacked this ready-made explanation, and were already in search of the *esprit* of their *lois*. The institutions of France confronted them with a problem requiring solution, and Pasquier's explanations are markedly nearer those a modern historian would give than are Seyssel's; but Fortescue and Coke had no problem.

As early as the *Songe du Vergier* at the end of the fourteenth century, it was pointed out by André Lemaire in 1907, the scholastic-civilian technique of tracing all laws back to an original transfer of power to the prince by the people seemed to be gaining ground over the idea of immemorial tradition. Only if it had been forgotten in what terms a kingdom was first 'ordonné et institué' need one 'garder la coustume qui a esté gardée pour tant de temps qu'il n'est mémoire du contraire'.[55] Whether or not this really represents a clash or contradiction between two attitudes to the past of institutions, Lemaire was on firmer ground in arguing that when the French king's relation to the law was debated among the tensions of the Religious Wars, the simple view that immemorial custom defined both the law and the royal

[52] Seyssel, *La Grande Monarchie de France* (Paris, 1541), ff. 1–11. See J. H. Hexter, 'Seyssel, Machiavelli and Polybius VI', in *Studies in the Renaissance*, III (New York, 1956), p. 75.

[53] Pasquier, *Les Recherches de la France*, enlarged edn (Paris, 1596), Book II, ch. 1, ff. 27^b–29^a, and ch. 2, ff. 29^b–31^a.

[54] Sir John Fortescue, *De Laudibus Legum Anglie*, ch. 17; Sir Edward Coke, *Reports* (London, 1826), I, Part II, pp. vii–viii (preface to *Second Reports*); II, pp. viii–xxiii (preface to *Third Reports*) and *passim*; Sir John Davies, *Irish Reports* (London, 1674), preface.

[55] Lemaire, *Les Lois fondamentales*, pp. 45–7.

powers, though it was asserted, could not be long sustained. Taking its place and driving it off the field, Lemaire distinguished[56] a 'courant scolastique', in which it was argued that all power was originally the people's, a 'courant autocratiste', in which the scholastic view was simply reversed and original power ascribed to the king, and – most interesting from our point of view – a 'courant historique'. In England the 'courant traditionaliste', which died out in France, survived to maintain that all law was customary and prescriptive and the past merely the antiquity of the present. But since this could not be maintained in France, Pasquier, du Haillan and du Tillet embarked on a study of archives and records to establish what had in truth been.[57] It was the role of the past to authorize and direct the present, but there was no easy way of seeing in what direction that authority should be exerted.

The intentions of the historians were conservative and even traditionalist; not only did they expect to discover in the past authority for the present, but to study the long history of both law and monarchy was to encourage a respect for both. What emerged from their work, however, particularly in Pasquier's *Recherches de la France*, was less a discovery of the true constitution than the first true constitutional history. Pasquier was a magistrate of the Parlement de Paris, and it may be said that his past-relationships were those of the Palais: in the documents he studied he beheld the royal authority working on a multiplicity of local laws and customs, and constantly remodelling its own central judicial organs to exert itself the better. To Pasquier the Parlement was the foundation of royal power, because it had been the main instrument by which the royal authority had been extended. His book is neither absolutist nor *parlementaire*, but a detailed historical analysis of the way in which the two have grown up together; and in his chapters on the different courts of the Palais, he is entirely modern in his ability to see signs of a court's former functions surviving as fossils among its modern usages.[58]

If Pasquier wrote a true history, he did not furnish models for the present. This role was usurped by Hotman, who in the most notorious of his writings, *Franco-Gallia* (1573), argued for the original rights of a Frankish popular assembly, which had survived in the medieval Estates General but had been destroyed by Louis XI. Lemaire observes how instant an influence this exerted on so sound a historian as du Haillan; it was as if the effort to reconstruct history had given way before the need for direct guidance and authority in the present.[59] But Hotman had not really provided that

56 Ibid., pp. 71ff. 57 Ibid, pp. 82–91.

58 Pasquier, *Recherches de la France*, ff. 31^b–43^b, 44^b–45^a, 51^a–53^b.

59 Lemaire, *Les Lois fondamentales*, pp. 92, 101–2.

authority; he left it quite unclear by what right, natural or substantive, the 'Franco-Gallic' constitution was to be restored. Any fundamentalist, it has been argued, who calls for return to a lost constitution must face the normative question 'By what right shall it be restored?' and the historical question 'How has it been lost?' Hotman answered neither, but his ideas were taken up again in the early eighteenth century by the Comte de Boulainvilliers, in whose writings the sometimes fruitful dilemmas of fundamentalism are interestingly revealed.[60]

Boulainvilliers justified the privileges of the *noblesse* by representing them as the descendants of the Frankish freemen who had won their rights by the sword, but he was little more able than Hotman to point out in what way this entitled them to their privileges at the present day. They could not claim them in law, for Boulainvilliers's whole theme was that the expansion of the royal courts had robbed them of their privileges; and a right of conquest divorced from any system of law is no right at all, as Sieyès was to point out. Nor was Boulainvilliers in any significant sense a racialist, arguing that the nobles' purity of descent entitled them to restitution of their privileges. The most he can say is that *sang* and *épée* render a man freer than any other claim to freedom, since they leave him under no restraint but that of his personal honour; a doctrine which may have helped Montesquieu with his formula that honour is the principle of aristocracies, but does not amount to a legal claim for restitution of privileges. In reply to the first of the questions distinguished above, Boulainvilliers came close to constructing a sociological principle; but the tone of his writings as a whole is elegiac rather than polemical, an account of how the *noblesse* lost their rights rather than a vindication of their claim to have them returned, and is consequently historical. Like Pasquier, he saw the unity of French history in the expansion of the royal authority, but he wrote that history from the point of view of the defeated. Since he saw the *noblesse* as a class whose life was based on honour and the sword, his history, like Davies's, was the story of a struggle between two ways of living: between *honneur* and *loi*, between nobles and men of the pen, in which the former had been not only beaten but transformed. At the end of his *Essais sur la Noblesse*, he told the aristocracy[61] that they had become leisured and civilized, but had lost their liberty; and left it to them to weigh the results of their bargain.

[60] Particularly in the *Essais sur la Noblesse de France* (Amsterdam, 1732), and the *Lettres sur les Anciens Parlements de France* (London, 1753). Cf. R. Simon, *Henry de Boulainviller* (Gap, 1940); I follow the familiar if inaccurate spelling. [Harold Ellis, *Boulainvilliers and the French Monarchy* (Cornell, 1988).]

[61] *Essais*, pp. 273–300.

Boulainvilliers's work, in a very different way from Pasquier's, crossed the boundary which separates historical explanation from the mere use of the past to justify something in the present. Since France lacked a common law which could be thought ancient, it was never easy to see in what way the present could derive authority from the past. Any appeal to the past, therefore, was likely to raise problems which necessitated explanations of what the past had to do with the present. Normatively, these explanations were likely to involve appeal to universal principles true in both past and present; historically, they were likely to involve the reconstruction of complex processes of interaction between different elements – the monarchy and the courts, the bureaucracy and the seigneurs. It is not surprising, consequently, to find in French thought both the extremes of unhistoric rationalism and an efflorescence of constitutional historiography. These are not antagonistic elements, but different products of the same situation. Their common antithesis is the traditionalism that lasted longer in England, where relationships with the past presented fewer problems.

V. CONCLUSIONS AND SUGGESTIONS

The greater part of this article has been an attempt to make some particular applications of the model worked out in section II. It seems to have been demonstrated that a sense of continuity with a past may arise, not from the possession of narrative histories, but from the workings of social institutions and the records of their workings in the past, and that when the traditional statements of such continuities are exposed to challenge, they may in certain circumstances be restated in the form of authentically historical explanations. Studying some cases of historiography arising in the field of law, we have seen that the nature of the continuity sensed with the past varies in accordance with the way in which the law is supposed to be organized and transmitted. A relationship with the past based on customary law differs from one based on the interpretation of a written law, and that again from one based on the expansion of a royal jurisdiction; and both the ways in which problems can arise, and the character of the historical explanations they will call for, differ correspondingly. Some past-relationships are harder to challenge than others: English thought, starting from a unified customary law, remained traditional longer than was possible for French thought, which started from a plurality of legal systems.

No attempt has been made to classify either the circumstances in which problems in past-relationship can arise, or those in which they may call for and receive genuinely historical explanations. But as regards the former, it has emerged that this may happen (1) when there is a fundamentalist movement for return to the original source of a tradition, or (2) when there is a plurality of tradition and two modes of continuity with a past or pasts have to be considered at the same time. There may be further cases of either (1) or (2) which would be worth investigating: what, for instance, happened when samurai scholars in Tokugawa Japan attempted to disentangle the original forms of Shinto from Buddhist accretions and the original powers of the emperor from encroachments by the shogunate?[62] It is worth emphasizing that discussion of a society's authoritative traditions may affect both its historiography and its political thought; indeed, the two so often develop together that when they do not – when a society is discussing the sources of political authority without some related discussion of its relationship to its pasts – it will always be worth asking how this has happened.

The emergence of a problem in past-relationships does not lead only, or even necessarily, to the rise of historical explanation. As the example of Hsun Tzu shows, if it is desired simply to reaffirm the past's validity as a guide to the present, some pattern of universal principles will probably suffice. But this will leave unsolved the problem of temporal continuity: when a tradition is simply accepted, the questions 'Why should the present follow the past?' and 'How did the past become the present?' are virtually identical and receive the same answer, but once a tradition has been challenged they become distinct. If the present is unlike the past, but we affirm that there are normative principles common to both, there remains unanswered the question of how the present came to be what it is, and if the means exist of providing an answer, some effort to do so will probably be made. Few rationalists are wholly indifferent to historical continuity, and the origins of the present will appear to have some significance and authority.

But it is necessary that the means exist, both of describing the past as it was unlike the present, and of offering explanations of how it was transformed into the present. This is where law comes to be of importance to the rise of historiography, because law makes articulate the formal organization of a society. If, therefore, we have the law of a past society and the means of describing it as it then was – though this last will probably come from outside the established modes of legal thought: e.g., philology in the case of the Renaissance jurists, the means of isolating the feudal component

[62] F. Maraini, *Meeting with Japan* (London, 1959), pp. 151, 377; R. Tsunoda, W. T. de Bary and D. Keene, *Sources of the Japanese Tradition* (New York, 1958), pp. 472–5, 479–88, 506–40. [I seem at this time to have been unaware of the writings of Masao Maruyama.]

in English law for Spelman and Brady – we can furnish a fairly detailed description of that society as it then was. Furthermore, the test of any piece of historiography is the complexity and verifiability of the explanations it provides; and when a historical explanation is being constructed in terms of changes in a legal system, competition or coalescence between two such systems, or the relations between a body of law and other aspects of the society it regulates, we shall have the means of combining very varied elements and checking their interactions upon each other. Hotman, Pasquier and Craig in the sixteenth century, Davies, Spelman and Brady in the seventeenth, Boulainvilliers and the Scottish school in the eighteenth, could all do far more in the way of constructing explanations than all but the rarest of contemporary narrative historians; and the reason must be very largely that more could be done with the laws of past societies than with their inherited traditional narratives. There was little to be done with myths but rationalize them, little to be learnt from formal humanist historiography but often rather stereotyped moral and political lessons; it was difficult in the extreme to see past them to the societies which had given them birth; but in the laws of older societies their formal organization was described in a way which made it, by definition if obscurely, of close relevance to the present.

But here the validation of a model gives place to a new conception of the rise and history of Western historiography. It seems that problems in the history of laws and institutions, involving the conscious attempt to reconstruct them in the context of a unique past society, were being discussed, intermittently and in limited fields, but persistently and systematically, as much as two centuries before the era of the historicist revolution, which we are accustomed to think alone made such endeavours conceivable. There is no need to attack the concept of the historicist revolution or to decry its importance; it was certainly at this era that it became possible to attempt the historical approach to every department of human life and to human experience as a whole; but a new dimension has been added to the problem and it seems that our conception of the state of historiography before the historicist revolution, and of the roots of that revolution in the period preceding it, may require some revision. In particular, we must look again at the widespread assumptions that until Enlightenment there was no historiography other than humanist narrative, and that the origins of historicism are to be found in changes in philosophical thought rather than in the work of practising historians.

Until the late eighteenth century, it is true, words like 'history' were used mainly of the Greco-Roman narrative form, and when Descartes,

Bolingbroke and Priestley wrote about history as a discipline it was this that they had chiefly in mind.[63] But when Vico attempted a philosophical vindication of historical knowledge, the data he had in mind were not simply those of 'history' in the narrative sense, but were rather the subject matter of what he termed 'philology',[64] the science of the words, oral and written, in which was transmitted to us all that men had thought, said and done. 'Philology' also meant the textual and grammatical techniques by which Renaissance scholarship had submitted everything in the literary heritage of Europe to a common scrutiny, divorced much of it from the traditional exegesis by which medieval men had sought to adapt it to their needs, and discovered much more that the medievals had never had occasion to adapt. Vico found himself faced with this huge and partly alienated heritage and with a philosophy which denied it meaning and value. In this he may be compared to Ibn Khaldun, who had also found himself possessed of a great inheritance of knowledge about the past, which had little obvious function or significance in his society and was not furnished with one by that society's dominant intellectual techniques. He had therefore set out to provide what was lacking and, perceiving that all this knowledge had to do with human civilization, had concluded that a science of civilization – to him, as to Vico, a new science – was what was needed.[65] To both men philosophy of history and historical sociology were one and the same; and if we may suppose that Vico's predicament – the need to make sense and value out of all this information – was shared in some measure by the sociologists and philosophers of the eighteenth century, it will follow that the roots of their problem, and perhaps of some of the answers they found to it, lay in the effects which philological humanism had wrought upon European past-relationships.

We are looking now at the phenomenon of universal history; its history is that of the concepts used to organize and control the whole body of information about the past, and the history of historicism is that of the process by which these concepts became in the full sense historical. It is generally assumed that this process was the result of changes occurring at the higher levels of intellectual abstraction, and that the art of writing history was revolutionized purely as the result of what occurred at these

[63] R. Descartes, *Discours de la Méthode* (1637), Part 1; H. St J. Bolingbroke, *Letters on the Study of History* (Dublin, 1735), *passim*; J. Priestley, *Lectures on History* (London, 1788), *passim*.

[64] *The New Science of Giambattista Vico*, trans. T. G. Bergin and M. H. Fisch (Ithaca, NY, 1948), Book I, Section II, X, pp. 56–7.

[65] Ibn Khaldun, *The Muqaddimah: an introduction to history*, trans. F. Rosenthal (London, 1958), 1, pp. 6, 9–10, 76–8, 80.

levels; the current ran all one way, from philosophy to historiography. On the first of these assumptions no comment will be made here; possibly the concepts of universal history changed only as the result of philosophical change, though as it seems to have been taken for granted that little serious historical thought in the modern sense existed before the Enlightenment, the possibility that historiography underwent autonomous development, or contributed to philosophy, has not been much studied. But the second assumption must be re-examined now that we know that humanists and lawyers were engaged in serious historical criticism in the late sixteenth century. The history of universal history and philosophy of history is not co-extensive with the history of historiography. As the result of the relationships which different legal and political systems had with their pasts, and of problems which arose within those relationships, numerous traditions of advanced historical discussion, numerous national and particular problems concerning the past and its meaning to the present, took shape during the sixteenth and seventeenth centuries, and these affected the development of historiography, which deals with particular pasts and particular problems as well as with universal ones.

CHAPTER 10

Time, institutions and action: an essay on traditions and their understanding

Societies exist in time, and conserve images of themselves as continuously so existing. It follows that the consciousness of time acquired by the individual as a social animal is in large measure consciousness of his society's continuity and of the image of its continuity which that society possesses; and the understanding of time, and of human life as experienced in time, disseminated in a society, is an important part of that society's understanding of itself – of its structure and what legitimates it, of the modes of action which are possible to it and in it. There is a point at which historical and political theory meet, and it can be said without distortion that every society possesses a philosophy of history – a set of ideas about what happens, what can be known and what done, in time considered as a dimension of society – which is intimately a part of its consciousness and its functioning. How these images and ideas of time arise, function and develop may be studied as part of the science of society.

An essential feature of society is tradition – the handing on of formed ways of acting, a formed way of living, to those beginning or developing their social membership – and the transmitter of a message cannot do without some image of a message which he has received and of the way in which he received it. Both images will be, in some way or other, conceptualizations of the mode of activity to be handed on, and it will be thought of as having been received by the transmitter from transmitters before him: his predecessors in a craft, his ancestors in a society, or both. Societies therefore look backward in time to those from whom 'we' received what we now tell 'you'; even the so-called 'timeless' societies described by anthropologists are not really exceptions to this rule. But the variety of the ways in which societies have conceived the transmission of their traditions is very great indeed.

[Published in Preston King and B. C. Parekh (eds.), *Politics and Experience: essays presented to Michael Oakeshott* (Cambridge: Cambridge University Press, 1968), pp. 209–37. Reprinted in *Politics, Language and Time* (New York: Atheneum, 1971; Chicago: University of Chicago Press, 1980).]

This is not surprising when we consider, first, that the image of an activity's continuance must vary both with the character of the activity and with the ways in which practice of it may be thought to be transmitted; second, that any society or social complex envisaging its own continuity must do so in terms of those elements of its structure of which it is sufficiently aware to consider them continuous. Social activities and structures vary widely, and it cannot be predicted with certainty what elements of them will become institutionalized to the point of having stable and continuous images. Even in very simple societies, extrapolation of the image of the social structure in time can produce accounts varying widely, from one society to another, of the 'past', that is of the way in which transmission has been and is being conducted. In complex societies, the past itself is complex; society consists of a number of patterns of behaviour, each of which generates its own 'past' and need not be thought of as continuous in the same way as its neighbour; there may be contradiction between these 'pasts', and even conflict.

Oakeshott has emphasized the extent to which a 'tradition of behaviour' is not conceptualized, whether because its transmission takes place unnoticed or because it would not be appropriate to conceptualize it overmuch, consisting as it does in 'intimations' and 'nuances'. Nonetheless conceptualization of tradition is constantly going on, as it must if tradition is to function among self-conscious and communicative creatures, and we are beginning to see that it may take place in a variety of ways and give rise to a variety of mental phenomena. The concepts which we form from, and feed back into, tradition have the capacity to modify the content and character of the tradition conceptualized and even the extent to which it is conceived and regarded as a tradition. There consequently arise a wide variety of attitudes and strategies which men may adopt towards society's consciousness of, and in, its political life. In addition, however, since so large a part of men's consciousness of environment and time is gained through consciousness of the frame of social relationships which they inhabit, the conceptualization of tradition is an important source of their images of society, time and history. The importance of these visibly transcends the political; we are looking at one of the origins of a distinctively human awareness.

In *The Discovery of Time*,[1] Stephen Toulmin and June Goodfield have performed the interesting experiment of taking as their starting point the consciousness of time to be expected of an archaic villager, limited to awareness of the continuity of his immediate social structure, and examining how

[1] Volume III of *The Ancestry of Science* series (London, 1965).

this consciousness was progressively transformed by the thought of physical scientists where this raised the question of the time-dimension of the cosmos, by geological, palaeontological and archaeological discoveries, and by changes in social theory occasioned by or occasioning changes in the time-scheme within which human society was conceived to exist. They convincingly show that there was two-way traffic between ideas about the character and processes of human society and ideas about the structure and processes of the physical universe; but their thesis is limited by the fact that it does not and cannot deal with ideas about time arising from the self-awareness of particular societies. The 'time' they deal with is geochronic and cosmochronic; thought about society can have contributed to its 'discovery' only to the extent – a very considerable one – that society was considered as a universal phenomenon, a central incident in the history of life, earth and cosmos. But what we call historical consciousness is social and subjective in its origins; it is a developed form of man's awareness of himself as existing and acting in a continuous context of social relationships, and must therefore begin with his awareness of a particular social continuity to which he himself belongs. But we have already seen that this awareness can take forms as many and varied as the social institutions with which it originates. We are following a line of inquiry distinct from that of Toulmin and Goodfield, concerned with an awareness of time that must have been multiple in its origins and its modes; we are forced to recognize that the history of historical awareness is necessarily distinct from that of the discovery of cosmic time, and that no unified 'history of historiography' is likely ever to be written. Since each society has its own mode of conceiving its past, the history of its historical consciousness must in principle be peculiar to itself – even when it becomes conscious of its role within a greater history, even when historical consciousness is imported or imposed from without. We cannot, then, treat the history of historical thought as a unity, a progressive accumulation of insights starting from Hecataeus or Herodotus as the history of science can be said to start from Thales. It is part of the history of social self-awareness, and is as multiple as the social forms and social experiences in which that awareness develops.

We are, then, concerned with the conceptualization of tradition, with the modes of social self-awareness and the attitudes towards tradition to which conceptualization may give rise, and with the complex awareness of continuity which we call historical consciousness as one possible outcome of changes in this kind of thought. To understand what happened to the time-consciousness of the archaic villager, we must consider the consciousness of social continuity which the village, the city, the empire, the church or the nation – to go no further – required of their members, and we must inquire after the origins and occasions of changes in that consciousness. When we put it in this way, it is clear that the problem could be studied in the context of social development; the individual's time-consciousness could be looked on as changing in relation to changes in the organization of society. But an alternative approach, which will be adopted here, is to elaborate and extend the model of a tradition which we have begun to build up, and attempt in doing so to discern the directions which conceptualization of a tradition may be expected to take, and something of the alternatives, choices and strategies which may confront minds engaged in such conceptualization.

A tradition, in its simplest form, may be thought of as an indefinite series of repetitions of an action, which on each occasion is performed on the assumption that it has been performed before; its performance is authorized – though the nature of the authorization may vary widely – by the knowledge, or the assumption, of previous performance. In the pure state, as it were, such a tradition is without a conceivable beginning; each performance presupposes a previous performance, in infinite regress. Furthermore, it may well be that it is the assumption, rather than the factual information, of previous performance that is operative; each action provides the grounds for assuming that it had a predecessor. Traditions of this kind, then, are immemorial, and they are prescriptive and presumptive; and this was pointed out by Burke, who was an acute analyst, as well as an eloquent expositor, of the traditional society and the traditionalist mind.[2] This is perhaps the simplest set of assumptions which we can ascribe to the traditionalist mind, when it is sufficiently self-conscious to have ideas and assumptions about what it is doing and the society it is acting in; but the full exposition of these assumptions requires a sophisticated mind and highly subtle language, as the writings of Hale and Burke bear witness. It can happen, in favourable circumstances, that a society may conceive all the activities of which it is aware, the whole pattern of its structure as it visualizes itself, in traditional terms. Such a society will conceive its past as an immemorial continuity, its structure as inherited from an infinitely receding chain of transmitters; timeless societies are those in which the links in the chain are no longer distinguished from one another, each transmitting

[2] 'Our constitution is a prescriptive constitution; it is a constitution whose sole authority is that it has existed time out of mind . . . Your king, your lords, your judges, your juries, grand and little, all are prescriptive; and what proves it is the disputes not yet concluded, and never near becoming so, when any of them first originated.' Burke, 'On a Motion Made in the House of Commons . . . for a Committee to Enquire into the State of the Representation of the Commons in Parliament', *Works*, ed. Bohn, IV (1866), p. 146.

ancestor being perhaps thought of as the reincarnation of his predecessor, and the process of transmission being compressed into a single timeless act instead of being drawn out into an endless chain. At a more sophisticated level of consciousness, the traditional society may insist that not only are its practices and usages inherited, but its conviction that they are so is itself inherited from an assumed chain of transmitters, so that its knowledge of its past is and can be no more than presumptive. It cannot even know – it can only presume – that it has always based itself on presumption, though with this self-validating chain of presumptions many societies have been enviably content. The traditional conception of society is in several ways of enduring value to social theorists. Any social act does in fact presuppose an antecedent degree of socialization, and it is conceptually impossible to imagine a social complex coming into existence at any single moment. Both in the seventeenth century and in the twentieth, it has been salutary to be reminded that society is indeed immemorial, and further that our knowledge of the social usages that have preceded us inherited from those usages themselves, from the assumptions they encourage us to make and the intimations they permit us to pursue. But in the present essay we are concerned less with tradition as an objective fact, a necessary mode of social life, than with the conceptualization of tradition, with what happens when a society forms an image of itself as a constant transmission of ways of living and behaving; and while it is possible for this self-awareness to take a strictly traditional form, for a society to envisage itself as immemorial, prescriptive, an inherited style of behaviour and thought, this is by no means the only form which conceptualization of a tradition may take, nor will it necessarily retain the form it has once taken. Now when a change in a society's self-awareness has become at all widely disseminated, that society's styles of thinking and acting have been irreversibly altered. There may still be much in its traditions of behaviour which has not emerged into consciousness and perhaps never will; what has changed, however, is its mode of being and becoming conscious of itself and its existence in time, and once this has happened a society is no longer what it was. We are studying its political and cultural individuality, therefore, when we study the form which its self-awareness has for the present assumed.

Moreover, when we say that a society's image of its own continuous life may take forms other than the traditional, we mean that it may not conceive inheritance as its sole mode of reception, transmission as its sole mode of action, or presumption as its sole mode of knowledge. There are other ways in which behaviour and knowledge may be envisaged, and a society's departures from a purely traditional self-awareness may be enlargements of its political and social, indeed of its human, vocabulary. Nor need human existence in time be envisaged solely as existence in a stream of transmission. Once men are thought of as thinking and acting in ways other than those appropriate to the traditional framework, it becomes possible to envisage their behaviour in social time as a complex series of interactions between different modes of behaviour, of which the traditional is only one. At this point the social framework begins to appear the result or product of human action, instead of merely its matrix; a historical mode of understanding begins to replace a traditional one, and what may be the most far-reaching of changes in a society's style has begun to appear. A society thinks of itself in purely traditional terms in proportion as it is aware of itself simply as a cluster of institutionalized modes of transmitting behaviour. We may, somewhat in the manner of Victorian anthropologists, envisage a simple kinship society, in which everything is learned from the fathers before the shrines of the ancestors; in such a society, it is evident, everything will be thought of as transmitted, continuous, immemorial and – since each father must speak on the authority of his father – presumptive. It is needless to point out that no society is as simply linear as that; the kind of self-image which the model conveys can be found even in complex literate societies, where the kind and degree of institutionalization have been favourable to its existence. In pre-industrial England, for example, all social and national institutions could be conceived as bound up with the common law, that law was conceived as custom, and the activity of law-making was conceived as the conversion into written precedents of unwritten usages whose sole authority was that of immemorial antiquity. Consequently, to the end of the eighteenth century it could be argued that the constitution was immemorial, its authority prescriptive and our knowledge of it presumptive. The character of English institutions, in short, was such as to favour the assumption that the only form of action was transmission and the only form of knowledge the inheritance of learning. But in sixteenth-century France we have the case of a complex institutional society where continuity in the past could not be conceived in terms of any single institution, but different institutions suggested the images of different modes of action. The *coutumes*, in force in some regions, suggested the authority of continuous usage; the Roman law, in force in others, suggested that of rational action; the royal jurisdiction and its *cours souveraines*, overarching and co-ordinating all, suggested an authority distinct from the other two but interacting with them; and by the end of the Religious Wars French scholars were saying that their institutions could be understood only in terms of a history of the royal power's expansion at the expense of customary, seigniorial and provincial jurisdictions.[3] *Les rois ont fait la France.* A society's institutions, it is clear, may be either consolidated or discrete, homogeneous or various; it may inherit dialogue, dialectic or conflict between its traditions, and the impulse to replace tradition, first with another image of normative action and second with history as the vision of interplay between modes of action, may arise from within the inheritance. There are seams, after all, in the seamless web; or it may appear so to those who receive and wear the garment.

Institutionalization, the necessary cause of traditionalism, may then be the cause of a society's tradition being conceived in terms other than purely traditional. But conceptualization has a logic of its own, and images and concepts of a non-traditionalist kind may arise from causes lying within the process of giving a tradition conceptual form. So far we have imagined tradition as the concept of an activity's indefinite continuity, arrived at by extrapolating the concept of its continuity in the present and – when this is done rigorously – imagined as immemorial or without a beginning. But the foundation myths of Greek cities, in exploring which Hellenic historiography was obliged to begin, provide us with examples of traditions of a different sort. These do now arise from the extrapolation of institutional continuities, but consist in ascribing a sacred or epic origin to the society conceived as a whole. In the late and sophisticated form which the Greeks gave it, this activity became what is known as historization; it was the historian's business to discover origins, preferably human inventors, for societies, institutions and arts.[4] But in its more purely mythopoeic form, this kind of 'tradition' has the value of reminding us that a society – whether tribe, city, culture-complex or civilization – is not necessarily imagined as a whole only in consequence of being imagined as a cluster of institutionalized continuities. There may be an awareness of tradition less precise but equally vivid, and when this occurs society's continuity may not be explicable in institutional language at all. It may have to be expressed in terms of whatever vision of the world human perception and fantasy have been able to conceive by means other than the conceptualization of institutional or even social traditions, and this vision may entail a very different image of time or none at all; in the great phrase attributed to Australian aboriginals, it may be 'in the dreaming'. But if institutional time and sacred time or non-time are juxtaposed, then society's time-consciousness is already a complex matter.

[3] The most intensive study of this, written from a historicist point of view, is that of V. de Caprariis, *Propaganda e Pensiero Politico in Francia durante le Guerre di Religione, 1559–1572* (Naples, 1959).

[4] See M. I. Finley, *The Greek Historians* (London, 1959), and 'Myth, Memory and History', *History and Theory*, 4.3 (1965), pp. 281–302.

To describe a timeless existence, a sacred origin or an immemorial continuity, are all ways of conceptualizing the continuous existence of society. The more precisely we imagine society as a series of concrete human actions in time, and time in terms of sequence of such actions, the more we seem to move away from imagining society in terms of the sacred, as our use of the words 'temporal' and 'secular' indicates. Nevertheless, complex interrelations between different ways of envisaging time, society and action are constantly found in the thought of societies. In ancient China, for example, there seems to have been equal emphasis on the idea that the *li*, or governing rituals, originated in the creative acts of sacred heroes called the Former Kings, and on the idea that the truth concerning the acts of the Former Kings could only be inferred by presuming their continuity with the traditional character of the *li* as inherited by the present. It is possible at one and the same time to extrapolate the present form of an institution back into a remote antiquity, and to realize (the mythopoeic mind need not even realize) that the beginnings of such an institution are exceedingly hard to imagine, if only because they cannot be conceived in terms of the institution's functioning. A system conceived in none but traditional terms must be conceived as immemorial, since antecedent tradition is necessary in order to account for its existence at any moment; but few societies have been bold enough to assert that they have existed *ab aeterno*, or sophisticated enough to assert that a prescriptive or immemorial tradition is merely one whose beginnings are not to be found in any single moment or moments. Most societies have their culture-heroes or founding fathers; but to imagine traditions of behaviour originating in specific actions is to imagine actions whose creative power is not explained by any antecedent tradition. Hence the charismatic figures who stand at the mythical beginnings of so many traditions – the gods, heroes, prophets and legislators, who abound in the legends even of highly institutionalized societies and provide the inheritors of tradition with occasion to imagine politics and other activities as consisting of charismatic (which here includes rationalist[5]) instead of traditional action, and time as a sequence of such actions instead of an institutional continuity. What stands outside tradition is charismatic; where time itself is envisaged as the continuity of tradition, the charismatic may stand outside time and become the sacred. But if an activity is seen as a succession of charismatic or sacred actions, then a new vision of time may be constructed in terms of moments of creation rather than moments of transmission. This no doubt was what Oakeshott had in mind when he described the ethics

[5] The purely rational founder of a society is always a heroic and miraculous figure.

of the self-made man as idolatry;[6] such a man must visualize his actions as unendingly creative and charismatic. It may nevertheless happen that the idea of a series of charismatic actions, even the vision of time as composed of a sequence of sacred acts, becomes part of the mental furniture of a society, so worn and domesticated with constant varying use that it may be described as belonging to society's traditions.

'A tradition of behaviour', Oakeshott has truly written,[7] 'is a tricky thing to get to know'; so much so, we now observe, that parts of it must be conceptualized in non-traditional terms. 'The pursuit of the intimations' of such a tradition will not be the simple unfolding of a consistently traditional 'style' of either thinking or acting. It will involve our envisaging charismatic figures, actions and styles of behaviour; these will run counter to the theme of transmission and continuity, setting up alternative images of action and authority. Within tradition there will be dialogue between the non-traditionalist and traditionalist voices with which it speaks, and the pursuit of intimations will involve us in conflict and contradiction, in problems of historical, philosophical and methodological interpretation, even in existential dilemmas of self-determination and self-definition. A tradition may be a turbid stream to swim in, full of backwaters, cross-currents and snags. Nevertheless the dialogue we have begun to depict has its logic and its strategies, and the next stage in our inquiry must be to map some of these.

A tradition, then, may stress either the continuity of the process of transmission, or the creative and charismatic origin of what is transmitted. The two are conceptually distinct and entail different images of action and of time; but they are dialectically related, and are often – perhaps normally – found together within the same tradition. A distinction may be drawn between traditions which conserve highly specific and significant images of the creative actions with which they began and of which they are in some way the continuation, and traditions which depict themselves as sheer continuity of usage or transmission and conserve little or no account of their beginnings. These two types are, respectively, the sacred, which lies outside time, and the immemorial, which refuses to admit a beginning in or outside it. Burke's 'prescriptive government' which 'never was the work of any legislator',[8] Oakeshott's 'tradition of behaviour' and his 'bottomless and boundless sea', are traditions of pure usage; but we have seen that traditions which admit to no beginning at all are rare and rest, where they exist, on the

[6] Michael Oakeshott, *Rationalism in Politics* (London, 1991), p. 35. [7] Ibid., p. 128.
[8] Burke, *Works*, ed. Bohn, VI, p. 148.

accident of a society's being very highly institutionalized in a peculiar way. The assumption that everything in English society could be treated as an inheritance from some earlier time was after all a myth – and Burke knew it[9] – resting on the further myth that everything in English law was custom. But if most traditions of usage make some acknowledgment to the idea of a creative origin, it is equally true that most traditions claiming to originate in a creative act have to admit that the authority of the initiating charisma has become merged with that of the chain of transmission through which it has been mediated – the well-known problem of the 'routinization of the charisma'. Traditions once conceptualized are complex mental structures, and in the dialogues that occur within them, what Oakeshott has called the 'abridgment' of tradition into an ideology is only one among a number of intellectual operations that may be carried out.

Ancient Chinese thought (in its Western translations) presents an interesting example of political ideas organized around a tradition more highly and consciously institutionalized than was ever possible for Hellenic thought. The *li* had supposedly been established in mythic time by the Former Kings, and to that extent charismatic figures and creative action formed part of Chinese imagery. But when Confucius, in a time of disorder, set out to intensify the impact of the inherited *li* upon society by eliciting a consciousness of the virtues which they contained, he did not associate these conceptualized virtues with the figures of the Former Kings so much as stress the continuity of their transmission from an ancient time which was known less by contemplating what the Former Kings had done in it than by presuming its continuity with the inheritance of the *li* in more recent times. When he called himself 'a transmitter, not a creator', he was not simply being modest about his own role; he meant that what he was teaching possessed the character of a tradition, whose authority was derived from the continuity of its transmission. But if transmission, not creation, was to be the central social act, then the role of the Former Kings, the creators, was liable to lose its importance. There are several recorded sayings in which Confucius makes it plain that we know what form the *li* possessed under Hsia and Yin, the earliest of the three dynasties which he thought historical, only by inference from our better documented knowledge of the

[9] 'In the matter of fact, for the greater part, these authors appear to be in the right; perhaps not always; but if the lawyers mistake in some particulars, it proves my position still the more strongly; because it demonstrates the powerful prepossession towards antiquity, with which the minds of all our lawyers and legislators, and of all the people whom they wish to influence, have been always filled; and the stationary policy of this kingdom in considering their most sacred rights and franchises as an inheritance.' *Reflections on the Revolution in France*, in *Works*, ed. Bohn, III (1901), p. 305.

usages of Chou, the most recent dynasty; and if we know Hsia and Yin only by presumption, the same may be true of the Former Kings. His confidence in his ability to know the past by inference and presumption was very high: he held that he could reconstruct what institutions had been like in the past by simple extrapolation from their form in the present, and regretted only that independent evidence did not survive to corroborate him. (In Jacobean England Sir Edward Coke advised antiquarians against venturing to reconstruct the history of institutions without taking the advice of lawyers, who worked on the presumption of continuity.) Confucius is also said to have declared that since we knew what Yin had added to Hsia ritual, and what Chou had added to Yin, we could predict what additions would be made by any future dynasty succeeding Chou – a doctrine which carries 'the pursuit of intimations' to a point where it becomes 'the poverty of historicism'.[10]

It was Mo Tzu, the first post-Confucian thinker to envisage the possibility of governing society by means other than inherited ritual, who declared to his adversaries: 'You are only following the Chou, not the Hsia dynasty. Your antiquity does not go back far enough.' A familiar if important contrast may be erected between the two positions. Confucius was a conservative; he was anxious to invest the present system with authority, and did so by regarding it as an inheritance from the past. Adopting a traditionalist position in a highly traditionalist society, he invested the present system with authority inherited from a former set of practices which themselves acquired it by inheritance from a remoter past... and so *ad infinitum*. In such a scheme of thought it is not necessary to know a lot about the mythical origins and founders; it may even be inappropriate to stress them overmuch. Institutionalization tends to reduce, if hardly ever to eliminate, the importance of myth; it replaces a mythic dream-time with a secular time of institutional continuity. It is important to have a well-established foundation in the recent past on which to presume continuity with the remoter past; but to attempt independent knowledge of the remoter past is in Burke's phrase 'preposterous' and in the Confucian Hsun Tzu's 'like giving up one's own prince and following another's'. Our knowledge of the past is based on the presumption of transmission, and the subtleties of historical awareness which may arise in this style of thinking consist largely in awareness of how much more there is in a continuous tradition of behaviour than we need or can know.

[10] For further treatment, see 'The origins of study of the past' (chapter 9, above), and J. G. A. Pocock, 'Ritual, Language, Power: an essay on the apparent political meanings of ancient Chinese philosophy', in *Politics, Language and Time* (New York, 1971), pp. 42–79.

But Mo Tzu was in the strict sense a radical: that is, he was adopting the posture appropriate to a rebel in a traditional society, which is that of a reactionary. He did not believe it any longer possible to govern society by the inherited means of ritual, and had an alternative set of arrangements to suggest; but it was nevertheless so far from possible in that society to forgo deriving authority from antiquity that he must suggest an alternative version of antiquity which would authorize his alternative arrangements. The appropriate location for his image of antiquity was the remotest accessible past, since there the presumption of continuity with the traditional present would be hardest to apply and, once he had occupied the headwaters of tradition, he would be in a position to maintain that the stream had been diverted from its proper course. Instances of this radical strategy, the advocacy of return to the roots or sources, abound in the history of argument within systems of authority. To take examples from English history, the Levellers opposed to the traditional constitution the image of an idealized pre-Conquest England after which all had been Norman usurpation; and Bolingbroke, followed by the early parliamentary reformers, adopted the Machiavellian tactic of ascribing to the existing constitution 'original principles' on which it had been founded, from which it had degenerated and to which it must be restored. To the latter argument, it is significant, two modes of reply may be detected. In one – represented by Lord Hervey and Josiah Tucker[11] – the past was repudiated as barbarous and no longer relevant; here the conservative's basic concern with the present was pushed to the point of brutal rejection of the appeal to history, a rejection, however, founded on a developed power of historical criticism. In the other, far more subtly traditional, Burke pointed out that an immemorial constitution can have no original principles, since a system whose knowledge of its own past is based exclusively on the presumption of transmission can never arrive at knowledge of them.[12]

[11] John Hervey, Baron Hervey, *Ancient and Modern Liberty Stated and Compared* (1734); Josiah Tucker, *A Treatise Concerning Civil Government* (1781). The same view was constantly advanced in the *London Journal*, which supported Walpole against Bolingbroke and the *Craftsman* in 1729–34.

[12] *Works*, VI, ed. Bohn, pp. 146–8. 'To ask whether a thing which has always been the same stands to its usual principle, seems to me to be perfectly absurd; for how do you know the principles but from the construction? and if that remains the same, the principles remain the same . . . On what grounds do we go to restore our constitution to what it has been at one definite period, or to reform and reconstruct it upon principles more conformable to a sound theory of government? A prescriptive government, such as ours, never was the work of any legislator, never was made upon any foregone theory. It seems to me a preposterous way of thinking, and a perfect confusion of ideas, to take the theories which learned and speculative men have made from that government, and then, supposing it made on those theories, which were made from it, to accuse the government as not corresponding with them.'

The radical's rejection of the traditional present forces him to adopt new positions. Once he has denied that the present derives authority from a past of which it is the presumptive continuation, three questions confront him. Since his image of the past as he sees it cannot be arrived at by presuming its continuity with a present it is designed to repudiate, how is that image arrived at and maintained? Second, since the past as he conceives it does not authorize the present, it cannot possess or transmit traditional authority; what authority does it then possess, or, in other words, why are we obliged to return to it? Third, if it possessed and still possesses such authority, how have matters so fallen out that it is no longer actualized in our institutions? As the radical was, initially at least, a normative writer seeking to give authority to his programme rather than a historical writer seeking to explain what had happened, it is likely to be the second question that concerns him most, but the means by which he endows his image of the past with authority must be intimately bound up with the means by which he constructs it; since the function of the image is to contain and convey authority, the authority must to a large degree define the image. Mo Tzu indeed seems to have been impelled to open the whole problem of the nature of authority and its place in political society, but he was clearly a man of unusual philosophical capacity. In a traditional society possessing only a highly institutionalized present and the presumption of its continuity in a past, it is likely that the radical desiring a past to return to will be obliged to erect a myth – an image of the past owing most to the creative imagination and heavily endowed with charismatic authority; for if we assume that action and authority conceived as outside the stream of tradition must be conceived as in some way creative, charismatic or sacred, the radical's solution must be dictated by this necessity.

Much obviously depends on whether the tradition already contains images of creative or sacred action[13] – on whether, for instance, it defines the nature of the sacred act with which it began – for then the radical has only to depict the tradition as a departure or degeneration from its own beginnings, and authority may be defined as a recrudescence of the original charisma in the present. It was a weakness in Mo Tzu's position that so little could be said about the Former Kings and the Hsia other than the presumption of their continuity with Chou usages. But great religious traditions in highly literate societies, which begin with detailed written expressions of inexpressible sacred events, will be in a peculiarly interesting position in

[13] On this point – as elsewhere in this essay – I am indebted to correspondence with [the late] Marshall G. S. Hodgson of the University of Chicago.

this respect. Protestant thought, for example, began by making an intensive scholarly critical endeavour to reconstruct the practices of the primitive church, as possessing the authority of revealed truth over the present, but later generated an increasingly illuminist attempt to attain though inspiration direct experience of the operations of the Spirit not only in primitive times but in all times. In Islam, where the reinterpretation of primitive documents is less possible, the radical Shia sectaries claimed that the charisma of the Prophet had passed to the hero 'Ali, and that those who did not give their allegiance to 'Ali were no true Muslims. In such cases as these a sacred charisma, never to be fully contained within the normal mechanisms of transmission, is thought of as awaiting outside time the faithful who seek or expect it within time. Apocalyptics develop elaborate schemes of prophecy, predicting the times and occasions on which the charisma will return to the temporal world; mystics pursue 'the intersections of the timeless with time', regarding their occupation as extrahistorical. But whether or not the operations of the timeless are conceptualized into a historic scheme, authority has been located outside time, and the strategy of return may end by abolishing its own necessity; 'if a man think to be saved by the report of Christ's dying at Jerusalem, he is deceived'. If the structure of time is the transmission of authority, an authority which may be had by direct contact with the timeless seems to abolish time altogether.

The strategy of return does not depend on the tradition's conserving any image of its sacred or other origins; if 'Ali and the Former Kings do not exist, the radical is often capable of inventing them. English common-law traditionalism repeatedly denied that the origins of tradition could be found at any specific moment,[14] but this did not prevent the Levellers locating in pre-Conquest England 'the birthright of Englishmen', or the Georgian democrats locating at the same period the realization of 'the original principles of the constitution' and erecting the figure of Alfred into that of the English legislator who had established them. The tradition contained no specified charisma which could be vested exclusively in the Anglo-Saxons, but if we ask what sort of authority English radicals supposed the vanished past to exercise over the degenerate present, we find answers in which the charismatic and the rational are blended. The Levellers identified the inner light of the spirit in every man with his natural reason and the freedom to exercise it; they could both assert with Lilburne that institutions

[14] See Burke, *Works*, VI, ed. Bohn, pp. 146–8, and Davies, preface to *Irish Reports* (1612): 'Neither could any one man ever vaunt, that like *Minos*, *Solon*, or *Lycurgus*, he was the first *Lawgiver* to our Nation . . . Long experience, and many trials of what was best for the common good, did make the *Common Law*.'

embodying that freedom had once existed in England and assert with Overton that it did not matter if they had not, since the authority of spirit and reason was independent of worldly happenings. The Georgian radicals had abridged the constitutional tradition into a Polybian-Machiavellian 'science' of mixed government, according to which every stable constitution must be founded on certain principles, from which it might degenerate and to which it must be restored.[15] Burke, as we know, contended that theories like these were always distilled from the constitutional inheritance which was then represented as degenerate from them, and that this was 'a preposterous way of thinking and a perfect confusion of ideas'. It might indeed be argued that the element of authority in each case did not belong to the common law and was borrowed from another strand of thought, Puritan or humanist, in the English inheritance; but in each case the authority vested in the past and enjoining a return to it was no longer located in a stream of transmission, but consisted in something – whether charismatic or rational – not dependent on time for its validity.

Here we seem to have established some fairly simple cases of 'the abridgment of tradition into an ideology'. The strategist of return, supposed to be making his departure like Mo Tzu from a situation of pure traditionalism, cannot invest the past in which he believes with the authority of tradition. He therefore borrows elements of charismatic or rational authority either from the tradition which he is criticizing or from some other strand in his society's inheritance – it is worth noticing that the stream of transmission must already be bearing along elements of charisma or rationality, or elements easily conceptualized as such – and concentrates them wholly in his 'past', in such a way as to deprive subsequent tradition of what now becomes a predominant form of authority, capable of commanding return to the past in which it was once fully actualized. But since traditional thought conceives time in terms of social transmission, an authority which has not been transmitted is not in time and does not depend for its validity on its having been actualized in the past. The strategy of return tends therefore to be self-abolishing.

The phenomenon is familiar enough, being that 'radical', 'rationalist' or 'ideological' thinking which has been criticized from Hsun Tzu to Michael Oakeshott by those aware of the reality and ubiquity of tradition; the outlines of their criticism are also familiar. But there is a foreshortening of perspective into which a vivid awareness of tradition should not be allowed

[15] For details of this abridgment, see J. G. A. Pocock, 'Machiavelli, Harrington and English Political Ideologies in the Eighteenth Century', in *Politics, Language and Time*, pp. 104–47.

to lead us. We should beware of supposing that the criticism of tradition by those in search of an alternative basis for authority necessarily leads them into ideological postures, so that every dialogue between the conservers and the critics of a tradition is like that between Burke and Paine. This is simply not so; traditionalism has its own naivety, which consists in exaggerating its own subtlety and the naivety of its opponents. It can be empirically shown that the range of strategies open to both the conservative and the radical is greater than we have so far allowed, and that in confrontations between them the awareness of history is by no means all on one side. If the abridgment of tradition is ideology, the criticism of tradition may be history – the ascription to the past of a relation to the present more complex than mere transmission. The ideologist and the historian may be closer partners than seemed likely at first sight.

A tradition in the pure sense consists of a set of present usages and the presumption of their indefinite continuity; the only modes of social action which it conceives or recognizes are use and transmission, and the radical critic is therefore driven to invent or import some other mode of action lying outside the tradition. But we have already seen that traditions of pure usage, containing no other concepts of action or authority, are on the whole rare. The majority contain some image of charismatic or other action, which the radical may employ to construct his strategy of return and develop into the foundations of his ideology. It further happens that few radicals find themselves confronted with a traditionalism so pure that it makes no other assertion about the past than that it is the indefinite antiquity of present usages. Factual statements are commonly made about actions taken or assertions of authority made in the past, and the basis on which these are made is seldom exclusively that of presumption. The character of these statements is all-important to the development of historiography. If they consist merely of allusions to sacred and timeless events, with no secular or institutional continuity with society's present, we are in a situation like that of the Greeks, unable to make any statement about the past which is not either myth or the rationalization of myth; if they consist merely in presumptions of the continuity of present usages, we are in the situation already described, limited to either the presumption of antiquity or the invention of a timeless myth of charismatic action. But if they are made in such a way as to facilitate discussion of what happened and what authority it exerts over the present, then critical discussion of past, continuity and tradition becomes possible. It is when two men – who may be the conservative and the radical – begin making contradictory but discussable statements about the past and its relation to the present that historical thought can begin. We should observe, however, that it may well be the radical who wishes to initiate such a discussion, and the conservative who denies that it can or should be held. It was the conservative and traditionalist Hsun Tzu who wrote: 'Abandoned incorrigible people say ancient and present times were different in nature . . . The Sage cannot be so deceived.'[16]

At this point literacy emerges as the force modifying the character of tradition. Should there have existed for a sufficient period the practice of conserving official records or literary expressions of what is taken to be the tradition's content, the conservative need not rely exclusively on the presumption of continuity, nor need the radical be confined to the construction of a charismatic myth. It will be open to the latter to re-combine and reinterpret the evidences of the past so that they present an image other than that of the tradition, just as it will be open to the former to construct an image of society in the classical and canonical perfection it supposedly enjoyed in some ideal past. The traditionalist, however, will always distrust the classicist, seeing in him the well-meaning author of a potentially radical doctrine. Words – the Chinese philosophers used to point out, referring of course to ideograms – are rigid in their form and yet endlessly debatable in their meaning; the tradition is that of the actual practice of the *li* and words should be kept in a subsidiary role; if they become predominant, there must be a ruler with authority to interpret them, and since the basis of his authority must be above words and outside tradition, it must be arbitrary and unintelligible. The fact is that a literate tradition is never a pure tradition, since the authority of written words is not dependent on usage and presumption only.[17] As durable material objects they cut across the processes of transmission and create new patterns of social time; they speak direct to remote generations, whose interpretation of them may differ from that of intervening transmitters of the tradition they express. If the position can be firmly maintained that documents are no more than occasional expressions of an essentially unwritten tradition, the doctrine that equates authority with simple transmission may survive; the concept of English politics we find in Burke is directly connected with the fact that common-law records were assumed to be declarations of an immemorial *jus non scriptum*. But every reader is a potential radical; non-traditional interpretations arise, and with them the question of the authority to be employed in reading and

[16] H. H. Dubs, *The Works of Hsüntze* (London, 1928), pp. 72–5.

[17] See Jack Goody and Ian Watt, 'The Consequences of Literacy', *Comparative Studies in Society and History*, 5.3 (1963), pp. 304–45.

interpreting documents; this authority may be thought of as traditional, rational, charismatic or simply mysterious. Books breed sibyls to read them, and the sibyl's authority, recorded on the various occasions on which it is exercised, now enters the tradition, which increasingly becomes a record of the different interpretations which have been made of items in the social inheritance and the different modes of authority which have been asserted in making them. All these recorded facts are next made available to remote generations in ways that are more than merely traditional, and society's conceptualization of its modes of transmission – which is to say its image of itself as existing continuously in time – becomes various, subjective and controversial. Documents tend to secularize traditions; they reduce them to a sequence of acts – whether the acts recorded, the acts of those recording them or the acts of those interpreting the records – taking place at distinguishable moments, in distinguishable circumstances, exercising and imposing distinguishable kinds and degrees of authority. They reduce time from a simple conceptualization of social continuity to that of an indefinite multiplicity of continuities, which – since in the last analysis they represent different ideas of action, authority and transmission – cannot be altogether consistent with one another.

The radical desiring to alter the traditional image of the past has now many strategies open to him besides that of constructing a myth and investing it with charisma. The past consists of many recorded actions and images of authority, of which the greater part must be acceptable to the conservative as well as to himself; these may be selected and rearranged so as to provide a new image of the past and the sort of authority it exercises upon the present, counter-interpretations may be put forward and their rival claims may be discussed. Since the discussion of alternative versions of the past and their relation to the present is what we mean by historiography, we may risk the hypothesis that the beginnings of historiography are to be found when, in a literate tradition, an attempt is made to alter not so much the received facts of the past as the kind of authority which they exercise over the present; for this will bring about the discussion of alternative versions of society's continuity as a means of transmitting authority. The concepts employed in constructing and discussing these versions will be various, and will not all seem to us such as historians have any business to be using. Depending upon what modes of authority are supposed to be inherent in the tradition under discussion, there will be timeless concepts of sacred or rational authority; there will be concepts of action and transmission peculiar to the tradition's institutional character, and taken for granted without critical investigation; there will even be uncritical or anticritical employments of the concept of tradition. But the possibility now exists of agreeing, first, that certain acts were performed irrespective of the authority which they exercise, and second, that certain forms of authority were asserted and recognized irrespective of whether they are or should be now acknowledged. There now exists the possibility of two further stages in the growth of historical thought. The first is that of a 'pure' or 'objective' historiography, meaning the reconstruction of a past irrespective of the authority which it exercises over the present. This stage, it should be observed, has sometimes been reached by accident; classicists and radicals have discovered, with a sense of shock, that they have reconstructed the past in such terms that it can authorize only itself.[18] The second is the realization of the complexity of tradition, the discovery that society's past contains and has transmitted all these modes of authority and of action, of which purely traditional authority and the activity of pure transmission form only one conceptualization, so that the tradition has become a dialogue between its more and less traditional – a dialectic between its traditional and its anti-traditional – modes of envisaging itself. If the former of these stages is more likely to be reached by radicals and classicists, the latter is more likely to be reached by conservatives and sometime traditionalists.

'The criticism of tradition is history' – a sentence the necessary counterpart of Henry Ford's 'History is more or less bunk. It's tradition' – is now seen to mean that historiography emerges from the context of a discussion of various ways in which the past can authorize the present. In this discussion many concepts by no means appropriate to pure historiography will be constantly in use, and though the tendency to eliminate them and convert the discussion from the level of politics to that of history will be very strong, there is no reason to suppose that it will ever reach absolute completeness. In these circumstances we have to avoid the temptation – which has flawed several brilliant Italian works of the post-Crocean school – to single out those aspects of thought which we consider 'historical' and in their light to condemn others as 'unhistorical' and writings containing concepts of the latter kind as less than 'history'. It is clearly wiser to consider pure historiography as one extreme of a wide spectrum of types of discussion, which will be intensified in proportion as modes of authorization come to be looked on 'objectively', i.e. in the same light as others. Since what we are concerned with is history, the light in question must be that of a common temporal

[18] A *locus classicus* of this sense of shock is François Hotman's *Anti-Tribonian* (1566). See J. G. A. Pocock, *The Ancient Constitution and the Feudal Law* (Cambridge, 1957), pp. 11–15, and Julian H. Franklin, *Jean Bodin and the Sixteenth-Century Revolution in the Methodology of Law and History* (New York and London, 1963), pp. 46–58.

context, and it should therefore seem – at least *prima facie* – that it will be hard to construct a historiography where the dominant mode of authority is and remains sacred. It is true that one of the main origins of modern historiography is found in the endeavours of sixteenth-century religious reformers to recover the exact text of Scripture and the exact institutional character of the primitive church. This led not only to counter-endeavours in the field of erudition on the part of their opponents, but to discussion of the modes of transmission of authority and the structure of the Christian community. The reformers' posture was radical; they meant to use their recoveries to prove that the historical church had failed to transmit authority and had consequently lost it; and like other exponents of the strategy of return, they faced the question of how to define the authority which had once existed and the authority by which they themselves claimed to know it. Since what was in dispute was an action of the sacred upon the world of time, the reformers claimed the authority of the sacred acting on and through themselves, their acts being conceived as opposed to tradition; they claimed both to interpret the past and to reform the present by personal authority and charisma, and the strategy of return duly proved, in a number of cases, self-abolishing. Their opponents pointed out that charisma was tending to replace transmission altogether, and advocated a return to the accepted modes of interpretation of the sacred origins, which were scholastic reason, institutionalized authority and prescriptive usage. The next step should ideally have been the construction of a vision of Christian history in which all these modes of authority and transmission were seen as acting together; but – apart from the political struggles which discouraged any such eirenic – so long as the Christian world is seen as an interrelation of the sacred and the temporal, the possibility of a Christian historiography depends on the extent to which that interrelation can be defined in terms which permit the temporal to be seen as the product of an inner dynamic. Once the sacred is defined as universal and extrasocial, it greatly complicates our task of viewing historiography as the outcome of the secularization of conceptualized social continuity. We therefore borrow from the great religious traditions such evidence as increases our self-limited understanding of the strategies of tradition.

In the emphasis which Richard Hooker laid on the church as a traditional community, transmitting its interpretations of original revelation in ways which invested them chiefly with prescriptive and presumptive value, we recognize not merely an appeal to tradition as a mode of authority sometimes preferable to charisma, but an intensified awareness of the traditional community which is often considered the ideal conservative response to the strategy of return. To the Shia fundamentalism which became a recourse to the charismatic figure of 'Ali, orthodox Sunni Muslims reply by declaring their loyalty to the Ummah, which is the historic Muslim community existing in time, somewhere containing all truth and, though it may contain imperfections and uncertainties as well, not to be broken up by those who are certain of their perfection. Here we have a heightened awareness of transmission as carried on in many modes and asserting many forms of authority; it makes possible – though this seems not to have been realized in Islam – that authentically historical awareness of the complexity of tradition as containing many modes of transmission which was mentioned earlier; and in its realization that different assertions of authority must be weighed against one another and that a certain relativism attaches to them all, prescriptive awareness of authority and tradition may be renewed on a higher level. This has already been defined as the species of historical awareness which the conservative is especially likely to achieve, but it is important not to credit him with it too hastily and to realize the complexity of the dialogue with the radical that must precede it.

We have so far defined the anti-traditional thinker, not as one who wishes to abolish the authority of the past or to impose a new conception of authority on society, but as one who, having denied that the past authorizes the present by vesting it with continuity, is obliged to create a new past and invest it with an authority which easily abolishes the necessity of referring to a past at all. His thought is therefore Janus-faced, but we should pause before emphasizing too ruthlessly the contradictions which it may contain. It tends to become unhistorical, in the sense that it devises a mode of authority independent of social continuity; but it contains an equally visible tendency towards the historical reconstruction of the past in a shape which, together with the authority which it possesses for the present, it is the radical's peculiar contribution to leave uncertain and discussable. In a documented tradition his 'past' will be a compost of assertions of fact and authority selected and rearranged from a common inheritance; he cannot help revealing, and leaving open to question, the methods by which he has done this. Furthermore, the more 'factual' and the less 'mythical' – these are not mutually exclusive categories – the past which he claims once existed, the more specific the authority which enjoins that it should exist again, the more he (or his readers, or his adversaries) may feel impelled to ask why it does not exist now: how has the unauthorized present come into being? He may reply, like Plato or Machiavelli, by averring that there exists a general tendency towards instability and degeneration in human affairs; but the more clearly he can differentiate the characteristics of his 'past' from those of his 'present', the more specific he may feel able to make his account of how the latter came to predominate. Boulainvilliers's account of the decline of the *noblesse* is more complex as a piece of historical explanation than his account of their original privileges;[19] the Georgian radicals, having erected the myth of a free medieval commonwealth of land-owning warriors, accounted for its decline by tracing the rise of government finance, professional armies and parliamentary influence in ways which passed through Hume to the Glasgow school.[20] The radical reconstructs the past in order to authorize the future; he historizes the present in order to deprive it of authority. Both operations may give him a bias in favour of historical explanation, which may emerge almost against his wishes from the very character of his enterprise; as with the radical legal humanists of the *mos gallicus*, who reconstructed Roman law in order to imitate it instead of following the glossatorial tradition, and then found they had reconstructed it in such detail that it could not be imitated. The conservative may profit by such mistakes, but never could have made them.

The repudiation of tradition, and the construction of a mode of authority owing nothing to time or continuity, need not – paradoxically enough – diminish a thinker's interest in the reconstruction of the past. Thomas Hobbes repudiated tradition and constructed a mode of authority which has nothing prescriptive about it. Consequently, it is said, he regarded the study of history as of limited illustrative or prudential value. He denied that the common law was Coke's 'artificial reason', based upon presumptive awareness of tradition, and said it was merely the commands of natural reason rendered authoritative by the sovereign. Yet it is precisely in his writings on English law[21] that we find him among the advanced historical thinkers of his day, conscious that the doctrine of immemorial custom could be refuted by reconstructing the law as it had once been, the feudal law of a feudal society. Nor did he adopt this line of argument for merely polemical reasons. There is a visible relation between his denial that the past was a source of authority for the present and his awareness that it could be explained as existing in its own right; and his reconstruction of the past was a piece of serious antiquarian thinking, not a mechanical application of

[19] Comte de Boulainvilliers, *Essais sur la Noblesse de France, contenans une dissertation sur son origine et abaissement* (Amsterdam, 1732).

[20] Andrew Fletcher, *A Discourse on Government in its Relation to Militias* (Edinburgh, 1698); Giuseppe Giarrizzo, *Hume politico e storico* (Turin, 1962).

[21] *Behemoth* and *A Dialogue of the Common Laws*, in Molesworth (ed.), *The English Works of Thomas Hobbes*, VI (London, 1839–45).

his abstract theories. Because his thought was unhistorical in one respect, it could be historical in another. A rationalist approach to authority and a historical approach to the past may be partners as well as opposites; this is only one of the complexities which follow from the radical's denial that authority is prescriptive.

In his now well-known reply to Hobbes on English law, Sir Matthew Hale raised the presumptive theory of custom to a new level of sophistication.[22] He wished to deny that law was a series of simple rational commands; he contended that law was custom, and that in a given custom nothing could be seen but the fruits of experience, shaped in a series of concrete situations to which no moment of commencement could be assigned, and thereafter tested in subsequent situations not identical with their predecessors but assimilated to them by practice. The details of these situations had not as a rule been recorded; the content of the law had been constantly refined on the presumption that it was being preserved; we could say of no item in the law when it had originated, nor could we trace the succession of contexts in which it had been shaped and modified. There was only the presumption that it had answered, and would continue to answer, in all the situations to which it was exposed; but this presumption was overwhelmingly strong.

Hsun Tzu had attacked the radical strategy of return by arguing that the past could not be known by means other than presumption. To know the ways of the Former Kings we must follow those of the Later Kings; to know those of the Later Kings we must follow the usages of Chou; to know those of Chou we must follow Confucius. Hale was attacking a rationalist theory of authority, which implied the possibility of independent knowledge of a past no longer prescriptive, by arguments essentially the same. It is important to observe how the traditionalist strategy shifts under attack. In a system of pure tradition, all knowledge is dependent upon transmission; the validity of transmitted knowledge can only be presumed, but since we have no means of knowledge other than transmission, this presumption must be made of all knowledge; the circle is closed. When therefore the radical, the rationalist or the antiquarian begins to assert that the past can be known by means that do not presume its continuity with the present, that the past does not authorize the present but enjoins another set of political arrangements, that authority can be found by means that do not locate it in the past, or that the past can be studied in ways that do not invest

[22] Printed in Holdsworth, *A History of English Law*, v (London, 1924), Appendix. See Pocock, *The Ancient Constitution and the Feudal Law*, pp. 170–81, and 'Burke and the Ancient Constitution: a problem in the history of ideas', in *Politics, Language and Time*, pp. 202–32.

it with authority over the present, the conservative's strategy is – at this stage in the analysis – always the same. Against the rationalist, he avers that nothing can be known of a social institution or its authority which does not stress its continuity with the past to the point where that authority becomes inescapably prescriptive; against the radical, the antiquarian, even the historian, he avers that nothing is known of the past which is not based on transmission and does not compel the presumption of continuity between the past and the present (or between a remote past and a recent past of which the present is the continuation). But both Hsun Tzu and Hale reveal that his position has in fact altered. The radical avers, in one way or another, that the past can be known, and however insubstantial his grounds, he forces the conservative to reply that it cannot be known; it can only be presumed. The radical constructs his image of the past by rearranging, modifying and occasionally inverting or contradicting the concepts and documents in which some part of the contents of a tradition is conveyed in easily manageable shapes; and since the elements of his structure are abstracted from a context of which they form part and with the other elements of which they have unstated and presumptive relationships, the conservative is able to point out that the radical's past is a construct, an abstraction, of limited validity. There is of course a sense in which all knowledge in a tradition is of this kind; Confucius may have intended this when he said: 'Shall I tell you what wisdom is? It is to know both what one knows and what one doesn't know.' But in Hsun Tzu the stress on 'what one doesn't know' is the stronger because assertions have been made about the possibility of knowing the past to have been other than the present, and in Hale the stress has become very strong and its expression very sophisticated. The past is a continuity, but a continuity of adaptation; the image of a body changing its cells, of a river changing its water, is more than once used; and we are being told that all we can ever know of the past is that it was unlike the present and yet continuous with it. Even this we cannot know so much as presume, for we cannot know what the past was like at any single moment. Such moments are inapprehensible. The tradition has become a flux, Hale's river that of Heraclitus and Cratylus.

No less than the radical, then, the conservative can think both historically and unhistorically. The radical asserts that the past can be known, but that some elements of it can be known out of their traditional context; the conservative asserts that all knowledge must be knowledge in a continuous social context, but denies to that knowledge any status more positive than that of presumption. It seems to be a sign of unconscious conservative bias in us, therefore, when we assert that Hale's thinking is 'historical' and that of

Hobbes 'unhistorical', or make similar comparisons between Guicciardini and Machiavelli. Hale and Guicciardini certainly possessed a greater sense of the complexity and intractability of historical events, but at the same time they denied that events could be known or governed, if at all, by any but the most rigorously presumptive methods: traditional conservatism in Hale, merging into scepticism and stoicism in Guicciardini. Their opposites in each pair were trying, by the aid of concepts abstracted from their historical contexts, to make history more intelligible and governable. But the conservative's strategies do not end with this union of scepticism and traditionalism, typically conservative though it is. The increasing complexity of non-traditional thought faces him with other challenges, to which he makes other responses.

It may for instance happen that the radicals have captured the past. That is, they may have succeeded in rearranging concepts about the past so as to form a pattern widely accepted as plausible and containing much that is acceptable and even dear to conservatives, but seeming to authorize in the present only a set of arrangements other than those actually existing. This seems to have happened in Georgian England, where the traditional image of 'the ancient constitution' had been revised to form a quasi-classical image of an 'ancient and balanced constitution', founded on principles from which, it was said, the present constitution was degenerate. In these circumstances there are several replies which conservatives may put forward. There is the traditionalist and prescriptive answer, advanced in this case by Burke, which denies that the principles of the constitution can be known, since they are nothing but continuities of immemorial usage. The more precise, however, the image of the past and its authority to which this answer is opposed, the harder it is to dissolve knowledge into presumption. There is the possibility of constructing a new version of the past, more persuasive than that of the radicals; but the more striking and original the intellectual means employed to do this, the less likely is it to furnish present arrangements with prescriptive authority. There is the further possibility of drastically denying that the past has authority over the present, and claiming for existing arrangements an authority derived from outside history. It should not surprise us to find this conservative radicalism in close alliance with historical criticism; so at least it was in eighteenth-century England. For the century following the Exclusion controversy, it was a standard tactic of the defenders of the Court – especially when the Court was Hanoverian rather than Stuart – to employ the feudal interpretation to deny the antiquity of the constitution, whether immemorial or balanced, and argue that since the past was mainly darkness and despotism the principles of government, such as they were, must be extrahistorical in their location and recent in their discovery. Until the advent of Burke altered the intellectual scene, a classicist appeal to the past was the weapon of English and American radicals, a critical rejection of history that of the Court. Nor is this a peculiarly eighteenth-century phenomenon. Against the 'abandoned incorrigible people' who argued that past and present times were different in nature, Hsun Tzu demanded: 'Why cannot the Sage be so deceived? I say it is because the Sage measures things by himself. Hence by himself he measures other men . . . by the Way he can completely comprehend things. Past and present are the same. Things that are the same in kind, though extended over long periods, continue to have the self-same principles.'[23]

If Hsun Tzu could pass from traditionalism to essentialism in a few brush-strokes, it might seem that all that has happened is merely a tactical reversion of roles; the conservative desires to defend things as they are, and it is simply an accident of the polemical situation which determines what argument he adopts. But to leave it at that would of course be superficial; there is in the conservative's mind a constancy of belief as well as of interest. His basic position is that the existing arrangements of society contain their own justification, that it is not justifiable to subject them wholly to be evaluated by some standard existing outside themselves; and since it is impossible to cease altogether from visualizing the existing arrangements as inherited, the element of tradition never quite disappears from his thought. Hsun Tzu's Sage does not resolve his 'Way' into 'principles' which he proceeds to substitute for it; the Way continues to be the practice of the *li* and the pursuit of the intimations which they contain, and what he is really asserting is that he can find no time in the past in which the *li* were not active and their intimations valid – and intimations constantly present and valid may be termed principles. In eighteenth-century England the position was more complicated. Ancient and present times were allowed to be different in nature, and the conservative school employed both historical and rationalist criticism to deny that the principles of government were to be found in the past; the same tactic was employed by Voltaire and other defenders of the *thèse royale* in France, against Montesquieu and the lesser advocates of the backward-looking *thèse nobiliaire*. Reversing the strategy of return, it was argued that the true principles of government had been discovered in England only recently, about 1689, and that once they had been discovered their effect was to render the past irrelevant. If

[23] This translation is that of D. Bodde, in Fung Yu-lan, *A History of Chinese Philosophy*, I (Peiping and London, 1937), pp. 282–4.

they were of recent discovery they were not contained in tradition, and we seem to be faced by a conservative argument abandoning the appeal to prescriptive sanction. But a pragmatic and a prescriptive conservatism are not as dissimilar in their intellectual style as may at first appear.

If the principles of government were of recent discovery, how had this discovery been made and what was the legitimacy of actions performed before – or indeed after – their discovery? It might be argued that the discovery was made as a result of the developing historical experience of the English people; this seems to be part of the very complex historical thought of David Hume.[24] But if actions performed before their discovery were not to be considered mere folly and barbarism, they must be explained and justified by something other than 'the principles of government', in which case these 'principles' could not be the sole source of authority for political actions. Unhistorical authority alleged by a conservative will be a different matter from unhistorical authority alleged by a radical. It will authorize an existing set of arrangements, whereas its radical counterpart authorizes one that must be brought into existence, even if this is to be done by a return to the past; and a consequence is that the authority of the latter must stretch further and do more than that of the former. The conservative demands less of his 'principles' and puts less into them; they will resemble less a comprehensive theory of government than a pragmatic justification of existing arrangements. Indeed, they may turn out on inspection to contain little more than the pragmatic statement that arrangements must be continued if they exist and must be made if they do not exist, and that somebody must attend to continuing or constructing them. There is certainly little more to the conservatism of that admirable eighteenth-century curmudgeon Josiah Tucker.[25]

The conservative in his pragmatic vein is anxious that practical steps shall be taken and existing arrangements upheld, without being subjected to excessive scrutiny in the name of abstract principle. To ensure this he will even repudiate the continuity of past and present, which his prescriptive and traditionalist brother is so anxious to maintain. But prescriptive action is undertaken on nothing more than an assumption, which its defenders are memorably reluctant to see replaced by an abstraction; and that assumption is no more than the presumption of its continuity with earlier action, which must also be presumed – as a matter of practical necessity – of the majority of actions undertaken in a purely pragmatic spirit. A pragmatic

[24] Giarrizzo, *Hume politico e storico*. [To this reference it is now prudent to add Duncan Forbes, *Hume's Philosophical Politics* (Cambridge, 1975); Nicholas Phillipson, *Hume* (London, 1989), and J. G. A. Pocock, *Barbarism and Religion*, II (Cambridge, 1999), pp. 163–240.]

[25] [See now the more intensive treatment of Tucker in chapter 9 of J. G. A. Pocock, *Virtue, Commerce and History* (Cambridge, 1985).]

action must have a context and make sense in that context. A prescriptive style, which appeals constantly to precedent, may have much in common with a pragmatic style, which appeals only to necessity; this is how it was that the conservatism of the eighteenth century could reflect the thought both of those who believed the Revolution justified by precedent and of those – the so-called *de facto* Tories – who believed it justified only by necessity. Burke was able to unite these lines of thought by demonstrating that neither entailed, and each rejected, the establishment of an abstract and recurrent principle of dethronement. Pragmatism is the establishment of a continuous style of behaviour which cannot any longer be presumed; this is the sense in which it is conservatism without traditions.

We may now see how it is that the conservative can unite the extremes of traditionalist veneration for a past and sceptical denial of the past's relevance for the present. He believes wholly in an established and continuous mode of behaviour, which contains within itself all the criteria by which it can be judged and so cannot be judged by any standard outside itself. The radical attempts to establish such a standard in the past, the rationalist outside it. The appeal to tradition can be used against the rationalist, to return all thinking to the context of a given social continuity. But the radical is in one way a more formidable opponent, because he has an alternative version of the prescribing past, and as soon as traditionalism becomes a means of denying that such a version can be reliably constructed, it becomes a mode of scepticism differing only in degree from outright denial that the past can be known or relevant. Historical scepticism becomes a conservative weapon when it becomes a means of denying that the present act or arrangement can be judged by some standard located as existing and emanating authority in the past. An act concerning which nothing can be said with certainty except that it must be presumed continuous with some antecedent act is not so very unlike an act of which not even that can be said, given only that it is our agreed purpose that a social continuity must be established and maintained. At this point it becomes a conservative interest to emphasize the discontinuity of history, its character as a series of discrete actions, where previously it was to his interest to emphasize the presumed continuity with which it transmitted authority and legitimation. If each act is unique it cannot be judged by comparison with any of its predecessors; but if its intent is to establish authority and continuity, it should be accepted as such and not condemned. A series of such acts will re-edify a presumptive tradition; and neo-conservative and neo-Burkean historians are seeking to reduce history once more to an esoteric and disenchanted narrative of the almost inscrutable acts of statesmen.

There is here an antinomian and anarchic strain in conservatism. Distrusting recurrence and regularity, it reduces history to a river into which one cannot step twice, with the consequence that it becomes difficult to step into it even once. It is interesting that the 'abandoned incorrigible people', against whom Hsun Tzu declared the steadfastness of the Sage's self-discovered nature, were probably not radical heirs of Mo Tzu but Taoists, since an affinity between Oakeshott's thought and Taoism has been detected by some critics. The assertion that 'past and present times are different in nature' is certainly to be detected in some Taoist writings,[26] but it does not seem to mean that the past may be reconstructed by historical technique and seen to be different from the present. 'Footprints', we are told, 'are made by shoes, but they are far from being shoes'; an utterance which seems to indicate that history escapes our knowledge. The Taoist insistence on the undifferentiated unity of all reality led them, it appears, to repudiate all attempts to pin exact definitions on it. If then you tried to assert that the present was known and properly governed, the river would slip through your fingers as you tried to net it. But this argument goes from Cratylus to Heraclitus: if you cannot step into the river once, you cannot step into it twice either; and no more than Hale did the Taoists believe it possible to determine the state of the tradition at single moments, past or present. They therefore abandoned the use of all concepts in government, even the concept of government itself. This view shocked Hsun Tzu, who was inclined to regard the transmitted contents of tradition as a body of authoritative institutions and dogmas, but it is a natural if extreme development of an integral part of the traditionalist style; indeed, it seems likely that the Taoists reached their belief that no moment in the Way was the whole of the Way, and that consequently no moment was like another moment, partly through reflection on the nature of tradition. Because the intellect cannot grasp the full meaning of any act in the sequence of a tradition, it cannot grasp the whole meaning of the tradition; and consequently it is very easy to think of action as the carrying on of a style, the continuation of a mode of behaviour whose character can be apprehended but never analysed, and which in turn is realized in action rather than in conceptualization. From this the Taoists went on to regard the whole of reality as a style – the Way – and to take that delight, which Oakeshott shares, in telling stories of craftsmen who could perform their tasks perfectly because they did not consider how to do them, who were perfect in their style because they did not conceive it as a style. But if politics is to be the practice of a

[26] Arthur Waley, *Three Ways of Thought in Ancient China* (London, 1939), pp. 32, 37–8.

pure style, the practical is in fact being absorbed by the contemplative, the pragmatic by the aesthetic; where the traditionalist legitimized his acts by presuming them continuous and the pragmatist acted to institute a continuity, the aesthetic statesman acts so that the continuous style of his actions may be contemplated and enjoyed. All three share a conservative style; they presume a tradition.

Disinterested historiography is possible only in stable societies, where the present is fortified by means other than the writing of histories. It is therefore part of the conservative style to emphasize that history is studied for its own sake, and in a well-known passage Oakeshott has compared the impure historian, who expects the past to teach him something, with the pure historian, for whom the past is dead, a beloved mistress whom he does not expect to talk sense. But if the past can be considered dead, this can only mean that society's relation with its past, which we have seen to be society's continuing structure and its own inner self, has been stabilized by means other than those of the historian. In less stable societies, Oakeshott's historian is an impossibility. For Machiavelli, who makes significant use of erotic imagery as regards the past, history is Fortune, a treacherous and savage virgin whom we can never fully possess, but who may well devour us if we do not master her; and the river may burst its banks in a devastating flood.[27] Even in a stable society, there is a certain cosiness about the Oakeshottian *ménage*. The point about a mistress is that we are not obliged to live with her; Oakeshott's historian and his past maintain separate establishments. But once we define society's awareness of its structure as its awareness of its continuity, of the complexity of its relations with its past, the occasionally enjoyed mistress begins to assume more serious, more terrible and more moral possibilities. To the Florentines she was the maenad Fortune, an irrational and irresistible stream of happenings. To the Romantics she was (and is) the Goddess History, of their relationship with whom they expect a final consummation, only too likely to prove a *Liebestod*. The conservative style leaves her in the role of mistress, but it has been the aim of this essay to show that traditionalism and its refinements form only one voice in a dialogue with and within tradition, out of which arises a constant discussion and redefinition of the modes of continuity and authority which link past to present and give the present its structure. In that dialogue the past is to the present something more like a wife: an other self, perpetually explored.

[27] *The Prince*, ch. 25.

CHAPTER 11

The historian as political actor in polity, society and academy

It seemed a proper inquiry for the Conference for the Study of Political Thought to investigate the character of history, as both a subject and a form of political thought, literature, discourse, or whatever term you may prefer. History is – or, more interestingly, histories are – invented (meaning both discovered and constructed) in political societies, as a characteristic and perhaps necessary activity, and then discussed, and disputed, by participants in those societies, including those specialists in the activity known as being historians. What manner of political action, or reflection, does all this entail? What kind of political institution, or phenomenon, is a history? What is done, to whom, by whom and by what means, when a history is constructed, communicated, debated, criticized, subverted and, subject to all these, written? What kinds of political practices go on and may be the subject-matter of theory; what kinds of political reflection, or theory, may the various forms of historiography constitute?

I proposed these questions – or rather, since they may need all manner of restating, this kind of question – to the speakers at Tulane University. It was apparent that they were questions about a great many ways in which history and historiography constituted political practice; and it seemed appropriate therefore – since we were in the first instance an assembly of political theorists – to conduct a re-examination of Michael Oakeshott's contention that history, properly understood, neither does nor should serve any practical purpose at all. It should be our business as theorists to recognize the importance of practice without subordinating ourselves to it. But the journey towards the philosophical point where practice itself comes under criticism proved to lie through a landscape, both political and historical, in which practice went on under conditions of great cultural diversity and

[Published in *The Journal of Pacific Studies*, edited at the University of the South Pacific, 20 (1996), pp. 89–112. An earlier version had been delivered to the Conference for the Study of Political Thought, meeting at Tulane University, New Orleans, in March 1996.]

of course cultural change. To consider the politics of history and historiography, therefore, it was necessary to pursue them through a diversity of cultural frameworks in which the very meanings of the words 'politics', 'history' and 'historiography' might change or disappear; with the further consequence that to discuss the cultural diversities of 'history' might itself be to perform a political act and even to reflect upon it.

I should like to begin, then, by proposing a modest programme for studying the politics of historiography in a stable and relatively familiar cultural setting; it being clearly understood from the start that this definition of historiography and its politics is even as I write being destabilized and rendered problematic. I shall imply that this is not an unprecedented situation, so that the target of destabilization has already its own means of restoring its stability; and of course, to choose a particular construct as the target for deconstruction is already to privilege it, implying that this and not some other is the thesis in temporary possession of the field. I do not think this gambit will be objectionable, given that I can set up a model of historiography sufficiently familiar to us all, including those who will wish to see it deprivileged. From that point I shall try to proceed in directions along which we may see it being changed.

In this simple situation there is a political society; it has a history; and there is an activity of narrating or otherwise expounding that history. Clearly, this is not to say very much; what we mean when we say 'a political society', and what we mean when we say 'a history', can differ enormously from one cultural situation to another. But we may presume that 'a political society' displays a distribution of powers and that the 'history' entails some narration of events taking place, or situations existing, in past time. Here it is as well to be careful. In New Zealand, we are assured, the Maori people do not speak of history as behind them, but before them; this, however, does not mean that they think it happens in time future, only that it possesses authority and may have to be re-enacted or re-experienced, in time now or to come. Whatever the tense structures or structurings of time in diverse cultures, we shall not go far wrong at this stage if we suppose that 'a history' normally entails a 'time of the ancestors' or 'time past'. It is a temptation, therefore, in constructing our model, to say that the 'political society' is a distribution of power, and the 'history' the past existence that power structure ascribes to itself for reasons that have to do with affirming, legitimizing and maintaining it. History, we find ourselves saying, is the memory of the state; history is past politics and politics present history.

That these dicta are now considered obsolete in our understanding of historiography does not mean that they are not useful for analytical or diagnostic purposes. Certainly, not all political societies are or have been states; not all histories have been laid down in the archives of a state's institutions or bureaucracies. The narratives or past-entailing propositions maintained by, let us say, the Yamanamo people of the upper Amazon may have more to do with the sheer existence of the Yamanamo as a people than with any particular power structure existing among them; and the activity of identifying and as it were isolating that structure, and demonstrating how the tribal discourse operates to maintain it, may or may not be a proper thing for the anthropologist to do to the Yamanamo. It depends on how far the Yamanamo have found it necessary or convenient to engage in this critical activity for themselves; the anthropologist is not necessarily entitled to do this for them. Or rather, to them. We find at this point that the activity of verbalizing, conceptualizing, criticizing, erecting a fabric of second-order discourse around a discourse of power, is itself a distribution of power; and this is true whether it takes place 'within' a society, i.e. between its politically accredited members, between those members of the society and those not so accredited, or between the members of a society and those external or 'foreign' to it. The world is now full of people who are tired of having their history written for them by others, whether those others be domestic or foreign; and the entitlements that may exist between those whose history it in some sense is, and those who presume to narrate it, are disputed in the politics of history, anthropology and human affairs in general.

The next step in developing our model is to make room for the possibility that this tension has always existed and may be integral to the politics of history. It is easy to say that power structures give power to some and not to others, and to present the 'historian' as telling a narrative that legitimates the power structure in which he is a beneficiary. But it is a little too easy for the intellectual to presuppose that the others are always the hegemons and she always the critic; that she is privileged (and at the same time martyred) to write the critical history that shows how the other histories have been produced by the power structure and have served to authorize it. To understand the politics of history we need to know what relations have existed within the power structure and produced both the construction of history and dispute over its construction, as well as what relations have existed between those within the structure that produced history and those subject or foreign to it. We take the step of supposing a power elite capable of both producing and supporting dispute between its members, and suppose further that within that elite different versions of history will be read and written, so that 'the historian' becomes a specialist in conducting the dispute as well as in authorizing the structure. To one subject to the structure things may well seem different; she is more likely to notice the consensus from which she is excluded than the dispute to which she is not admitted; but if we want to know what has been and is going on, we need to see things in both ways and ask whether these are connected.

Adam Smith, lecturing at Glasgow in the 1760s, noted that 'modern' (i.e. post-ancient) historiography differed from 'ancient' (i.e. Greek and Roman) in that it was far more litigious.[1] It was concerned with rival systems of jurisdiction, which based claims to authority on assertions that certain events had occurred and had been of a certain character; so that the historian was condemned to spend much of his time debating both the authenticity of the events and the modes of their authentication. Smith thought it questionable whether this was 'the historian's' business, though he was engaged in altering the meaning of the word 'history' so that it should be; he thought it hard to reconcile with the 'ancient' understanding of the word, meaning the recounting of an exemplary or edifying narrative. But he clearly did not think that Thucydides or Tacitus had been retelling tales whose factual and moral content had been beyond dispute. Their business had been to penetrate the springs of action and the relations of cause and effect, to the point where these might have to be left mysterious; this was what was edifying about them, and the role of exemplary narrative might be to display the great difficulty of knowing or of initiating an example. If feudal and ecclesiastical culture had been litigious and disputatious, city-state culture had been agonistic and tragic. 'The historian' had become something other than a functionary, or expositor of the ruling values, at the point where he appeared in the role of sophist or rhetorician, since it was the business of the latter to know that actions and their value could always be presented in more than one way. This could be a criticism of agonistic values, but it could be part of the *agōn* itself. Historians in this sense were not simply divided into functionaries and critics, upholders and subverters of the ruling order; the historian as agonistic citizen was actor in and commentator upon the system whose history he narrated. It was at this point in ancient history that historians went one way and philosophers another; Plato does not mention Thucydides, or Thucydides Socrates. If we ask for the first historian martyred by a political system he loved and honoured, the answer may be Ssu-ma Ch'ien rather than any Greek or Roman.

We enter upon an interesting tension between 'history' and 'historian'. Political societies, we find it easy to say, 'invent' or 'produce' or 'construct'

[1] Adam Smith, *Lectures on Rhetoric and Belles-Lettres* (Indianapolis: Liberty Classics, 1985), p. 102.

history that legitimizes or authenticates or in the last analysis 'invents' their activity and their continued existence; so do groups, both privileged and oppressed, that exist within a political society and may be thought to constitute it. This 'history' commonly takes the form of a narrative, and we have begun considering the politics of what happens when 'the historian' offers to retell that narrative. Before we do so, it seems appropriate to ask more questions about what the political society has been doing in producing that history, and what it offers to the individual privileged by the society to act and reflect upon himself as actor; I shall perform the experiment of calling that individual 'the citizen'. We are encouraged, not to say enjoined, to speak of the history as being or having been 'constructed' or 'invented'. These verbs imply the relative specificity of the actors doing the constructing, and the relative rapidity or instantaneity of the action of doing it. 'The invention of tradition' is a phrase that encourages us to find an original set of inventors, specify their intentions or motives and the circumstances or context in which they acted, and to suppose that we have thereby reduced the 'tradition' to historicity. So, it may turn out, we have; but we may need also to enquire what relations existed between the inventors and other members of their society who may have been involved in the action, and we need to enquire whether the invention was indeed instantaneous or took place over time. The longer it takes to 'invent' a 'tradition', the more will the words 'invention' and 'tradition' become interchangeable; the greater the number of members of a 'community' who are involved in 'imagining the community', the more will the 'community' and the 'imagination' become indistinguishable.

The value of the terms I have been analysing is that they oblige us to remember the existence, and try if we can to adopt the perceptions, of those who were not party to the 'invention' or the 'imagination', and find themselves its subjects rather than its agents. These, we may say, were not properly members of the political society at all, and we may privilege them (or ourselves acting in their name) to subvert the society or the history it has constructed. But it should seem that, to understand the politics of history, we need to include the actions and perceptions of those who are members of the society, and inventors and imaginers of its history. Otherwise, alienation too easily becomes a privilege we permit ourselves.

At this moment we should remember that there are an enormous and indefinite number and variety of ways in which a political society may be constructed, may generate a culture, and may 'produce' or 'invent' a history; and consequently, that the meaning and content of the term 'history' may vary as widely. In talking about 'the history' of a particular society, therefore, we may have to spend a great deal of time discovering what that term means, perhaps in a cultural and mental world sharply different from our own. That means that there are risks involved in asking, as I mean to do, what the 'history' generated by a 'political society' possessing some stability means to the 'citizen' of that society; in performing the abstraction I intend, I risk carrying over some cultural assumptions not appropriate to every 'political society' and 'history' we shall want to consider. In order to move ahead, however, it seems worth the risk.

Let us suppose that the citizen is satisfied with his political society to the point where he identifies himself with his membership of it. (I use the masculine pronoun because things are probably biased that way.) It may be that this means of establishing a self is among the principal benefits offered by the political society, and outweighs the others. Let us further suppose that the society has constructed a history that not only legitimates but authenticates its existence, presenting it as existing in an extension of time; and that it offers, not to say imposes, this history as a further means whereby the citizen may identify himself, as a member of the society's history as well as of its other structures. He may accept this invitation, or he may not; the society may be sufficiently plural and complex to satisfy his need of a self by means other than its history; or the history it has to offer him may be complex and agonistic to the point where this need is better satisfied without it. Happy, we say in either case, is the society that has no history. Before we consider cases of these kinds, however, it seems important to consider the simple case of the citizen of a polity possessing a history – one somehow constructed – that authenticates both it and him, or that he supposes to do so. What are the politics of his situation with respect to that history? We may say that he possesses it, in which case he may affirm some kind of right or property in or to it. Or we may say that it constructs and defines himself to himself, in which case we may need to ask how far he is, and in history has been, either an agent or a critic in constructing the history and his self. If we decide that he has been neither agent nor critic, we may decide that both the history and the self it invents are inauthentic. There will be a politics of asking what title 'we' have to decide this for him; very different from the politics that will arise if 'he', the citizen, comes to this decision of inauthenticity for himself.

But I am already presupposing the contestability of the history that offers authentication to the structure of the society and the identity of the citizen. This contestability may arise in either or both of two ways. It may arise from competition, conflict, or agonistic relations among the citizens themselves, in which case there will exist more than one version of history, and these will be in contest with one another. Given that the political society possesses some capacity to present itself as an exercise in conflict resolution, or in ruling and being ruled, this need not prove intolerably disturbing to the citizen; he is presumed capable of recognizing himself as an agonistic being and his society as possessing a past and a present of agonistic relationships; he may recognize this society, and himself in it, as continuingly capable of conducting contestation, and the continuing contest between more than one version of its history as part of the politics that affords him a political identity. We ourselves, as critical intellectuals, have to recognize the terrifying power of universal and hegemonic constructs without presuming the citizen other than ourselves capable of living only within one of these constructs, since if we do so, we presume neither him nor ourselves capable of citizenship at all; he can only be a subject and we can only be critics. There are cases, however, where our presumption that he can sustain the burden of living in a conflicted society becomes the demand that he set about living in a society where there will always be two histories incommensurable with each other. We need to ask ourselves in what circumstances, and with what entitlement, we find ourselves making this demand of the citizen.

A second possible genesis for the contestability of history resides in the mere presence in the scenario of the actor we call 'the historian'. This term denotes someone who has made it his particular concern, his independent, autonomous or specialized activity, to retell histories, which may include those the polity has authorized because they authenticate it; and a point is reached where he begins to tell them in terms not identical with those in which the citizen is used to hearing them told or to telling them himself. This does not happen simply because the historian as citizen becomes aware that the same story can be differently told by the protagonist and the antagonist; we are assuming that the citizen as agonist is capable of knowing this for himself. It happens also because the historian, as sophist, as rhetor, as critic or as philosopher – the last case is rather rare – becomes aware for reasons ultimately linguistic that there is always more than one way of telling the same story, and that this is indefinitely extensible, to the point, perhaps, where it feeds back into his awareness as citizen that the springs of human conduct in agonistic relationships are arcane, mysterious and capable of no final retelling. But he may also make this assertion as specialist intellectual; and I seem to have suggested that historians are the heirs of the sophists rather than the philosophers. Their pedigree is Latin as much as Greek, however, and it is safer to say that they are the heirs of the rhetoricians. At a later moment in the history of historiography, the term 'history' ceases to be confined to the narrative of past political actions and begins to denote the archaeology of past states of culture and society, achieved through the interpretations of the vast archive of texts – literary, legal, governmental, ecclesiastical – accumulated in scribal societies like those of late-antique and medieval Europe. 'The historian' now acquires the capacity to declare that the actions of authenticated history can and must be interpreted in the 'contexts' of past states of culture which he is able to reconstruct, and that these are indefinite in number, so that – once again – there are an indefinite number of ways of telling and retelling any story. A further stage is reached when the historians enter the academies, and their activity becomes professionalized, and within fairly severe limits cosmopolitan, so that there exists a guild, estate or republic of historians, whose business is to discuss with one another, and in their own autonomously generated language, the terms in which they are constantly telling and retelling both the histories that have been the property of the citizens and, interwoven with these, histories of which the citizen has not previously heard and in which he is not accustomed to recognize and authenticate himself. This does not mean that the historian has acquired complete autonomy; his involvement in both society and state has almost certainly increased with the general increase of specialization; but it does mean that he is in a position to claim autonomy, or to find it ascribed to him by those who may very well resent his supposed possession of it.

Up to this point I have been considering the relation between the historian and the citizen, that is to say the historian's fellow-member of political society. The situation will alter sharply if we consider his relation to the state: if we suppose that entity to have intervened in the authorization of narratives that support its authority. Will the historian be a functionary, a dependant, a beneficiary of the state; will the state enjoin its readings of history on the citizen and the historian; in what ways will the state look upon its authority as contingent upon certain readings or structurings of history? This is as good a moment as any to point out that the 'histories' generated and authenticated by political societies do not only consist in narratives and interpretations, but entail structurings of experience, memory and time – world-views as it is perhaps too easy to call them – reflection upon which may carry us rapidly into the realm we term that of philosophy; the relations between political history and political philosophy may be more intimate than the apparent mutual indifference of Thucydides and Plato (speaking for Socrates) would suggest. Perhaps, however, it will be convenient to return to the citizen, as a means to understanding the politics produced by the advent of the historian.

We supposed the citizen to know and to value certain accounts of history, as authenticating and authorizing the political society of which he is a member. If we suppose that society to be a certain distribution of authority, or of power, we may suppose that it assigns some measure of either to the citizen, and that he sees the authorized history of his society as underwriting whatever power or authority he exercises. There are other ways in which he may derive reassurance and value from his society; we have considered the possibility that it may offer him assurance of his social and even his personal identity; but I have emphasized the component of power because it conveniently dramatizes what may occur when the historian appears and sets about retelling the authenticating histories in terms that are unfamiliar to the citizen and over which the latter may have no control. Let us suppose, as we have already, that the historian does not appear simply in the role of one citizen propounding to others a version of history other than that they accept and find familiar. The historians are plural and they are professional. They have organized themselves into a guild or academy, in which they constantly retell and reinterpret histories including those that citizens and state employ to authenticate themselves. Their dedication is to the proposition that stories can always be retold and reinterpreted, that there are always new contexts in which they can be situated, and new meanings they can acquire, that each new meaning is a potential criticism of some other, and that there is a similar diversity of value-judgments that may be implied or pronounced. They are carrying to extremes the requirement that the state be a liberal state, that is, one capable of operating on the assumption that all its institutions and values shall be contestable, contextualizable, and interpretable in more than one way. In order to continue a process of historization that appears to be ongoing and without any possible closure, they have created a specialized but still public space within the public space of the polity, in which they conduct a discussion of history couched in a highly professional language, one made up of the second-order terms in which a language conducts discussion of itself; one esoteric not in the sense that it is kept secret, but in the sense that in order to speak it you must learn it well enough to qualify as a member of the guild. This space is the academy. Its inhabitants – who are not of course exclusively historians – require of the polity that it be considered both free and privileged to speak in its own ways, but at the same time continue to regard it as public. The historians discuss matters of public concern, and consider their debate part of the debate among citizens. They assume – often without very close examination – that there will be communication of some kind between their specialized academic speech and the speech in which the citizens seek to maintain their understanding of history, so that any changes in that understanding that the historians may advocate will trickle down to the citizens sooner or later, having been translated into the language that the latter find appropriate for their concerns. But their commitment is not solely to the proposition that a self-determining society shall be capable of rewriting its history at need; it is also to the proposition that no matter how the society chooses to tell or retell its history, there will always be some other way of telling it. They have enlarged the liberal proposition that no decision be considered final into the Socratic proposition that anything may be subjected to question and that any question may expect an answer. They do this as historians, not as philosophers, but they have joined the philosophers in establishing the academy: that space in which anything may be questioned and the language spoken is a second-order speech in which the questions may themselves be questioned, but is assumed to be open on all sides to two-way communication with the space in which the citizens use language in their own way. We have returned to the problem of the academy and the character of its speech, a problem posed at the beginning of Greek political philosophy and again at the beginning of German; and I suggest that many of our discussions may have to do with the political preconditions that must be met before the Socratic proposition can hold good.

The received histories that a polity may decide to regard as authoritative at a given moment – 'four score and seven years ago', or however they may begin – have in the last analysis to do with autonomy. Not only do they assure the citizen that his autonomy and that of his polity are established and legitimate; they give effect to that autonomy, in the act of determining what past history the polity shall deem itself to have had. Why should we consider this slightly ridiculous? If it is the mark of an autonomous or sovereign polity that it can determine, or have a voice in determining, what is to be its future, it is no less necessary that it be free to determine its past. Out of the multiple choices that must be made in constructing a history, it is both reasonable and necessary that a society or an individual be free to situate the self in a certain history, to declare where one thinks one has come from in the act of declaring where one is going. Choices of this kind may be incoherent or even immoral, and it is important to be able to say so; and there is the question of the authority exerted in making such statements. In New Zealand, a certain narrative of a historical event in the past has just been enacted by a parliamentary statute, and one must ask just what is the force and binding power of such a statement. But if we regard all public determination of history as tending to be absurd, it is because we are situating ourselves in the academy first and the polity second; and it may further be because we have mistakenly moved from considering all decisions criticizable to regarding all attempts at autonomy as absurd. The world we live in encourages us to make this move, for reasons not as conducive to the liberty of thought as we may suppose.

I am saying that the citizen is concerned, and has a stake, in what happens when he finds historians rewriting his history for him. If his history is part of his autonomy, such a rewriting entails some reconstruction of his autonomy, and he is entitled to ask whether this is being done to, for, or by him. If he finds his discursive world being reconstructed by forms of discourse to which he does not have access, his situation is analogous to that of those whom we call subaltern, as finding themselves included in worlds to whose discourse they have no access at all; but it is not identical with theirs, for the obvious reasons that (a) the academy exercises no manner of state power or coercive authority, and (b) there is a world of political language that the citizens share with the academy, but within which the academy has erected itself as discoursing in a second-order language or metalanguage so far specialized that the citizen must learn it, and to that extent join the academy, before taking part in a conversation that may have consequences for him. There are public spaces in which the two languages meet, and here they may collide; the citizen, feeling that the language of the academy is being intruded upon him, may try in response to intrude his language on that of the academy.

There have been recent cases of this order, some of which raise the interesting question of how the discursive spaces, or theatres, in which these language collisions take place are constituted when the subject-matter of public discourse is history. It may be said that the citizen is not much disturbed when authenticated history is reconstructed by someone writing a book; is it the case that the medium of print creates a public space that is easier to join or leave alone, so that the citizen is less likely to feel threatened by a discourse in which he has no part? In United States culture it has recently been exhibitions and monuments that have been involved in collisions; does this mean that the installation or visible arrangement of real and symbolic objects creates a form of space in which the citizen feels more directly situated, and so exposed or threatened, and in which it is harder to establish a dialogue that comforts him by the existence of its rules? Such spaces, moreover, are – more obviously than those created by print – maintained at the public expense, and there arises a question including but exceeding that of freedom of expression: whether the citizen or the state is required to subsidize a discourse in which some of the participants claim freedom to disregard the practical consequences of what they may say for others. We find a politics of space, a politics of medium, a politics of maintenance; and behind them, what looks like the historian's variation upon the politics of philosophy and practice, with which we are already familiar. Like the philosophers, the historians have set up an academy, in which they may discuss the histories of their society without any limits other than those imposed by the rules of their discourse, retelling, reinterpreting and recontextualizing them without any limits for which they will answer to any but those obeying the rules of the academy. Yet they do not deny that their speech is public, or that it has consequences in the world of political practice; on the contrary, the politics of discourse within the academy, the politics arising from its second-order speech or metalanguage, are intensively predicated on the practical consequences of historical interpretation, some of which are such that only historians perceive them. It would be easier for all if the historians could say, with Michael Oakeshott, that historiography is a purely contemplative or aesthetic discourse that can or should have no practical consequences whatever. But there seems to be a practical world, which the historians do not even desire to escape, since much of the subject-matter of their discourse is public property, which concerns others, and in which others – in this case the other political beings – are affected by discourse and have a claim to speak. It would also be easier if the citizens could dismiss historical discourse – as they can always, but never quite successfully, dismiss it – as conducted in a language or a universe that deprived it of practical significance. It is conceivable that recent debates could lead history in America to being treated as Americans treat religion: to being publicly guaranteed its freedom so long as it is not expressed or debated in spaces so public that the polity is responsible for their maintenance. This solution to the problem of religion, however, is based on the Enlightenment assumption that the state does not have to generate a religion, or a sacred dimension of its own existence. Whether it can escape generating a history, or secular dimension of its existence, seems less certain; the problem is one for post-modernists to confront.

* * *

There are then extensive fields in which to discuss the politics of historiography in established and functioning political societies, supposed to have generated authorized and authenticating histories, to have rendered them discussable within parameters compatible with the polity's continued functioning, and to have generated an academy in which they may be discussed without direct regard to political practice. I could clearly have spent very much more, indeed all, of my time analysing ways in which such societies (usually but not always states) have generated histories (both narratives and larger orderings of the historical universe) and invested them with political significance; and ways in which the discussion, contestation and interpretation of these histories, increasingly by those termed in some special sense historians, have generated discourse perceived as being of both political and philosophical significance. I chose, however, to lay emphasis on the relations between citizen and historian as separated beings, because it afforded a bridge to the second part of my paper, which attempts to look at the politics that arise when a history is affirmed, or claimed, or demanded and constructed by those who declare that they have not been members, either fully or at all, of the polity that has generated the history by which they are confronted. What will be the history such voices construct? Will it be a political history, or the history of an anti-politics? What will be the politics of confronting it with the history so far maintained by a political society, and with the political society that has maintained that history? In pursuing these matters, we may find ourselves disposed at times both to employ the feminine pronoun, and to take up the historiography of multiple and post-colonial cultures.

We have been supposing a society whose inhabitants possess, in some degree of commonality, a set of political institutions and practices that generate histories. They will also possess a shared culture of some kind compatible with their politics; and the moment has come to say what should have been obvious all along, that their authenticating histories will relate their culture as well as their politics. It may also be worth repeating that their history may be one of contestation between alternative political forms and competing cultural groups supporting these alternatives, and that the politics it narrates may be the story of how those contests have been managed; histories generated by the ruling structure may be dialogic as well as monolingual. Let us now suppose the discursive world to be entered and challenged by persons who affirm that they and those for whom they speak have been excluded from the political structure on grounds including the cultural; the usual triad of religion, race and gender will do as a first definition. We now ask: what kind of history may we expect such persons to construct? What will be the politics of constructing it, in particular the politics of its relations with the historiography of the politics from which its constructors have been excluded? They have had no politics, at least in the sense in which we have been using the word; what kind of history will they construct in the attempt to acquire one?

Prima facie, it might seem that, having no history, they will proceed without one, on the basis of some claim to pure right, pure will or pure identity.

But such claims are hard to construct without alleging some history – even Sieyès's Third Estate, which was nothing and might be everything, was said to be driving out the descendants of the conquering Franks – and the more our insurgent group is conscious of an identity, the more likely it is to furnish itself with a past and use history as a means to authority in the present. Much will now depend on its programme with respect to the political structure from which it has been excluded; does it seek to join that structure, to modify it, to destroy it, to replace it? At one end of the spectrum it is content to re-narrate the existing historiography; at the other to subvert and delete it; but to the extent that the insurgent group has been excluded from politics, it has no political history to narrate except that of the politics of its exclusion, and must look elsewhere for the materials of a history that will authenticate it. The next question to ask is whether and to what extent the group excluded from the political structure and its history has also been excluded from the culture that accompanies the politics. In the case of gender, it is easy to imagine that women display a high level of participation in the culture that confines their role within it, though we must pay attention to those who contend that they have maintained an autonomous culture alongside it. I mention the case because it dramatizes the alternatives we have to consider. The more the politically excluded share the culture of those who have excluded them – let us now propose – the likelier it is that they will adopt a strategy of shifting the focus of historiography from the political to the social or the cultural, finding in the extrapolitical the basis both of a history that authenticates their existence and of a claim to admission into the political structure on revised or reversed cultural grounds.

This move from political to cultural or social history is one of the older tactics in the politics of modern historiography. It may be said to recur every time there is a call for a 'new history', as happens about every thirty years and is traceable back to 1751, when Voltaire declared that the history of monarchy was worth studying only in so far – which was in fact very far indeed – as it formed part of the history of *les mœurs et l'esprit des nations,* and d'Alembert went further in declaring that the only histories worth studying were those of kings, most of whose actions were destructive, and those of *les gens de lettres,* who did most to preserve what was constructive.[2] Just who they were, and what d'Alembert intended by thus privileging them, need not detain us; the point is that this outward movement, this broadening

[2] Voltaire, introduction to the *Siècle de Louis XIV* (1751) and the *Essai sur l'Histoire Générale* (1756); d'Alembert, *Discours Préliminaire à l'Encyclopédie* (1751).

of the field from the history of state to the history of society, has often been the work of historians challenging the political structure in order to broaden its membership, though it has just as often been the work of those strengthening the political structure by connecting it with the culture and society it maintains and governs. The dichotomy continues to this day; I expect we all have colleagues who hold that political history is politically incorrect, and that everything that is not 'cultural history' (the buzzword of the moment) is 'traditional history' and therefore to be discouraged. If we have, I know what we reply to them.

At this point it may be desirable to introduce the concept of alienation. There is an impressive body of literature explaining that we write history not because it authenticates us but because we are alienated from and by it; that the very act of writing, thinking or living history alienates us from the past and from our former selves. This is the consequence of the process of historiography as we have been describing it: the discovery that the past can be interpreted in many ways besides those that make it relevant to the present, including those that may have made it relevant to itself. This is the point at which we discover *The Death of the Past* and that *The Past is a Foreign Country*[3] or Oakeshott's dictum that to study the past for practical purposes is to engage in necromancy.[4] The politics of a historiography viewed as self-alienation very easily becomes a politics of self, and there were many strange and disastrous consequences of this development. But in my present attempt to establish a fairly simple politics of historiography as a relation between selves, it is sufficient to point out that a history written out of exclusion from the political entails to that extent a historiography of alienation. How is one to write the history of an activity from which one was excluded, in which one was subject or subaltern but not actor? How is one to write oneself into a history that is that of the diminution or alienation of one's self by exclusion from action? One solution, as we have seen, is to discover or invent an activity possessing a history other than that of politics, in which one has been an actor and which forms a context for the activity of politics, conditioning the latter's nature. This activity may be culture; if we have not been Romans we may have been Greeks. But this does not quite do away with the problem that the activity of politics has already narrated its own history, and that as historian one has to face the question of how to narrate it. One may have recourse to a kind of

[3] J. H. Plumb, *The Death of the Past* (Harmondsworth: Penguin, 1969); David Lowenthal, *The Past Is a Foreign Country* (Cambridge: Cambridge University Press, 1985).

[4] Michael Oakeshott, 'The Activity of Being an Historian', in *Rationalism in Politics and Other Essays* (London: Methuen, 1955), pp. 137–57.

counter-history, in which one narrates the action as it looks when one was excluded from it and it was done to rather than by one; or narrates those actions to which one was a party as defined by one's exclusion from the full selfhood of politics; or narrates the actions of the political masters as if they were qualified at all times by the act of excluding one from them. One has moved into writing history as the narrative of a master–slave relationship, and it is a tempting strategy for the not-altogether-emancipated slave to perpetuate that relationship in writing, so as to deny the master the chance of emancipating himself from it. (All my life I have been listening to the charge that liberals are fascists in disguise.) But the flaw in this strategy is that the author remains self-cast in the role of slave; those who are forever emancipating themselves will never be free.

If the masters are to recognize that the slaves made themselves a world in which they were not altogether slaves, the slaves must perform a reciprocal recognition for the masters. (It was after all easy for the masters to be free and equal with one another; freedom was what slavery was for.) Historians who narrate a history from which they are excluded with no intent but to subvert it will necessarily deny it autonomy; whereas historians constantly retelling the story will know both that the slaves were not only slaves and that the masters were not only masters – that they possess a history not all of which the slaves may condemn. The diversity of history helps to legitimize it; but here we risk discovering that the genocides were not only genocides. To contextualize may be to palliate, even to legitimize; we are on treacherous ground, where the historian may be a danger to all parties. Meanwhile, the polarization into masters and slaves has disrupted the culture that we were supposing those excluded from the political structure shared with those included in it; Caliban is at the point of telling Prospero that his consciousness is a false consciousness because it can only be the consciousness of a master. This charge may be true or itself false; Prospero will seek to narrate his history in reply to it.

Let us turn back from this extreme to the case of one excluded from politics who affirms membership of a cultural group of the kind we call ethnic, and can claim that it possesses a history that can be narrated. This actor – who may be placed in a post-colonial situation – may be talking self-authentication, self-alienation, or some mixture of the two. That is: one may affirm that one still possesses one's culture, that it has a present and lays claim to a future, and that it possesses a past from which one derives authority for acts and speeches in the present; or one may affirm that all this once existed but has been destroyed, that one's condition is anomic, and that one has no choice but to subvert the existing structure through the violence that arises from one's lack of a civic personality, until – somehow – political and cultural personality is restored to one. Caliban imposes on Prospero the information that he can only curse until he finds a new language. The role and even the meaning of 'history' will clearly be very different at these two extremes, and there will be many intermediate conditions.

We shall be discussing two of the positions along this spectrum: first, that occupied by the kind of people we term 'indigenous', who can claim to recollect a pre-colonial identity and culture, and to reconstruct its history under post-colonial and indeed post-modern conditions; second, that occupied by a people whose past is entirely circumscribed by enslavement and transplantation, and whose history must consequently be written in quite a different way. The former typically operate by claiming to be indigenous, autochthonous, in Maori *tangata whenua*: people possessing a relation to the land that antedates European colonial settlement and was not established by the mechanisms of appropriation fundamental to the European sense of property, polity, economy and history as established in the early-modern classics. From this relationship and its narrative – very often both established and expressed in terms rather poetic than prosaic – they derive an authority, a legitimacy, a history, and a claim to what they challengingly call sovereignty, initially incommensurate with those expressed by Europeans, in particular with European settlers. These, however, claim to have been living in the land and occupying it in their own way – which includes but is not limited to the expropriation of the indigenous people – with the result that there is established an adjudication, and very possibly a treaty relationship, between the two, whose politics become the politics of bicultural relation.[5] It is now found that two histories are being written, of which each authenticates a different set of actions in the past and present and between which negotiation must take place if there is to be negotiation in the present; but that each authenticates a different set of legitimacies, so that the negotiation must be between two different perceptions of what negotiation is – since histories authenticate politics, different histories may authenticate different politics. It further appears that the negotiating peoples, who have been interacting since their first encounter, have been living in a minimum of two histories, even in two perceptions of what history is and what it means to live in it; and that actions in the past, which one owns

[5] Hugh Kawharu, *Waitangi: Maori and Pakeha Perspectives on the Treaty of Waitangi* (Auckland: Oxford University Press, 1989); Andrew Sharp, *Justice and the Maori: Maori claims in New Zealand political argument* (Auckland: Auckland University Press, 1990); Paul McHugh, *The Maori Magna Carta: New Zealand and the Treaty of Waitangi* (Auckland: Oxford University Press, 1991); Andrew Sharp and Paul McHugh (eds.), *Histories, Power and Loss* (Wellington: Bridget Williams Books, 2001).

as one's own and performed in one's own history, have been performed at the same time in another's history and must be interpreted as that history offers means of interpretation. It may very well be that the colonized know this already and the colonizers still have to learn it.

Problems now arise that go beyond the simple problems of double-standard judgment. These may be severe enough. It is an obvious strategy, and by no means an unreasonable one, for the colonized to declare that history as they perceive and have suffered it invalidates history as the colonizers have perceived it: that the latter is based on bad faith and has no meaning beyond its use for their expropriation. The colonizers may reply that they are being told that they have no history and consequently no culture of their own; but that there is more to their history than their expropriation of the colonized, which they are now prepared to admit only to be told that they have no moral foothold from which even to admit it. It may further be the case that the culture of the colonizers is a guilt culture, well equipped to condemn itself; and that the historians of this culture, being among its intellectuals, carry their function of rewriting its history so far as to delegitimize it altogether. In declining – of course quite rightly – to delegitimize the culture of the colonized, they may go so far as to represent it as guiltless, and even without the capacity for guilt and self-condemnation. This propensity may be traced, in the history of our culture, as far back as Rousseau and Diderot and the opposition between history and innocence. It raises the problem that to ascribe all guilt to ourselves and all innocence to the others is not to establish an equality between the two; yet how is this to be done?

We have to consider the politics of histories in encounter. In an important work, recently published, Judith Binney has shown Te Kooti Arikirangi, a Maori prophet and warleader of the nineteenth century, singing into existence as he enacted it a prophetic history in which he and his followers thenceforth acted, and in which the actions of others, both Maori and pakeha, have to be understood if we are to know how they appeared to others though not to themselves.[6] Binney, who is herself pakeha, has consulted the elders of the Ringatu church Te Kooti founded to ensure that her representation of their history is authentic to them; they are not unanimous about that history themselves. It is a remarkable achievement; yet it gives rise to the thought that Te Kooti was not the only prophet re-creating Maori in histories of their own, and that others – pakeha as well as Maori – created histories in which Te Kooti, like any other, must be interpreted in scenarios

[6] Judith Binney, *Redemption Songs; a life of Te Kooti Arikirangi Te Turuki* (Auckland: Auckland University Press with Bridget Williams Books, 1995).

not of his own making. What is to be the society, the conversation, among such a multiplicity of histories? To take an illustration from another recent work of importance, let us consider the crew of shape-changing mythical beings who occupy the Haida ship on the cover of James Tully's book on the constitutionalism of multicultural situations.[7] Each of these has a myth to recount, a song to sing, and there is a priestly figure who hears all the songs together. But we must suppose that they desire to debate as well as to sing, to require one another to see themselves in one another's histories; that there is more to this than singing one's song and reciting one's genealogy, since one must criticize one's song and hear it as others hear it, as well as singing it. This relation between histories in encounter has political prerequisites, and at this point the till recently colonized will certainly tell the till recently colonizers that these prerequisites have not been met yet. Cases have occurred in which 'indigenous' students in 'multicultural' universities have demanded the establishment of courses in their culture in which they will determine who gets to be admitted to the class and how much of the content of the course may be disclosed outside the classroom. Universities have rightly replied that esoteric learning must be conducted off campus, since the university operates on the Socratic premise that anything may be questioned and any question may expect an answer. The indigenous have as rightly replied that the Socratic premise presupposes a political equality between questioner and answerer – that something is done to a culture when you ask questions about it – and that they are declaring that such an equality does not yet exist. When it does not, the difference between comprehension and appropriation becomes elusive and perhaps illusory. Judith Binney is scrupulous in refusing to interpret Ringatu history in pakeha terms; yet in rendering both Maori and pakeha historiography historically visible, she may be situating both in a history that up to now only pakeha historians have attempted to construct. Reciprocity and equality will not be achieved until a Maori historian appears who attempts a sympathetic understanding of pakeha historiography in the context of history as post-colonial Maori understand it. The politics of that situation are not easy to predict, and there can be no guarantee that it is going to happen. An Irish writer has remarked that you have to be fairly sure of yourself before you can afford self-doubt;[8] and we are in fact supposing that a decolonized people will reach a point where there appears in their culture the academy, the space occupied by

[7] James Tully, *Strange Multiplicity: constitutionalism in an age of diversity* (Cambridge: Cambridge University Press, 1995).

[8] Frank McGuinness, in *The Economist*, 10 February 1996, p. 83.

historians free to reinterpret their society's history, in the assurance that the society can and will endure the restatement of its history for purposes independent of authentication.

The appearance of the academy is guaranteed by neither politics nor history, and we cannot be too sure that it is a prerequisite of that noble dream of reciprocity (as it might be called) that we are imagining: that relationship in which two incommensurate cultures, of which one has hitherto dominated the other and driven it to alienation, become capable each of writing the other's history and situating its historiography in the context of history as the speaking culture constructs it. In theory, the political negotiation we have imagined – the negotiation of sovereignties and identities by means including the affirmation of histories by both parties – might be thought capable of generating this relationship by its own workings; and certainly the academy is not going to generate it, for the reason that its inhabitants are hitherto all on one side of the negotiation, and their capacity to interpret the indigenous culture as well as their own has hitherto been an aspect of the latter's power over and appropriation of the former. But for this reason in turn, the political negotiation is hitherto at an impasse; the indigenous culture, seeking sovereignty over and by means of its own history, is likely to be interested in the dominant culture's history only to delegitimize it – in which the intellectuals of the dominant culture are all too anxious to join – and is likely to make its own history a monologue in which others are not permitted to speak. Negotiation, notoriously, consists largely of a jockeying for power by repeated refusals to negotiate; in this case, refusal of dialogue of the kind we are imagining.

The academy, then, if present in this situation, cannot do much more than rectify its language, maintain the Socratic premise while trying not to falsify it by imposing it on others, and make itself useful by holding out the image of dialogue and reciprocity as we have depicted them. If we sustain the definition of the historian as one committed to the principle that there is always another way of telling the story, it is not too much to add a recognition that this requires a society of story-tellers – who must however share the historian's premise that there are ways other than their own – and that no one voice or chorus is going to speak for all of them. The historian thus defined is not going to be unduly alarmed by the prospect of the academy's becoming an intercultural dialogue of interpretation; it will have to be a dialogue, not a collision of monologues, but the academy is defined as dialogue. The difficulties are intimidating because they are metacultural and metahistorical; the academy has been invaded by those alienated from their own historical speech, and any one of the positions from which the historian may attempt to empathize with the construction of history by others may be pervaded by a perception of history that one ought not to be imposing on those others. But the historian as defined is not unaccustomed to evaluating one's own position; one knows the hermeneutic cycle fairly well from the inside; one never did share the noble dream of objectivity;[9] and one's purpose is not to be a philosopher-king, but to take part in the intelligent dialogues that may be instituted inside the cave. I return to that starting point of historiography among the sophists and the rhetors, who understood paradiastole and had no wish to abandon it.

Let me then conclude with the politics of history considered as politics of the academy, that erratically self-steering fifth wheel on the political hearse. I have defined the historian as one committed to the proposition that there is always something more to be said about the past, conceived as the subject of an open-ended discourse. To maintain this commitment one need entertain neither a noble dream of objectivity nor a solipsistic vision in which interpretation has no limits; the historian is also committed to the proposition that others beside oneself have in fact existed, and is anxious to draw as close to objectivity as the nature of one's subject permits, by setting up and observing canons of criticism and falsification made as tight as they can be. One may justify one's pursuit by alleging values that are aesthetic: the delight and instruction to be derived from multiplying one's interpretations of a historical occurrence, and knowing that there will always be more interpretations that can be constructed and vindicated. 'The one duty that we owe to history', Oscar Wilde apparently said, 'is to rewrite it.' Wilde was an aesthete, but he did say it was a duty. The historian – far from alone in this – offers this delight and duty to one's fellow-citizens in the open society. But one does not escape politics; one only diversifies them. Any reinterpretation the historian offers will have political consequences and effects, which one may or may not intend; the premises from which one offers it will be informed by all manner of political implications, of which one may or may not be aware. Speaking from within the cave, the historian tries to be as conscious of one's assumptions and intentions as one can be, and aims or should aim to attend to inputs of all kinds, received from fellow-historians, fellow-citizens, and often resentful subalterns and strangers.

There are kinds of histories constructed to authenticate, to legitimize, to subvert, and otherwise to perform upon one's fellow-beings. There are no

[9] Peter Novick, *That Noble Dream: the 'objectivity question' and the American historical profession* (Cambridge: Cambridge University Press, 1988).

historical statements that may not have effects of this kind, including those that the historian may make without any thought of producing such effects. In a universe of practice, even the statement 'This statement has no practical consequences' is self-falsifying; there will be practical consequences if one says that. The historian, however, does intend to make statements that have unintended consequences, and that situate practice in the unintended and unpredicted universe of history, where there is always 'more in this than meets the eye'.[10] The purpose of making them is more than prudential; more even than that of supplying the practitioner with irrelevant information, in order to remind him of the limited relevance of what he is doing himself. It is to make statements that are not merely practical, though they never cease to be such; and to consider the aesthetic and perhaps philosophical, and the political as well as the practical, consequences of making them in historical and political conditions.

[10] I adopt this phrase as a key to historical study from the late David Joslin of St John's College, Cambridge.

CHAPTER 12

The politics of history: the subaltern and the subversive

There is a kind of history, of great though not exclusive significance, which is the creation of a political society that is autonomous, in the sense that it takes decisions and performs actions with the intention and effect of determining its character and the conditions under which it exists. That history is both the record of those decisions and actions (here the society both makes its history and narrates it) and the narrative and myth of how the society is said to have come into being and acquired the capacity for autonomy in the same sense just stated. Together, they form what I shall term the 'constructed history' of the society. This construct will, of course, be the work of the dominant members of the society. But in so far as some of them are the equals of others, it will record contests and come itself to be contested between the antagonist equals. And it is possible that it will record the resolution of these contests and come to be the narrative of a state of affairs in which equals rule and are ruled by one another.

At some point or points in the construction of this history, there appear historians who, whether as functionaries or volunteers, are specialists in narrating its component narratives or the master-narrative they compound. Whether in consequence of the character of narrative itself or of the political conditions under which narrative goes on, these specialists discover that narrative is an open-ended activity. A narrative can always be re-narrated by modifying its assumptions or its values, the systems of authority or the contexts of reference in which it is situated, and there appears to be no theoretical limit to this constant modification and re-narration. This does not set the historians free. As functionaries or as citizens, they are constantly drawn back into the construction of the history that expresses

[Published in *The Journal of Political Philosophy*, 6.3 (1998), pp. 219–34. Earlier versions had been presented to seminars at the Australian National University and as the third of a set of lectures given as Sir Isaiah Berlin Visiting Professor, Oxford University, Michaelmas Term 1997.]

and legitimates the being of the society; as advocates and as partisans, they are as constantly drawn into the contestations and factions among the citizens, which are pursued by means that include the writing of histories from this standpoint or from that. The historians, nevertheless, retain the freedom which specialists derive from the surplus of energy they invest in their function. They are always liable to find that they have written more, or other, than their function required of them, and perhaps it is in the nature of narrative, or of the multiplicity of contexts in which it goes on, that this should be the case.

But they find themselves, as a rule not unwillingly, involved[1] in a duality and complexity of function. They may be unruly members, but still they are members, of the society and culture within which they write, and whose history they are as a rule in some sense writing. Nor is that society's capacity to absorb and reinvent its history to be discounted or underrated, even under the conditions obtaining at the end of the twentieth century. The historians may re-narrate the story of the society's dissensions and decisions, even of the piecemeal growth of its capacity to endure dissensions and take decisions, as a narrative far more contested and contestable than their fellow-citizens find agreeable. They may show the society to have existed in a world larger than itself, far more complex and disorderly than it has ever managed to control. And yet, in so far as that society is a sophisticated and supple one, able to bear shocks and recognize its own limitations, their narrative will become part of the history of that capacity and will even reinforce the capacity itself.

The toughness of societies which are in this sense 'political' is not to be underrated, and for this reason the centripetal power of political histories is very strong. To diversify the narrative is to strengthen the narrative; to diversify the society is to strengthen the society; and for these reasons every history of the politics of a society tends to become and remain the history of the groups and individuals composing that society, of the relations between them that constitute the internal structure of its politics, and of the contexts and situations these politics have brought together. The more the narrative is designed to represent this structure as complicated and precarious, the more it will become the history of the circumstances by which it was beset. The history of a political society has an almost irresistible bent towards becoming the history of its own autonomy, and towards reabsorbing the

[1] Only some would call it 'entrapped'.

histories, and the historians, who re-narrate and diversify a history designed to control diversity itself.[2]

It follows that every political society tends to maintain and recount what may be termed an autocentric history, a history of itself so far as it has succeeded in maintaining itself. (There are even histories, like Machiavelli's of Florence or Pietro Giannone's of Naples, which are histories of selves which have persistently failed to maintain this autonomy, and yet have persisted in the very act of failure.) Autocentric history cannot be said to be illegitimate, but it is open to the reproach that others will appear in the narrative only as alien beings who act and suffer in the history of the central self. Can there be a political genesis of a heterocentric history, in which others will appear as constructing and narrating, erecting and criticizing histories of their own and of themselves? Can we write the histories of others than ourselves?

For this inquiry we need an elementary heterology (to use the name of a science carried to meta-existential lengths in a literature I have not read). It is the study of the creation and subsequent behaviour of Others (to use a term which has unfortunately become a buzzword, held menacingly over our heads as a means of displacing our existence). Nevertheless, our world is full of those who are not ourselves and with whom we may or may not share membership; and we need means of studying how we think of them, what this does to them and what they may do in response. Here I shall limit myself to categorizing those others who do not form part of 'our' society and its history, and it seems at first sight that these may be subdivided in two distinct yet overlapping ways. First, either they may exist outside our society, yet constantly subject to its attention; or they may exist within it, yet be denied full membership in the society that calls itself 'we'. Second, at an ideal point at which the analysis begins, either they may possess already-formed histories of their own, or they may not. These distinctions are not clear-cut. There are enormous grey areas between their positive and negative poles. Yet I shall make use of them in moving towards the situation I most desire to explore, that in which 'we' who have a history are required to live at the same time in a history other than our own.

To begin, then, there may be an 'other' consisting of a people and society as sovereign as we ourselves and possessing a history as autonomous and interior as our own, yet the narrative may be so related as to reveal that

[2] Thus, the historian finds it a good deal easier to be a liberal than a dissident – for those who know the difference between the two.

both we and other have been shaped and made our respective selves by our constant interactions. This might be termed the West European situation, as it was through the first half of the twentieth century; there existed a British history, a French history, a German history, and others, each consisting of an *Innenpolitik* which was a history of self-formation and an *Aussenpolitik* which was a history of relations with others.

Neither writing nor conducting such a plurality of histories proved to be an easy matter. The practical experience of living it has in fact been one of enormous catastrophes. There has therefore arisen a demand for a new kind of history, not located in competing sovereignties. In these new histories the formation of selves shall be shown to have been more contingent, interactive and incomplete (and the self's sovereignty over its own formation less so) than used to be considered the case when history was held to consist of the self-formation of states and an academy of professional historians was held capable of narrating it with neutrality and objectivity.

When 'we,' then, are faced with an equally sovereign 'other', the choice seems to lie between narrating a history of histories existing independently and in interaction – probably through the classical relations of war, treaty and commerce – and constructing (if that is the right word) a new kind of history in which the sovereignty of selves, and therefore their independent existence, shall be broken down and replaced (by what is not yet clear). If we find that a history of state formation and self-formation has nevertheless occurred, we may find ourselves reiterating its narrative, but now as that of a Bad instead of a Good Thing.

Let us consider another range of cases, which might be said to constitute the British as distinct from the European situation. Here there exists the history of an association, confederation or union of states, which may or may not have produced a 'we' who consider its history 'ours'. Within this coalescence of selves and their histories, let us suppose one society and its history which has exercised hegemony over others to the point where it identifies its history with that of the whole – saying 'British' but meaning 'English', in short – but cannot find ways of merging that history with that of the larger association. Let us suppose another society, whose participation in the larger association has been to a considerable degree voluntary but has left it dissatisfied, on the grounds among others that its history has not been and perhaps cannot be narrated as independently shaping the history of the association. And let us suppose a third, whose participation may convincingly be represented as involuntary and enforced and whose history may be related as that of a series of more or less successful attempts to break away from it. Clearly, I have been depicting, in more or less idealized form, the English, Scottish, and Irish cases within the contest of what is currently termed 'British history', and is written both as the history of association and separation between these entities and as the history of any entity which may have been formed as a result of the former history. This history is complex and interesting,[3] because it entails the partial realization and partial interaction of histories rendered autonomous by the existence of institutions of self-government. Each component entity desires to narrate its own history, as formed internally by the interactions among its members: the English, at one extreme, because they have believed to the point of excess in their own historic autonomy; the Irish, at another, because they have not finished struggling to affirm it (war and treaty have been going on over the frontiers of the self there to be determined). All three put up stubborn resistance to any attempt to re-narrate their several histories in a pluralized narrative in which they shall appear to have been formed, not by their self-affirming actions alone, but by the actions and interactions by which they have shaped one another. The need for such a narrative is obvious, since we are at a point where British and Irish history cannot be understood or continued unless in terms of their interactions; yet, on the other hand, histories of self-formation must continue to be written alongside these histories of heteronomy. We begin to appreciate the complexity of living both in one's own history and in that of another, a complexity whose dangers cannot be dismissed by airy proposals for the abolition of the self.

Let us resume our heterology. The Irish case may be considered in two ways, between which there is a vigorous contestation: as that of an independent nation with its history, discontented with its former subordination to another nation and history; or that of a predicament in the full sense 'colonial' or 'post-colonial',[4] where identity has been imposed by alien domination and by the struggle to escape imposed identity, to the point where one is as unsure who one is as Captain Macmorris in Shakespeare.[5] The colonial or 'subaltern' identity may then be considered as the next in order of those formed and existing outside the sovereign identity which narrates the primary history. But the problem of self-identification provides an equally valid reason for considering it along with those others who are formed by inclusion within the sovereign order but exclusion from its politics and its history.

[3] [For further inquiries into its character, see J. G. A. Pocock, *The Discovery of Islands: essays in British history* (Cambridge University Press, 2005).]

[4] I do not necessarily vouch for the clarity of either of these terms.

[5] William Shakespeare, *Henry V*, III, ii.

Let us therefore consider the cases of those excluded from the political order on economic, or ethnic, or gender grounds – slaves, barbarians and women, for example, as they appear in the writings of Aristotle – and ask concerning them the questions peculiar to the present inquiry. Will they have histories, and if so of what kind will these be? Will they construct histories for themselves, and if so of what kind, in the act of claiming voice for themselves within, outside or against the political order? What impact will their speech and actions have on the internal relations between citizens constituting that order, and on the history which the latter construct and narrate of themselves? With what choices and challenges will the historian, whose business we have said is to re-narrate narratives and constructions, be faced by the multiplication of narratives and kinds of narrative that may now arise? In what history or histories will the post-colonial individual find himself or herself – gender has now become central – obliged to live?

We suppose that this 'they', or these Others, have not been included in political life and cannot therefore narrate its history as 'theirs', that is, as one which they have made or in which they feel involvement. It is now possible that there is either some kind of history or some social activity other than the political, which they can recover, reconstruct or invent (at this stage in the analysis it need not matter which) and narrate. We are presuming, however, that the political narrative from which 'they' have been excluded is in a strongly hegemonic position, so that they must contend with its power to exclude, marginalize, silence or otherwise subordinate them. The relation between it and any history they may construct of and for themselves will therefore be, or include, a contest for power. We suppose them appealing from the history of the political to that of some other activity conducted elsewhere in the structures of society, and therefore to be termed 'social'.

This appeal – a strategy open not only to the excluded, but also to the dissatisfied within the included – from the political to the social is itself a political act. It is designed to empower those hitherto disempowered, to admit them to the political, and to change the structure and even the concept of the political in the course of doing so – which may mean, it should by now be evident, changing the concept of history as well. It is important to note, in parenthesis, that the strategy sometimes entails denying the separate or the central existence of the political, and that this is not without its effect on the exercise of power. When Hellenistic philosophy set about replacing the polis by the *ecumene*, many human energies were liberated, but the ability of free citizens to challenge the power of military rulers was diminished.

In the politics of historiography, then, we observe a turn from the political to the social, which has itself political intentions and effects. This turn may be the more effective if political history is in process of making itself – if, as in the case of Enlightenment historiography, the political narrative seeks to mitigate and reinforce itself by including, and at the same time contextualizing itself within, the narratives of social activities (in the Enlightenment case, manners and commerce) not previously deemed to form part of the political. This raises the possibility that new capacities and new groups may be accommodated, by means including historiography, within a politics capable of modifying itself to include them; we may call this the liberal possibility. The line between co-optation and competition, however, is a shadowy one, and those seeking to empower themselves may not wait to be co-opted.

There is a recurrent phenomenon calling itself the New History, which occurs at irregular intervals as a challenge to both political and narrative history. (The historians may encourage the latter challenge as well as the former, if their search for ever more precise contextualization has led them to break down the narrative into a succession of discontinuous moments.) It is a temptation to those excluded from the political narrative to deny the primacy of narrative as well as of politics, and to find the meaning of their historical existence by situating themselves in an infinite series of micro-narratives, micro-moments and micro-managements. The enlargement of the field of study from the political to the extrapolitical paradoxically enhances this tendency towards microscopy, because it vastly increases the variety of contexts in which micro-moments may be found. Whenever it appears, the New History offers to displace and replace political history in favour of history written on some other scale, the designation of which varies with the condition of the intellect and its culture. Not long ago, it was 'social history' to which everything was to be subordinated, but now the buzzword is 'cultural'.[6] The liberal historian, who believes that nothing human is alien to the historical narrative and that there is a politics of saying so, therefore welcomes such enlargements, until one finds that there is a contest for power going on and that the narratives and contexts one constructs have been targeted for proscription. At this point one is living in a politics of contested power, existing perhaps because those who have been

[6] In some universities you were till recently liable to be told that if you were not doing 'cultural' history you were doing 'traditional' history and were therefore condemned to the dustbin. Those who talked this nonsense were valued colleagues, doing valuable work. Given that the business of the historian is re-narration and the discovery of new contexts, the enlargement of the field towards the 'social' and the 'cultural' is greatly to be welcomed.

excluded from power wish to claim it for themselves and are unwilling to negotiate the terms of their admission to it: the politics, in Yeats's language, of the stone in the midst of all.[7]

The New History can be dated back to 1750, when Voltaire and d'Alembert, among others, proposed the abandonment of a neoclassical historiography in favour of one of *les mœurs* and *l'esprit humain*. In this case the group to be empowered was the *gens de lettres* or intelligentsia. An interesting response came from the young Edward Gibbon, who saw in d'Alembert's proposals the latest in a series of moves through which, since the beginnings of Western intellectual history, one or other of the faculties of the human mind had sought hegemony over all the others.[8] In d'Alembert's case, he thought, it was the mathematical. Gibbon hoped that this endless rotation of Fortune's wheel might be replaced by a *governo misto* of all the faculties engaged in the literary study of the culture inherited. But this liberal ideal is not easy to achieve, and it may be invidious even to praise it when the preconditions of its attainment are lacking. Gibbon and d'Alembert were both, even if variously discontented, members of the privileged elites of their culture. Gibbon came to share Burke's view that the self-assertion of the *gens de lettres* had done enormous harm in preparing the way for the cultural disaster of the French Revolution. But if there is truth in this, it indicates that the liberal solution, to which historians are predisposed, faces daunting obstacles in proportion as there are stones in the midst of all, who feel no obligation to pursue it. Burke expressed the belief – in itself Enlightened – that the human mind by itself is capable of rebelling against society and overthrowing it. We do not have to go so far in investigating the question of what happens to politics and history when there are those present who believe that they derive nothing from the historical order but the denial of their identity.

We need to consider such cases, if only because they furnish the two key words in the title of this article. 'Subaltern' is, I believe, a term derived from Gramsci, used to denote the culturally subordinate and, in particular, those having no identity except that which they can derive from the fact of their subordination. 'Subversion' is a strategy in which they and others may engage. We have been thinking of history as a means to the creation of identity. But it is possible that the Self cannot be created without the

7 W. B. Yeats, 'Easter 1916', 'Sixteen Men', and 'The Rose Tree', in W. B. Yeats, *Collected Poems* (London: Picador, 1990).

8 Edward Gibbon, *Essai sur l'Étude de la Littérature* (London, 1761). [J. G. A. Pocock, *Barbarism and Religion*, I: *The Enlightenments of Edward Gibbon* (Cambridge: Cambridge University Press, 1999), chs. 8–9.]

simultaneous invention of Others, whose history is that of the creation of the Self, but who have no part in it. Since this is an ideal type or pure case, it is hard even to imagine, and harder still to discover, as we travel in space or time, in unmitigated reality, though we shall find many cases of which it is close enough to being descriptive to make its employment urgently necessary. If the Other is not absolutely the creation of the Self, however, there may be a history of the Other which is not the history of the Self. Caliban, who complained that he had no language except that which Prospero had taught him, could nevertheless remember Sycorax, his mother, and speak of her;[9] and Sycorax, had she still been present, might well have addressed Prospero in terms more telling than any her son could lay his tongue to. It is hard to invent a human being, as Mary Shelley pointed out; especially hard so long as we inhabit a world of society and history, not like Frankenstein's of technology. There is a philosophy which takes off from the point that this can no longer be guaranteed.

So we the Selves invent Others, neglect to provide them with a history (as perhaps we cannot), and withhold from them the autonomies of speech and action which are necessary if they are to make histories for themselves. I am speaking from the point of view of a Self, and am therefore interested in emancipation rather than revolution; like not a few Others, I am pursuing the liberal solution. How is the Other to acquire a history and become my equal? I would rather have equals about me than subalterns in a state of insurrection. Among the strategies of liberal society, what can be done with that capacity for re-narrating my history with which the historians have unsettled yet enriched my political being? Can it be exploited by the insurgent, so that the narrative with which she or he constructs an identity is also a retelling of my history, in which I can join while continuing to reconstruct my self? And can we arrive at a condition in which Self and Other retell each other's histories in the course of retelling their own? If we arrive at such a condition, will it constitute us a We, or only a You and I, the best we can aspire to after having been a Self and Other? These seem to be the questions to which we are directed by the current emphasis on a politics of difference.

Slaves, barbarians and women in antiquity; the class other, the ethnic other, and the gender other in what I had better call post-modernity (though in using that term I accept no obligation to explain what modernity was). Each of these others has had a history imposed upon it while being excluded from making it. And we imagine each trying to reconstruct history in the

[9] William Shakespeare, *The Tempest*, I, ii.

process of acquiring an identity from which to act in the making of history – but doing so, we had better remind ourselves, under global conditions which render it doubtful how far any of us will retain the ability to do that.

To review the predicament and assess the resources of each of these others in turn would for obvious reasons be too huge a task for a single article. All I shall attempt is a few theoretical propositions and distinctions. To begin with, it is either true or false that the Other has no history except that imposed by the dominant structure. In theory, even this is too simple, since if it were true the Other would have been absorbed into the self-governing history and would have ceased to be an Other. We are, rather, saying that the Other has no history except that of exclusion from the history of the dominant structure, no history other than the negation of the latter history. From this point dialectics arise. The subaltern (I use that term as defining the predicament just stated) may use total exclusion as the basis for a total negation of existing history, and hope to achieve total power over it, wiping the slate clean and beginning history again. What was the Third Estate, asked Sieyès? Nothing. What had it the capacity to be? Everything. What did it desire to be? Something. This formula rested, first, on the assumption that the history from which the Other had been excluded was about to exhaust itself and stop. In revolutionary situations this does appear to be what happens. It rested, second, on the assumption that there exists outside history a realm in which the Other can rediscover itself and discover in itself the true agency in the making of history; so that history begins where previous history ends. There are, it needs no repeating, assumptions which we no longer accept. We see in them the point at which the Fox is tempted to believe himself a Hedgehog. And when the Age of Revolutions (1789–1989) ended, it was evident that revolution itself had become the paradigm of a dominant history, and had exhausted its power to maintain itself by the invention and exclusion of Others.

We therefore abandon the hypothesis that the Other may have been excluded from history altogether and may discover outside history the means of rebirth: the noble dream of revolution. It seems to follow that we abandon the further hypothesis that the Other has no identity but the negation of the identity imposed by the ruler. Caliban was mistaken in claiming that all he could do with the language Prospero had taught him was to curse; that he was so far subaltern that he could attempt only the subversion of language by blasphemy, obscenity and transgression. He was not so far into the linguistic turn that he could not remember Sycorax and speak of her. And resurgent indigenous peoples, of whom we make him the type, are everywhere remembering Sycorax to considerable effect. Whether

Sycorax is a memory or an invention is not the immediate issue, though it becomes one once the pakeha ask the question. What matters to the *tangata whenua* in their search for a recovered autonomy is how they will remember Sycorax, or live with themselves as remembering or inventing her, once that autonomy has been to any degree recovered.

We say, then, that there is no realm outside history, none in which language may not find a subject-matter. The proposition that there is no subject-matter beyond language's capacity to invent one is of more metaphysical than practical interest. There is no zone of exclusion, it follows, in which the excluded may not be discovering and making some history of their own. To find an exception we must go to the death-camps, in which nobody lived long enough to continue or transmit any history initiated by their own actions. In transgenerational human societies, everybody dies, but they live long enough to conduct history. Even in the absurdist world of Samuel Beckett, it is going on. The assumption is that human language, and human social context, are rich and various enough to be of indefinite extension, so that it is not possible to control, define or negate the whole of it by any one act or combination of acts. Caliban is mistaken, therefore, if he says he can do nothing with language but curse. The statement is its own negation. What he (or she) may be saying is that the situation it describes is too close for comfort: that it is not true, but that one is entrapped in a situation which is as if it were true, with no way out. Caliban articulates this predicament by inserting blasphemy and obscenity in every word he utters; we know his voice quite well, and it is a question whether it is doing him or anyone else much good.

The Others are situated somewhere in society and its many histories, if outside the politics that determines its own history and identity. It follows that when some category of Others begin to feel that they have a Self and seek for a Self to affirm, they find that they have a history of some kind in addition to the negative history of exclusion from Self which they articulate in the person of Caliban. Perhaps there was a making of the English working class, or perhaps there was a world the slaves made, to use the language of two major romantic-Marxist historians of recent times[10] – heroic narratives in which a culture was created under the most adverse of conditions, and Caliban ceased to be the persona of a principal actor. Radical historians deny, when they can, the merely victim status of their protagonists, and though this confuses the liberal narrator, who finds himself damned if he

[10] Eugene D. Genovese, *Roll, Jordan, Roll: the world the slaves made* (New York: Pantheon Books, 1974). E. P. Thompson, *The Making of the English Working Class* (London: Gollancz, 1963).

denies victimhood and damned if he affirms it, the response is sound. The enormous condescension of posterity comes in many forms, and we have not finished with them yet. But in the depths of subaltern history may be discerned those who were never anything but victims, so utterly disregarded that they were not even Others and found what selfhood they had merely in suffering. It is a tragedy for the subaltern historian that these cannot be even retroactively empowered. How to write history for those who never had any? All the more important, one can only add, not to impute this status to those who made themselves worlds of some kind.

The ability of the subordinated or subjected to make and invent histories of their own is partly a matter of social space. Thompson's migrant workers and factory workers occupied, though they did not possess or control, fairly extensive spaces in which to create a culture of class; the slaves on Genovese's plantations found patches of space and time in which to make a world in some measure their own. A very different situation, perhaps the most universal and enigmatic of all, is that of the gender other, whom the separation of public from domestic space causes to be present, if just out of the sight of narrative and archive, at nearly every moment in the creation of the public history from which she is supposedly excluded. The history constructed by her on her behalf is very much a history on the other side of the looking glass, less a matter of the space she occupies than of how a doubly defined space looks to her, and may look to men when they catch sight of her looking in.

This formulation will not satisfy; but then, none should. Women are to be found at all levels of society from the powerful to the powerless, and sometimes occupy positions of power whether formal or informal. They are therefore in principle, if not always in practice, well placed to write histories of power viewed from unexpected angles, in addition to the strategies already considered, those of contextualizing the political and microtizing the narrative. Theirs is also, for the reasons just put forward, a history well placed to raise the question next to be considered; that of the politics to obtain between the political history which the rulers tell of themselves, and the anti-political history by the telling of which the ruled define themselves outside of politics, and at the same time enlarge, modify or subvert the political by claiming for themselves, thus defined, a voice within it. Is the new history simply an antithesis of the old, or is there more than this antagonism to both of them?

The world the slaves made interacted with the world the masters made, the latter oppressing the former, the former constantly reminding the latter of what it was and what it could not do and thus consciously rendering it insecure. Extensive plantation literature testifies to this. If histories come into being on each side – but slaves cannot create connected histories until they have advanced some distance in emancipation, and even then it is very difficult – they may continue the relationship of oppression and subversion. It remains necessary to imagine one history which is the negation and inversion of the other. At this point the relation of Self and Other has become what it was potentially, the relation of Master and Slave; and the process of emancipation may involve a complex game in which it is the Slave's strategy to deny the Master any opportunity to be other than a Master, or to escape from a relationship he may by now desire to give up, except on such terms as the Slave is willing to impose. The Slave will not accept emancipation at the Master's hands and constantly frustrates the latter's attempts to give it him. The Stone appears in the midst of all. Patrick Pearse insists on taking by violence what he might have had by negotiation, because otherwise he cannot believe that it is truly his; and any history the Stone may write will be one in which the former ruler can appear only in a purely diabolic role – a history in which there may be much truth but can be no exceptions.[11]

It is, I am taking for granted, the historian's function to insist that there are always exceptions. If this be true, the Master–Slave relation can never exist in absolute purity, and its violence and injustice consist in its constant thrust towards a purity it cannot attain. Thomas Jefferson once remarked that the trouble with being a slave-owner was that you could not behave decently in that role even if you wanted to: but then there must be a history of your wanting to, as well as of your not being able to. Such a history can be written from the slave-owner's point of view, if not actually by him. The history written by or for the slave will probably emphasize the bad faith of the slave-owner's position, to the point where even his best intentions will be presented as inauthentic. It seems possible to ask, however, whether or how often the Master is obsessed with his own role to the point where he cannot see himself outside it, and needs to be emancipated from this tunnel vision. The alternative is that he can see himself outside it, and needs to be told that he can only escape from it by giving it up.

There have been master castes so obsessed with their own mastery that they could think of nothing but their own slaves as Others. But against this we should set one of the more alarming insights of Niccolo Machiavelli, who points out that the rule over others of a free people is the hardest

[11] P. H. Pearse, *The Story of a Success: being a record of St Enda's College, September 1908 to Easter 1916*, ed. Desmond Ryan (London: Maunsel, 1917). William Irwin Thompson, *The Imagination of an Insurrection, Dublin, Easter, 1916: a study of an ideological movement* (New York: Oxford University Press, 1967).

to be endured, and the most difficult to escape, for the reason that the rulers are not imprisoned in it. In so far as they are free – it is a condition of their internal politics – they are satisfied by their equality with one another, and to that extent do not need their rule over others, which they keep as a matter of expediency only. They may be persuaded that it is expedient to give it up, but not that it is essential to their own being to do so; and when they emancipate their subjects, it may be for the ultimately insulting reason that they do not and never did care what might become of them.

Interesting historiographic situations now arise. Such a ruling free people will possess a history of itself as free; it will be an internal history, narrating the interactions between members of the society that make it a free political system, as well as of its attainment of sovereignty over itself that is no less necessary to its freedom. In either of these narratives, its rule over subject peoples, whose history is not the history of its freedom, will appear contingent and occasional rather than necessary. This is how the history of Britain has come to be the history of England, in which that of a non-entity called 'the Celtic Fringe' puts in an occasional and unnecessary appearance. But the internal history – the history in this case of England – is valid as far as it goes, and to that extent it will not be possible for the histories of the subject peoples, as they come to be constructed and written, to subvert and unmake it. It has been both enacted and written, and cannot be written out of the record. The ruling free people has to be persuaded that there is a history of its rule, which it may not know or want to know, as well as of its freedom, which it does know and wants to go on affirming. It is not necessary to persuade it, because it is not true, that the former history is the absolute subversion and negation of the latter; but what the relation between the two histories is remains to be debated, and the debate entails the self-constructed history of the ruled as well as the rulers.

We have moved away, however, from the simple geometry of Self and Other, Master and Slave, in which the Self cannot be without constructing and dominating an Other, and the inauthenticity of the latter compels the Self to subvert itself. In the world of history, we have begun saying – with the ironic support of Machiavelli – there is always more than one situation obtaining; and in consequence the Master–Slave relationship is constantly being approximated, but is never attained. The Master is always something else than a Master; does it follow that the slave is always something more than a Slave? If so, subversion is a political tactic, but not a condition of existence, and historiography has reassumed the liberal role. It has done so by means of its usual tactic of multiplying the contexts.

To the extent (which can be neither guaranteed nor eliminated) that there has been a world the slaves made or its equivalent, the excluded Others are also able and obliged to furnish themselves with a dual history. There will be the history of their subalternity, of how a false identity was imposed on them by their rulers and they went through the agonizing experience of recognizing its falsity and searching for some other identity that should not be false – impelled sometimes to assert its veracity by acts of existential homicide. But there will also be the history of whatever autonomy they found in making for themselves a world which was not merely the negation of the world imposed upon them. Since hegemony and domination have occurred in a great variety of historical contexts, these two kinds of history will appear in a great many shapes and combinations: here is another liberal implication of the view of history and historiography that I am putting forward. There are, then, two dual histories face to face with each other, and with themselves. On each side there is a history designed to affirm a self and a history that scrutinizes and re-narrates that self in its relation to an Other, or seen as itself Other. And there will be a politics interior to each of the dual histories, as well as a politics of the relations between the two.

I want now to consider this problematic in a particular context, that of 'post-colonial' politics, in which I shall suppose the presence of a free and formerly ruling people, with a history of its own, and of a people till recently subject to political and cultural domination, now asserting the autonomy necessary to resume, re-narrate and re-enact a history similarly its own. I have several reasons for choosing this theoretical situation. One is that it exhibits in a particular way the politics of history and sovereignty. Another is that it leads back, for historical reasons, to the historiography of Enlightenment, about which Isaiah Berlin has taken a number of positions. A third reason, partly contained within the first, is that it raises and may illuminate the question of debate between two histories and two views of history beyond Berlin's principle of the plurality of values.

There is then a self-conscious group – a group of which some are conscious and in which they feel membership – which has been enclosed within a ruling structure and its history, and for which there is now being claimed the autonomy to assert a past, present and future. That assertion, conversely, is a means of establishing the autonomy. There is the memory, whether constructed or transmitted, of a past before contact or colonization; and the form in which this past can be affirmed now, and affirmed to have existed then, varies with the character of the culture concerned. It may have been an ancient literate culture, in which there exist, or from which there have survived, documents in the form of narratives or archives relating a past – histories in the sense in which I have been developing the term, though how much these will resemble the histories employed by the ruling culture is another question. I am going to assume, as empirical reality encourages me to assume, that the ruling culture is European and that the establishment of its power over other cultures coincided with the growth of that complex historiography of European culture which I have been describing in simplified form. That empire coincided, among other things, with Enlightenment. It is a question whether the historiography of other literate cultures resembled European historiography, and if not, whether either historiography should be taken as the norm.

There is another possibility: the formerly subjugated and now reassertive culture may have been of the kind we now call 'indigenous', 'aboriginal' in Anglo-Australian, '*tangata whenua*' in Maori-Aotearoan. Such a culture will not present documents which may be criticized and rewritten as history, since it was before contact non-literate. It will conserve or construct the image of a pre-contact economy, neither agrarian nor monetary, and of a pre-contact imaginative culture broadly to be termed 'animist', which spoke of the human society as sharing a spiritual substance with the non-human environment. This language, however, is highly abstract in comparison with that of myth and ancestry in which the *tangata whenua* effect the identification of people with earth (and, perhaps, sea). There may exist, then, as inheritance or as invention, an indigenous world-view or ideology which is rather a cosmogony than a theism, philosophy or history in the West Eurasian senses of these terms. It may claim the status of history as a valid way of remembering and relating a past, but may not present that constant, critical and restless re-narration of the past which we have made the characteristic of historiography and of the culture which conceives its history in historiographical terms.

Indeed, the indigenous have good grounds for regarding 'history' as an instrument of alien domination, since this is the form in which it was proposed to and imposed upon them. European settlers came and said that agriculture, commerce and capitalism as they practised them were the means of breaking with the cosmogony of the pre-contact cultures, which they termed 'primitive', and entering the history of the progress of mankind. They used 'history' as an ideological justification of their dispossession and disruption of indigenous cultures, though the terms on which aboriginals and *tangata whenua* were admitted to history, or in some cases vigorously asserted their action and autonomy within it, varied very widely from one colonial history to another.

It is easy to say that the ejection of indigenous peoples from cosmogony and into history was effective, and that their present assertion that history has been unjust is nothing other than their means of acting within history and not cosmogony. Even revolution, were such a thing still possible, would be no more than an essentially European instrument of self-modernization on neo-European terms. Yet cosmogony remains an instrument by which modern or post-modern indigenous peoples criticize history itself even as they practise it. Europeans remember and in certain ways still practise it, and even where the indigenous are obliged to reinvent it, having lost it in the history imposed upon them, they accuse the history which has been the means, as well as the narrative, of their dispossession from it.

The political dialogues now going on in lands of settlement where indigenous peoples are reasserting their identity and claiming autonomy are, therefore, of considerable theoretical interest, since they entail debates between histories and counter-histories.[12] Suppose that the history of one's society (one is tempted to say 'one's country') is revealed to have been that of interaction between two peoples, each living in a history not reducible to the terms used in recounting the history of the other; so that the citizen (and with the citizen the historian) is required to live, speak and act in two non-reducible histories at once, and in the interactions between them. Can there be a politics, a citizenship, an autonomy and its history, a means to identity, in a life lived on these terms? And will its political form be that of a commonwealth or only a confederation? The problem is that of autonomy, identity and sovereignty in a multiplicity of histories – and we have to consider the possibility that these histories may be a means to their own undoing, and that we may be (or more probably are not) passing into a post-historical (or even 'post-human') condition.[13]

But before reaching that point, let us return to some questions situated in the history of our own culture. These will be problems in the history of the Self, that is, of the culture to which we may all feel that we belong. But since it has long been a characteristic of that culture that it asks whether the Self can much longer be maintained, it co-exists interestingly with histories that challenge the Self by affirming the Other. These counter-histories interpenetrate one another. As the Enlightenment history imposed upon

[12] Meaning by the latter term not only alternative historical narratives but alternative understandings of the term 'history', and even alternatives to the concept of history itself.

[13] [See further J. G. A. Pocock, 'The Treaty Between Histories', in Andrew Sharp and Paul McHugh (eds.), *Histories, Power and Loss* (Wellington: Bridget Williams Books, 2001, pp. 79–96; republished in Julia Rudolph (ed.), *History and Nation* (Lewisburg, PA: Bucknell University Press, 2006), pp. 137–65.]

the *tangata whenua* is both antagonist and protagonist in the histories they must construct of themselves, so the cosmogony of their animist past and present finds resonances in Enlightenment thought. It finds them in Rousseau, who thought of a natural innocence against which all civil society and its history were an aggression; it finds them in Herder, for whom history resided in the many self-imaginations of disparate cultures through incantation and myth. These Counter-Enlightenments, I argue, arose within what we call Enlightenment rather than from opposed sources, and they arose precisely as Enlightenment history was being imposed on the *tangata whenua* and Enlightened minds were wondering what this meant. I am in need, then, of some narratives of what is going on in Enlightened historiography, additional rather than opposed or even alternative to that narrated by Isaiah Berlin or John Gray.[14] To relate these narratives will serve various purposes as well as illuminating or complicating the matter of indigenous historiography. It will bear on the problem of the definition of Europe, and of Britain's place in Europe. It will bear out, and put into practice, my contention that historiography consists in the multiplication of narratives, between which there may exist a variety of relationships, many of them political. And it will lead back to the problems of living in a world where one finds oneself involved in a plurality of histories, each one of them potentially the means of defining a sovereignty, and yet both sovereignty and history are widely regarded as marked out for demolition.

[14] Isaiah Berlin, *The Age of Enlightenment: the eighteenth-century philosophers* (Boston: Houghton Mifflin, 1956). John Gray, *Enlightenment's Wake: politics and culture at the close of the modern age* (London: Routledge, 1995) and *Endgames: questions in late modern political thought* (Oxford: Polity Press, 1997).

CHAPTER 13

The politics of historiography

Mandell Creighton, in whose memory these lectures are given, was a sound and productive historian; perhaps best remembered for his debate with Lord Acton on the question of moral judgment in history. Acton, we recall, insisted that sin was sin and must be reported as such, regardless of mitigating circumstance or what we might now term cultural relativism. Creighton, a bishop, was not so sure. We might reasonably attribute this, in part, to the close relation between the Church of England and the Anglo-British state, making the bishop of London aware of the ever-present casuistry and reason of state inherent in the performance of the political actions of which history, then and even now, was so largely the record. It would be possible, however, to attribute his position in the debate with Acton to a rather different perception of the historian's function: that it was to narrate and explore the action in all its complexity – what we should now term its multi-complexity – neither mitigating crime and sin, of which there would always be plenty, nor making them the endpoint of historical inquiry and narrative.

I mention this matter for two reasons in embarking upon this lecture. In the first place, the prominence of this moral debate in our recollection of the distinguished historian I am to commemorate should not be forgotten, while I explore some theses in the theory of historiography, rather than join most of my predecessors in expounding some specific historical problem or process. In the second place, the perception of historical narrative that I have ventured to attribute to Mandell Creighton is by no means without its bearing on the topic I begin to identify in the title of this lecture. I have offered to discuss 'the politics of historiography', meaning by that term not the internal politics of the historical profession – entertaining in the

[This article is a revised version of the Creighton Lecture, delivered in the Beveridge Hall, University of London, on 3 November 2003. Published in *Historical Research*, 78.199 (February 2005) by the Institute of Historical Research.]

usual way though that subject would prove to be – but a more abstract and theoretical subject, the political theory of historiography, meaning in the first place an inquiry within the theory of politics into what it means to have a history; into what these words mean, into what manner of *Lebensform* (if I may venture the word) 'we' must be to have one, into what this 'history' we supposedly have must be, and into what it means to this 'us' to have or not to have the kind of history my argument will develop. I shall be speaking as one who was once a political theorist as well as a historian and has in some measure been a historian of political theory ever since.

I have already begun to use words in a tendentious manner. In the first place, I have used the word 'historiography', indicating that history is something written and that one way of understanding it is to inquire how others have written it and how we write it. In my own work of recent years, I have been increasingly concerned with studying the constructions of history by those who have written it at certain periods in the past, and have found this history of historiography to be a very different thing from the history of the philosophy of history which has been allowed to dominate it. In the second place, the writing of history, in the periods with which I have been concerned, was very largely a matter of the construction of narratives, and I have allowed the notion of narrative a continuingly important place in the account of the historian's activity I shall present. The idea that history is necessarily narrative has been often, and often justly, challenged, but I intend to retain it while proclaiming the importance of recognizing alternatives to it. That is, I shall suppose the historian centrally concerned with the questions: 'What has been happening? What kinds of things are these that have been happening?', and I shall presume that happenings are things that require narrating. Part of my inquiry into the politics of historiography, therefore, will be an inquiry into the consequences of supposing politics to consist of happenings that require to be narrated in a historiography; into what happens to political life when it is reduced to narratability.

A further tendentious statement is, of course, implicit in my title. By speaking of 'the politics of historiography', I have implied that the content of history is necessarily political, and have drawn close to the ancient formula that 'history is past politics, politics present history'. This statement is not in itself false – both parts of it are often and importantly true – but it is false to utter it as a definition of a subject and say that past politics is history's only and essential subject-matter. But it is also false to claim or assume that one cannot make the first statement without also making the second, and that to emphasize history as a political narrative is to suppress or marginalize the importance of histories that need not be political at all. This is not so;

history has many subjects as well as politics; but there also arises the truth that to depoliticize history is an act that has political consequences, that these may have been intended, and that not to speak of politics may be a political act. This has been the case with most of the proposals to write a 'new history', with 'new' subject-matter – social, economic, cultural – that have been put forward since they first appeared in the mid-eighteenth century.

I wish to redirect attention from historiography as a narrative of politics to historiography as a political phenomenon; but it has usually become the latter by a process of becoming the former. Our next step should be to suppose a political society, and then to inquire in what ways it may acquire a historiography and what kind of history this will narrate or otherwise affirm. This is not an easy inquiry, least of all at the level of theory. There are too many kinds of political society, and too many to which the term 'politics' cannot be applied without clarification or modification; and there are too many ways of conceptualizing a society's existence in time, and indeed the time in which it exists, to which the word 'history' is not applicable as we ordinarily use it. From these difficulties there emerge certain simplified assumptions that we find it easy to make. We readily suppose that the conceptual structures – possibly the narratives – that arise at this point serve only the purpose of legitimating the society and its authority system; and we suppose that these structures will admit of no dissent or alternative, and will be expressed in forms to which the notions of truth and falsity are themselves alien. We say, in short, that they will be myths, that the function of such myths is to uphold the continued existence – or that dreaded word the 'identity' – of the social structure that generates them, and that any narrative or image formed to carry out that function is itself myth, defying criticism and even verification. In a culture like ours, which sets an extremely high value on criticism and on the opposition between authority and the individual, it may be very hard not to imagine historiography as either the invention or the subversion and explosion of the myths upholding authority; but while there will always be many such myths that invite subversion, to stop short at this definition of historiography leaves it difficult to see how this activity arises in the course of political life or how it is related to the latter. It is worth inquiring, therefore, whether a political society is capable of generating a historiography definable in terms that do not limit it to myth.

We most easily do this by defining 'political': that is, by setting limits to it in ways that permit us to suppose a non-political, perhaps a pre-political or an extrapolitical. This is, of course, an unsafe thing to do; we shall be justly reminded that the non-political and the political co-exist and penetrate each other, and that to define the 'political' is to privilege those who are members of it by excluding as 'others' those who are not. We may reply that this is perfectly true, but that most political societies have in fact been constructed in this way and this is how their history needs to be understood and narrated; the construction of histories of the excluded is a necessary, but not an identical, activity, and does not remove or simply invalidate the histories of the political. These have happened and there is a need to know them; and although they will have been conducted, and written, with a view to maintaining the domination of those included in them, that may not be all there is to be told by re-narrating them. It is, I shall argue, a characteristic of the political that it leads to the re-narration of its history – including its myths – with consequences that are not always predictable. Let us then erect a simplified account of the political and see if it will generate a historiography.

Let us say that a political society will see itself as performing acts and maintaining institutions; after which we may look at ways in which acts and institutions may lead to a concept of history. The acts may be legislative, in the classical sense that they are seen as constituting the society and providing it with norms for future action; but this is a large assumption, especially if we prefix to such a foundation a time of the ancestors, or a dream-time, in which all norms were uncreated and independent of human action. It is important, although unsafe, to observe, however, that the foundation myths of Greco-Judaic civilization presuppose not a dream-time but a catastrophe: the expulsion from a garden, the fall of a city, the wanderings of a fratricide, matricide or parricide hero, the dispersion of peoples in a world deprived of language. In the nineteenth century this anti-mythical mythology was taken – perhaps it was by some of my predecessors in giving these lectures – as indicating a dynamic creativity and historicity which rendered our civilization superior to others. As a result many peoples in the world today see their history as a catastrophe imposed by us upon them. This may well disempower me from saying how such peoples did, do or should construct histories, if that is what they are to do now; but it does not alter the fact that we did construct our histories in this way and still do.

The founding legislator, then – Moses, Solon, Romulus, Confucius – is thought of as acting in an imperfect or fallen world, one of conflict, in which his laws will be favoured by many but must be communicated to, imposed upon, and resisted by others. There will be a narrative of this action or *agōn*, from which the laws may emerge with absolute and even sacred authority, but in which there will have been conflict and the conflicts will appear as contingent circumstances. At this point we may say that we have arrived at history, in the sense of a narrative presupposing a contest in which it is possible – even if we are discouraged from thinking it – that what happened might have happened otherwise. The narrative explains itself, but does not explain everything; as historiography ceases to be ancient and becomes modern, the causes of legislation's success are found less in the hero's actions than in the contingent circumstances in which they might conceivably have failed. What, however, are the sources from which we construct our accounts of what these circumstances contained or might have contained?

Ancient historians developed a rhetoric of 'fortune', meaning a world of random contingencies surrounding human action, in which chance might at any moment have injected a circumstance by which the action would have been frustrated. Monotheists opposed this, but the actions of God did not direct a history that human writers could speculatively investigate; and the history of modern historiography is the record of how we filled the circumambient world with circumstances whose being and operations could be understood, to the point where they became processes that were substituted for divine, heroic and legislative action as explanations of the latter's success. We now look for a source, in the politics of historiography, for this increasing richness of circumstantial explanation; and I suggest we find much of what we seek in the operation of institutions.

Institutions – let us elaborate our model by saying – are structures of regulated action, in which agents are directed to act in certain ways when they find themselves, or can claim to be, in certain circumstances. For this they need memory, and in literate cultures establish archives; documents accumulate which record the actions, decisions and speech acts of a past, together with the circumstances in which these actions were performed and the rationales which led to the premise that these circumstances were of the kind with which the institutions were programmed to deal. There can be found in archives a good deal of circumstantial information, which may tell either for or against the proposition that the society has 'always' been situated in certain circumstances, and has 'always' sought to control them by the same responses. This is a principal way in which societies have acquired pasts, dimensions of their own continuity which the narrative of human action is not necessarily concerned to construct, and have regarded these pasts as either historic or unhistoric as we now use those two words.

It has been important to the history of historiography, at least in our highly historical culture, that the narrative of political action has merged with, or been supplemented by, an archaeology of past states of society, so that there has arisen a further species of narrative recounting the process by which one state of things was replaced by another. What I am calling archives have been essential to the latter development, for the reason that they have supplied the contexts – the sets of social, cultural and historical conditions – in, under and upon which political actions have been performed. These contexts have been of great diversity, and it has been possible to construct a corresponding diversity of narratives of change (or the lack of it) in each of them. Given that the archive records information as to the circumstances in which an action was performed or a decision taken, there is no theoretical limit, although there may be severe practical constraints, on the kinds of context it may record. I have so far presented the institution as governmental in character; it may well have been judicial, and the archives of judicature – theoretically enlarged, it is significant to note, into the literature and philosophy of jurisprudence – have supplied a very large part of both the information and the sensibility to it on which the most sophisticated historiography has been built. It has been of equal importance that the culture shaped in the West European provinces was strengthened and burdened by a literary archive derived from Rome, Greece and Israel, and that it was a highly multilingual culture; for the consequence was that language itself became an archive and a record of contests, and that philology came to rank beside jurisprudence as a source of information regarding society, economy and, above all, culture in a past of process and change.

I could continue to elaborate a history of historiography along these lines – I have obviously said nothing about the church and the encounter between history and the sacred – but the project with which I have charged myself and you is to consider the politics of historiography rather than its history. What has the emergence of historiography, as I have so far imagined it, done for the political society in which I have imagined it emerging? I have imagined historiography as the construction of narratives – to which the construction of contexts for narrative must now be added – concerned with certain sorts of action (including acts of speech and speculation) performed in certain kinds of context, the latter defined very broadly and perhaps universally, in terms that range from chance through contingency to circumstance and from the random to the predetermined. The context is always partly, but never wholly, the product of the actions performed in it, since the society may now be thought of as seeking to extend its control over the circumstances surrounding it. Part of the history of a society is the history of what it has done; to which we may add the history of what it says it has done, and the history of how it has come to say it – to tell this particular history.

We reach a point where there is a temptation to maximize the truth that the historiography we are examining will always be in some measure fiction: it will consist of statements made with intentions other than the establishment of truth, by agents whose motives can be discovered. We are at present beset by mentors who contend that there is nothing to be done with a statement about history but to unmask the conditions that make it a fiction; in some cases they proceed to the conclusion that the unmasking of fiction is itself a fiction or fictive statement, so that there is nothing to do but imagine stories about the imagining of stories, and so *ad infinitum* in the library of Babel. But to the historian, and even to the political actor or citizen, the historical world appears to be one in which things happen without waiting for us to invent them and we may have to do something about them. As R. G. Collingwood once put it, 'man's world is infested by sphinxes, demonic beings of mixed and monstrous nature which ask him riddles and eat him if he cannot answer them'.[1] A great many of these 'beings' are human constructs, begotten by human actions and very often by human imaginings in the sleep of reason, not children of a natural or non-human world. This, however, is not enough to make them fictions; they may appear at any moment, and not all of them are our own nightmares – even if they are somebody else's. If we know their names and can narrate their histories, they may softly and suddenly vanish away, but not all of them will. The history of a political society, even if reduced to a history of human imaginings or constructs, will not prove to have been imagined solely by the society's present inhabitants who imagine or are led to imagine it; 'we' – if that pronoun may be used at all – shall find ourselves dealing with the actions and imaginings of others in the past, of others within as well as without the society, and even of ourselves in roles other than those in which we imagine ourselves. Let me now turn to ways in which the historiography developing in a political society may, and probably will, enhance its citizens' capacity to recognize this kind of history.

I have so far presented this historiography as originating in two ways; the construction of narratives and the exploration of archives. The narratives may record tales and myths of origin, or the actions performed in, by or for the society as a structure of agency; if the society has interacted with

[1] R. G. Collingwood, *The New Leviathan: or Man, Society, Civilization and Barbarism*, rev. edn (Oxford, 1992), p. 12.

those outside it, actors external as well as internal, strangers as well as citizens, will appear in the story, acting in ways other than those recorded and expected of citizens. Such narratives will have taken shape in a great variety of ways, but I will now suppose the intervention of those specialized actors known as historians. This had to happen sooner or later; I do not mean that historians are the only or the necessary agents in the construction of historiographies, but in the history our civilization remembers, and not in that alone, they have been present for a long time and form part of the process I am relating. They appear in many forms, but may be presumed members – in some sense – of the society acquiring the historiography. They may have been functionaries, required by the state or some other institution to furnish it with the narratives it required for some reason; but in our classical recollection they have commonly been citizens, writing their narratives in what was known as 'leisure', a condition freeing them from immediate instituted duties. They will have compiled their narratives because there is some demand for them, possibly originating among those who themselves are at 'leisure'; sometimes they have been travelling rhetoricians, appearing to meet this demand in a city of which they are not citizens after all. There will be interaction between the functionary and the leisurely; even the temple scribe may have and need time and space in which to construct his narrative, and in this space the needs of personality may assert themselves; if the historian is a citizen these needs may be both legitimated and enlarged. We encounter the problems of individuality and even liberty. The primeval martyr, the Socrates of historiography, is Ssu-ma Ch'ien, grand historian of China, a functionary if ever there was one.[2]

Ssu-ma Ch'ien desired only to write what was proper and even preordained for one in his office to write, but found that powerful factions might disagree on what that was. A historian in a more civic society may believe that he is writing the truth, when he is in fact writing what asserts the beliefs and the interests of a party or a class. In either case what matters is that there is conflict as to what has happened, ought to have happened and should be happening; there is conflict as to the history because there is, and may for a longer or shorter period have been, conflict in the politics. The next step is for the historian to know this and, with or without being a partisan, narrate the history of the society as the history of its conflicts. The demands of narrative itself may bring it about that, even as a partisan, he may write in ways differing from those in which the members of his

[2] B. Watson, *Ssu-ma Ch'ien: grand historian of China* (New York, 1958), pp. 54, 57–67.

party would have written; narrative breeds perspective before it breeds detachment. He will know that the narrative he is recounting could have been, and has been, recounted differently by those of other persuasions.

If he is required – as historians in ancient societies commonly were – to construct accounts of events occurring in his own time, he will discover the difficulty of recounting the same event from the reports of different participants, and may become aware that he must use his own judgment, and cannot do better than use his own judgment, in reconciling two accounts of the same event. In two ways, therefore, historians are likely to discover that there can be more than one history of events within the society, and that any event may be part of more histories than one, since those who remember it differently live in the histories they remember. The historian who has access to both lives in a multiplicity of histories, and informs his society that its history is contested, debatable and multiple.

What is the political significance of this? First, let us note that the consciousness of complexity is not limited to the historian; the citizens are aware of it in their own ways and look to the historian to help them deal with it. They are disappointed only when – as will happen – the community of historians becomes engrossed in its own second-order or specialized discourse to the point where this is not immediately, or foreseeably, shared with the community of citizens. Second, I have supposed that the consciousness of complexity arises from the richness of memory and interpretation created by the interactions of narrative and archive. The acts and experiences constituting the society's past are now seen as having happened in many contexts and as entailing many concurrent narratives. About these there may still be vehement and bitter divisions; but to the extent that the political structure still exists – and it is almost a premise of the existence of a historiography that it shall have persisted – its existence provides the context in which the past is perceived as having happened and as still going on. What explains the past legitimates the present and moderates the impact of the past upon it. There is a political structure capable of recounting its own history, not of unifying it but of diversifying it; and this critical and competitive capacity becomes part of the state's sovereignty – meaning by the term its capacity to manage, confront and continue its history. Even if that history should have been one of bitter, confused and revolutionary self-formation, the ability to write more than one version of that history, and to admit that there can be more than one version, is reinforced by, and actually reinforces, a present in which political institutions are legitimized and stable – I have noticed the phenomena I describe during travel in the Republic of Ireland. The politics of historiography have a strong bent towards conservative liberalism; they tell us that there are many stories to be told of ourselves and many ways of judging them, but that there exists a normative structure within which we can continue to judge ourselves and give effect to our decision.

There is a plurality of narratives because politics is a contested activity, in which actors have diverse goals, tell different stories, and, to some degree, live in the narratives they succeed in relating. If these narratives are altogether irreconcilable, there is no political society; if there is one, a diversity of narratives in some way and some degree persists. I could now unfold a scenario whose polar ideas are repression at one extreme and toleration at another; but I would rather study a situation in which a society is continuously informed that there is more than one history to be narrated, and that attention has to be paid to both. This was the case for a long time in the history of early modern England, and the reasons tell us much about the history of the civil wars of the seventeenth century. While this continues to be the case in the model I am constructing, archives as well as narrative histories are playing their part in the making of a historical consciousness. It was Adam Smith who pointed out that modern historians used footnotes and gave their references where ancient historians did not, for the reason that modern history was largely a matter of conflict between jurisdictions, where claims had to be supported and allegations of authority verified. It did not follow that a single objective or scientific narrative was expected to emerge; rather, the public had to make up its mind which narrative it was going to adopt, in the knowledge that its decision would continue to be challenged. This was one among several reasons why Edward Gibbon concluded that the two faculties of the mind most engaged in the study of texts, and therefore the writing of history, were the imagination and the judgment. The reader of history – especially that of a society in which the reader is a member – is in the position of a juror required to arrive at a verdict.

The archives of law are not only judicatory. As Donald Kelley has pointed out,[3] they contain sophisticated ideas of authority, continuity and society itself, which have done much to supply history with what we term its philosophy. Beyond or rather before all this, they record the activities of humans in all the varieties of social action in which conflicts may arise and require adjudication; they thus anchor the narrative of the past in the contexts of society as well as of political structure. I have mentioned the ways in which jurisprudence came to be supported by philology, and the history

[3] D. R. Kelley, *The Human Measure: social thought in the Western legal tradition* (Cambridge, MA, 1990).

of literary and artistic culture came to multiply the contexts in which political history was seen as going on. The history of political acts and institutions was not expelled from the contexts growing up around it; one could claim that it was enriched by this contextualization, and we have not yet reached the claim that it becomes irrelevant among them – a claim, as I said earlier, which is itself political.

Let me now mention – with a brevity that even pressure of time cannot excuse – the growth of two further and enormous contexts in which a society's narrative of its own structure and history comes to be situated. Should it have encountered, or even contained, a structure of action and authority concerned with the sacred – as in the Christian history of church and state – its history will recount the actions of those moved by values highly distinguishable from its own. And should its history record – as it almost invariably will; some would say there could be no history if it does not – its encounters with humans not included in it – strangers, barbarians, enemies, neighbours; internally, women and the governed classes – their actions, necessarily not to be understood as regulated by the increasingly complex norms by which the narrators live, act and write, will often form a context with which the central narrative intersects. At this point we could invoke a current catchword of our culture and speak of the 'Other'; it would seem, however, that 'Others' appear in many shapes and forms, and in many patterns of relationship or enmity with the narrators, and that it is a mistake to reduce them all to a common level of alienation. Let us suppose our society possessed of a vocabulary for regulating its dealings with varieties of 'Other'.

What has by now happened to the politics of the society we have been providing with a history? We have supplied it with an increasingly complex body of discourse, rendered so by our application of the notions of contest, context and encounter, which is necessarily a narrative centred on the society's actions, institutions and dealings with others. This informs the members of the society (as I shall venture to term them) of a present in which they act, and a present collectivity in which they are members; and it furnishes both these presents with pasts, complex, contested and quite possibly violent, tragic and in many ways problematic, in whose continuation the citizens are invited and obliged to see themselves living. This discourse is not ineffective; it is harder than we are sometimes told to imagine a society with no sense of past, and those who suppose themselves indifferent to history will probably turn out to entertain ideas about it, no better for being unexamined; and lightning may at any moment strike and compel them to think about it. They may not be as important in their politics and culture as they think they are. I have no great difficulty in imagining a society whose citizens are educated to a level where it is quite widely known that their politics and their history are complex, problematic and even insecure; to sustain this knowledge, however, they must have some level of confidence that their institutions, their elites and they themselves have some capacity for dealing with complexity, problems and insecurity, and that, if they doubt that capacity, they have ways of seeking to improve it. As critical intellectuals, we are educated to doubt even the latter capacity; the question before us as citizens is what comes after the doubt.

I have reached a point, towards the end of this lecture, where I am able, and perhaps required, to deal with two concepts much debated in our time: identity and sovereignty. The former has become a catchword and to no small extent a cant word; writings abound which offer to inquire into it and very commonly proceed to interrogate it and thereby to deconstruct it. They proceed on the Sphinx's assumption that it will not be able to answer the questions put to it; alternatively, that to ask a particular culture how its 'identity' was 'made', 'created' or 'invented' is to establish that it owes its being to particular contingencies and acts, and that since the historical circumstances of this isolated act of origination have disappeared – as of course they have – the necessary conditions of 'identity' have disappeared with them. Thus, the British, and by a further consequence the English, are told that they possessed 'identity' only so long as they possessed 'empire', and that since they no longer have the latter they no longer have the former, and must set about becoming something other than they have hitherto either believed that they have been, or possessed the authority to make themselves.

This fashionable argument appears to rest on a series of fallacies. In the first place, 'empire' historically meant not only sovereignty over others, but sovereignty over themselves; an important point to whose theoretical meanings I shall return. In the second place, 'identity', I shall suggest, means what we mean when we say 'we'; and in my model I have supposed 'we' to denote a society capable of public action and public speech, and of using the latter to provide its structure with a past, composed of complicated narratives that can be rendered more complex through re-narration and critical contestation and inquiry. 'We' therefore have this history, and if we can continue to narrate it and re-narrate it, there is an obvious fallacy about interrogating it in search, or in criticism, of our 'identity'. This consists of having the history 'we' possess by narrating it; and if we criticize statements which have been made to us about who we are and have been, or if the history we narrate informs us that our 'identity' has always been contestable or contested, then 'we' are the continuously existing society which has been debating its identity and is prepared to go on doing so.

The model I have presented is visibly that of a 'nation-state', and this in current cant may be enough to damn it. We should note, however, that the 'state' may be author of the 'nation'; that is, an awareness of shared membership – it is this which is miscalled 'identity' – may in principle spring from the possession, and history, of shared political institutions, to which considerations of ethnicity and culture are inessential without being unimportant. An examination of post-modern rhetoric against the continued existence of the 'nation-state' will show, I believe, that in many cases its true target is not the nation but the state; what it aims to destroy is the finite and self-determinant political society, exercising power which it often misuses, but determining its past, present and future history by the voices of those having voice within it, who may or may not constitute it a democracy. I have deliberately replaced the word 'identity' with the word 'history', partly because I think it better to have the latter and know it than to be sent in search of the former, but for the larger reason that I have aimed in this lecture to inquire what happens to a political society when it furnishes itself with a history and what manner of 'history' this may be. I have tried to present this 'history' as composed of two contending elements; on the one hand myth, designed to furnish the society with origins, continuity, 'identity' by all means, and heroic narrative; on the other, contestability, contextualization, and the many forces which render the historical narratives re-narratable and in the end criticizable – it is from the tensions between narratives that our capacity to inquire into their veracity may in part arise. Professional historians – who rank among that irritating class of beings who may follow the logic of their discourse even at the cost of their loyalties to society – discharge the function of asking their fellow-citizens what happens if their narratives should prove untrue, unverifiable, or such that there is no final way of determining their veracity. The fact that their rulers and co-citizens will resent these questions shows that they do care about their history, not that they do not, and that they can be induced to take part in the enterprise – of which the historians have no monopoly – of determining what this history has been and shall be. The society's – and the nation's – sovereignty over itself entails a capacity to decide on its history, both by writing it and by enacting it.

This implies that the public speech – the speech of the state – has both the authority and the duty to declare what it takes the past to have been. There are obvious dangers here, but we are not immediately plunged into *1984*. When the parliament of New Zealand declared by statute – in an enacting clause, not a preamble – that the invasion of the Waikato in 1863 was unjustified,[4] it did not forbid anyone to argue to the contrary; it declared that the policy of the state henceforth was to act on that premise, and that a time had come when it was the state's duty to re-narrate one of the historical narratives on which it had previously relied. Happy the society where this does not need to be done often, but doing it diminished neither the liberty of the mind nor the state's sovereignty. It was an exercise of the latter, and a declaration of what sovereignty may entail. In rectifying a past it endeavoured – probably with success – to govern a future.

In learning to have a history, which is the history generated by the society in which they live, the members of a state or nation learn that its sovereignty exists in a history of problems and contingencies; it may have dealt disastrously with many of them, but the history of its dealings is the history of its sovereignty. However, sovereignty is exercised over society as well as contingency, and many of the problematic narratives constituting this history will have been problems in the relations between its members – including the problems of who these members were, and whether they were willing members. In proportion as the society has been successful in continuing to exist, the information constituting its history will be information in which its members have a particular interest: memories and narratives they are accustomed to reiterate and debate, assumptions and implications which it is not always necessary to articulate or explicate.

At this point we return to the intimate relationship between 'history' and 'identity'. It is a consequence of the ways in which histories are formed that the historiography of a finite society will be autocentric; it will be told to, of and by the members of that society, in terms which must be partly those of the public language that society has formed for itself and has a particular need and capacity to speak, write and understand. Consequently, this society has a peculiar interest in this history; it is more interested in it, and more adept in articulating it, than any other; the history is largely for internal consumption, not for communicating to the members of other societies with other histories. 'They' will be reluctant to face the difficulties of understanding 'our' history, as 'we' will be of theirs. Living as we do with a global information explosion, which has consequences both peaceable and warlike, we know that this is a dangerous as well as a difficult state of affairs, and a rhetoric has arisen, and is increasing, which demands the

[4] Waikato Raupatu Claims Settlement Act, 1995, pp. 12–14. (See A. Sharp, *Justice and the Maori: the philosophy and practice of Maori claims in New Zealand since the 1970s*, 2nd edn (Auckland, 1997), pp. 299–300).

supersession and liquidation of particular histories and particular identities. It must be asked, however, whether the fact that something is dangerous means that it ought not to be difficult. Why should not the history of one long-established political culture be difficult for the inhabitants of another to understand? Why should it not present difficulties which only its inhabitants have either the need or the means to understand, which others may come to understand only as their needs and means direct and enable them? As myself an immigrant to a certain political and historical culture, I do not mind learning that I must understand it in my own ways, which are not those of the natives, and that even to understand how the natives understand it is not to understand it as they do. Acculturation may come, and may even come quickly; but this does not challenge the premise that the history of a given political society – I am now calling it a culture – is and ought to be difficult for even those belonging to it to understand, and difficult for a distinct set of reasons for those belonging to others – or uncertain to what they belong – to understand either. What makes it difficult to understand is, in all these cases, although for differing reasons, what makes it both necessary and valuable to understand; although this means that I am saying that the existence of widely diverse political cultures, with widely diverse histories and widely diverse understandings of what politics and history are, is valuable as well as dangerous. Will this statement hold up under conditions of post-colonial warfare? Time will tell.

Index

Printed in the United States
By Bookmasters